Welcome Home! Robert R[...]

The
Beauty Path

A Native American Journey Into One Love

By

ROBERT ROSKIND

Cover Portrait

The cover portrait is of past Iroquois Tadodaho (Firekeeper of the Haudenosaunee) by *Leon Shenandoah (1915-1996)*

Leon, among other wisdomkeepers whose words speak through this book, truly represents the wisdom and love we sought on our journey.

His portrait is part of the *Great Law Series* by gifted artist **Marcine Quenzer**

Prints of this and her other work are available at:

www.marcinequenzer.com

Copyright 2006 by Robert Allen Roskind

This edition published in 2006 by One Love Press

ISBN: 1-56522-100-1

One Love Press

PO Box 2142

Blowing Rock, NC 28605

(828) 295-4610 FAX: (828) 295-6901

email: roskind@boone.net

Website: www.onelovepress.com

Books by Robert Roskind

Rasta Heart: A Journey Into One Love

The Gathering of the Healers: The Healing of the Nation

*In the Spirit of Businesss: A Guide to Creating Harmony &
Fulfillment in Your Worklife*

In the Spirit of Marriage: Creating and Sustaining Loving Unions

Memoirs of an Ex-Hippie: Seven Years in the Counterculture

*Building Your Own House: Everything You Need to Know About
Home Construction from Start to Finish*

Before You Build: A Preconstruction Guidebook

The Complete Disaster Home Preparation Guide

I-dication

This book is "I-dicated" to all the Native American Wisdomkeepers whose words bring this book to life:

Leon Shenandoah (Iroquois)
Roland Manakaja (Havasupai)
Supai Waters (Havasupai)
Radford Quamahongnewa (Hopi)
Dawn Mapatis-Quamahongnewa (Hopi)

Thanks
To my wife, Julia, for her constant support and for taking these journeys with me

Author's Notes

All the events and people in this book are accurately portrayed. The dialogs and conversations are transcribed directly from video footage and are the speakers' *exact* words.

Throughout the book, I use the terms "white man," "white culture," "European," and "Anglo." There is only for clarity sake and I do not mean to imply anything discussed is due to one's skin color but rather is due to decisions by individuals and the cultures we live under - which can bring out the best or worst in us all.

I love a people who have always made me feel welcome
   to the best they had.

I love a people who are honest without laws,
   who have no jails and no poorhouses.

I love a people who keep the commandments without ever having
   read them or heard them preached from the pulpit.

I love a people who never swear, who never take the
   name of God in vain.

I love a people who love their neighbor as they love themselves.

I love a people who worship God without a bible, for I believe
   that God loves them also.

I love a people whose religion is all the same, and who are free
   from religious animosity.

I love a people who have never raised a hand against me, or stole
   my property, where there was no law to punish them for either.

I love a people who have never fought a battle with white men,
   except on their own ground.

I love and don't fear mankind where God has made and left them,
   for there they are children.

I love a people who live and keep what is their own without locks
   and keys.

I love a people who do the best they can.

And oh, how I love a people who don't live for the love of money.

—**George Catlin** (1796-1872), world famous Indian artist who
   lived among the Native Americans for years and visited forty-
   eight tribes.

Contents

Chapter 1
The Hopi Way

"Each of us are put on this earth to do some task, which is to fulfill our life purpose. We come at different times, with others to follow us just as we followed those who had gone before. They say we come to this world just to visit. Our behavior is tested and then we go to the next phase or sequence of life. Some of us leave good marks, some do not."
—The Hopi Elderly Elders in their newsletter, Techqua Ikachi

"By and by, Jah show every man him hand and Jah has shown I mine."
—Bob Marley

For five years, from 2000 to 2005, my wife, Julia, our teenage daughter, Alicia and myself, made many journeys to the island of Jamaica to seek out the roots of One Love - unconditional love - that was reflected in the island's music, especially that of international superstar Bob Marley and other conscious reggae musicians. During this time we wrote two books on our spiritual odyssey, *Rasta Heart:A Journey Into One Love* and *The Gathering of the Healers:The Healing of the Nations*. We also organized and hosted 54 free "One Love Concerts" on the island, most held in inner-city schools, to reflect back to them their message of love and forgiveness. Many reggae recording artists performed for free at these concerts. Little did we know that this path would eventually take us on a similar journey through several Native American tribes in our own country. This book is the story of that journey into One Love.

It began in July of 2003, while we were still working on *The Gathering of the Healers,* our second book of our Jamaican journey. Julia and I decided to visit the remote Havasupai Indian Reservation isolated on the floor of the Grand Canyon in Arizona to try to learn more about a Jamaican-Native American link. We had read that many tribal members revered Bob Marley as a prophet and had been embracing his music since the mid-1970s. For many Havasupais, Marley's music had become their tribal drumbeat.

(Bob Marley's music is considered by millions worldwide as a spiritual path leading us, as one author wrote, "from one state of consciousness called 'Babylon' to another state called 'Zion.' " The *New York Times* called him "the most influential artist of the second half of the twentieth century." From 1976 until his tragic death at 36 from cancer in 1981, his concerts were sold out, especially in Third World countries where he was seen as a symbol of hope for eventual liberation from oppression and poverty. He could draw 180,000 in Milan one night and 100,000 in Dublin the next. In one twelve-city tour, he performed for more than a million fans. Jack Healey of Amnesty International claims that Marley, more than any other figure, remains "*the* symbol of freedom throughout the world.' "

Conscious reggae, often referred to as "roots reggae," was birthed in Jamaica by Marley in the 1970s and early 1980s. There are now many conscious reggae recording artists, mostly Rastafarians from Jamaica, continuing his legacy. Reggae is perhaps the only music popular in *every* country in the world. To many of the world's illiterate masses, it is a lyrical form of social, political and spiritual communication. Reggae's "one drop" rhythm matches the human heartbeat and its message is a cry for justice and an end to oppression - both by individuals and by governments. It also carries a message of love, forgiveness, healing and spiritual freedom. As Bob Marley sang, "Emancipate yourself from mental slavery. None but ourselves can free our minds.")

On our way from our home in the Blue Ridge Mountains of North Carolina to the Havasupai reservation, we decided to stop at the Hopi Indian Reservation about two hundred miles east of the Grand Canyon. Though we had no idea if there was any connection between reggae music and the Hopi, neighbors of the Havasupai, we thought it would make an interesting stopover. A few days before leaving on the trip, I had bought two books, *The Hopi Survival Kit* and *Hotevilla:Hopi Shrine of the Covenant*, written by a 102-year old Hopi Elder Dan Evehema and American author Thomas E. Mails and had been reading them as we traveled. What they said was fascinating.

Their name, "Hopi," which in their language is "Hopisinumu," meaning "peaceful people," also refers to *any* people that are peaceful. Other interpretations include "one who follows the path" and "one who walks in the right direction." "Hopi" also has a deeper meaning. It is "a way of life which can continue endlessly." Some view that being Hopi is more of a *goal* rather than a present reality. There is a constant awareness that no one is perfect and yet through good behavior people are trying to *become* Hopi.

The books I bought explained that the Hopi, like all tribes, were very spiritually-oriented and perhaps the oldest and clearest guardians of ancient Native American beliefs and practices. As Peter Matthiessen writes in his book, *In the Spirit of Crazy Horse*, "The Hopi traditionalists are looked to by other Indians all over the continent for guidance in the quest to rediscover and maintain those roots of the Old Way that might still nourish the Indian people."

To this day, the Hopi have been able to retain their cultural and religious ways to a much greater extent than other Native American tribes. This is especially true of the Hopi living in Shungopavi on Second Mesa, the most traditional of the three Hopi mesas. Due to their physical isolation, they were far removed from the path of the new American society as it steamrolled from east to west, driven by its commercial desires, fueled by its belief in "Manifest Destiny." Hopiland was so barren it offered nothing for the dominant culture to seize (until coal was discovered in recent years). They were also the tribe that most vigorously resisted abandoning their religious beliefs and land, knowing that it would break sacred covenants they had made with Maasaw, the Creator's messenger. In fact, they believed it was their keeping of their sacred covenants that kept the world in balance.

Turning off Interstate 40 three days out from our home, we drove two hours towards the Hopi reservation, passing only a handful of small ranches and only one intersecting road. There were no stores, towns or other signs of civilization. The road is a two-lane blacktop - straight as an arrow and passing through beautiful but desolate country. It is mostly flat and barren with a few rolling hills. The ground is covered with scruffy grass, sage, a few low bushes and an occasional tree. Along the way you pass some magnificent earth-colored formations, some rising several hundred feet above the ground. Off to the west, the San Francisco Peaks, just north of Flagstaff, Arizona are visible on the horizon. These mountains, the highest in the area, are considered sacred by all local tribes including the Hopi and Havasupais. The land feels ancient and powerful with petrified trees, dinosaur tracks over 200 million years old, 12,000-foot high dormant volcanoes, and a huge crater made by a meteor that struck 50,000 years ago.

Hopiland, their ancestral home as well as their present reservation, is a collection of eleven small villages, nine with dramatic views as they hug the edge of the high cliffs of the Black Mesa. Another village, Moencopi, lies fifty miles to the north. Their "Mother Village," Shungopavi, is thought to be the oldest continually inhabited places in the Northern Hemisphere (some believe their village of Oraibi is the oldest).

As we drove across this barren desert toward Hopiland, I couldn't help but wonder why the Hopi had chosen to live here for centuries. Unlike most of the other indigenous tribes, there was *never* any abundance in their lives. The land was prone to drought, extreme heat and cold and sand storms. There is no surface water - no lakes, streams or creeks. In ancient times, there was no secure water sources and villages were established - and abandoned - according to water availability from a few small springs. Before modern wells were dug and large holding tanks installed in the villages, the women had to walk several times each day a mile down the steep mesa to a small spring to fill their water jugs. Water was precious and there was never enough. From infancy, Hopi were taught to use it sparingly. In times of drought, they ate scraps of food or walked 250 miles to work as temporary laborers for a neighboring tribe - just to get enough food to eat. And yet they have stayed.

Around mid-morning, we arrived at First Mesa. This part of the reservation is made up of First, Second and Third Mesa, finger-like protrusions of the Black Mesa, a sixty-mile long, 2,500-square-mile, 6000-foot diamond-shaped high plateau that rises fifteen hundred feet above the desert floor below. Everywhere you drive, the views are breathtaking, with hundred-mile vistas. Most of the modest houses are clustered together in the small villages, which are separated by barren emptiness and a few scattered dwellings.

We pulled into a small shopping area that included a modern-looking grocery store, a small cafe and an architecturally-designed gift shop. As we walked toward the gift store, there was a large poster on the bulletin board with a picture of a well-known reggae artist: "From Jamaica - Mikey Dread! -July 19 at 8PM at The Hopi Veterans Memorial Hall."

Pleasantly surprised, we went into the small gift shop and immediately began talking with the owner, Pauline Secakuku.

"I see you're having a reggae concert here in a few weeks," I said. "We've been writing books on Jamaica. Is reggae big on the reservation?"

"It's *very* big here," Pauline replied. "In fact tonight and every Wednesday night we have a reggae radio show, Rez Rasta Riddums, on our National Public Radio station, KUYI. Karen Abieta is the disc jockey. It's our most popular program, especially with the younger generation."

We soon learned there had been almost 60 reggae concerts at the Hopi Veterans Memorial Hall since 1984, including such artists as Culture, Burning Spear, Third World, and Steel Pulse. Given the tribe's roots of peace and love, and its history of oppression, it really should be no surprise that the Hopi would be drawn to reggae. We also learned that many Jamaican reggae artists, to express solidarity with other oppressed people, often stopover to perform for Native American tribes when they are touring. There are even several Native American reggae artists and groups including Casper and the 602 Band, Native Roots, Uproot, and Native Elements.

We talked awhile longer and then headed out to check into the lodge and explore before trying to linkup with Karen Abieta later that night at the radio station. Our motel, the only one on the reservation, was at the Hopi Cultural Center on Second Mesa. The Cultural Center is a complex including a meeting hall, a 26-room lodge, a restaurant and a small museum and gift shop.

After checking in, we decided to head over to the ancient village of Oraibi, about fifteen minutes away. The village sits on the edge of the mesa, which drops dramatically to the valley below. Everywhere you turn there are views of the desert. It is a village of a hundred or so structures, mostly low, squat homes made from hand-made sandstone and mortar and in various states of disrepair. Most looked abandoned. Most of the adobe buildings had small windows and doors, with earth roofs. There were no telephone or power poles, no paved streets or large water tanks as we had seen in the other Hopi villages we had passed. A few had been upgraded somewhat with modern materials such as plywood and concrete blocks - a rather incongruous touch to a very roots community. There were a few satellite dishes and a small generator was running in the background.

Even with this limited modernization, you felt as if you have stepped back in time. This was one of the oldest continually inhabited villages in the Western hemisphere, but now it was in a very advanced state of decay. Somehow that seemed appropriate. It was more like an archeological ruin than an inhabited village. It had a strange, almost eerie, but powerful feel to it. If you looked at certain areas where there was no moderniza-tion, it looked just as it must have 900 years ago. This village was old and decrepit - totally removed from time. The lightening-struck steeple of the old Mennonite church a short distance away seemed to symbolize that spirituality, in all forms, no longer had a place here.

The village seemed almost empty, with few homes showing any signs of life. There were only two or three vehicles around. We parked and walked across the dusty road to a two-story house that had been modern-ized, and looked to be the largest in the village. Noticing the "Welcome - Gift Shop" sign, we entered the home and were surprised to find ourselves in a large open and rather modern kitchen. It appeared to be the center of activity. There was a small table with a few beaded crafts for sale and some small plastic bags with piki bread, the traditional paper-thin blue corn bread that is a staple in the Hopi diet. A middle-aged Hopi woman, in modern dress, approached us from the rear of the kitchen, joined by a young girl about ten and her eight-year old brother.

"Welcome," she said with a big smile. "We have a few items to sell and some piki bread. Or if you want the children can take you on a guided tour of the village but no pictures or videos are allowed."

"That sounds great and we'd like to buy some of your bread," I said.

We headed out with the children for our tour. First, they showed us a large ceremonial kiva, one of fourteen that once existed in the village. Kivas are underground Hopi sacred ceremonial chambers, each belonging to a different religious society. There are as many kivas in each village as there are religious societies. About a third of the kiva protruded about six feet above the ground. It was about thirty feet in diameter with a large pole ladder sticking out of a square entrance built into its flat dirt roof. Inside, the kivas are supposedly pleasant, with plastered walls, earth-tone colors, subdued lighting and a center fire pit.

"This is a sacred building," the little girl said. "You cannot go in it or on top of it. Only society members. We have not even been inside."

As we walked, we got a little of the children's story. They had only recently moved here from California with their family, who had wanted to return to their ancestral roots. They were rather bored after living a faster-paced life and said that there was little for kids to do here, not even a swimming hole on the reservation. They told us only eight or ten families still lived in the village and none of them had children, so when school was out, they could only play with each other. Some tribal members returned to their village homes on celebration days, but even this was waning.

"We can take you to visit our grandfather Stanley," the little boy said after we had viewed most of the village. "He is the Oraibi chief and one of the oldest Hopi."

"That'd be great." I replied, delighted to have "stumbled" across a tribal chief. I knew from my readings that Oraibi had a long and complex history. It was often attacked by the Navajos, their larger and more aggressive neighbors who now greatly outnumber and surround the Hopi. Also, inter-tribal conflict had played itself out almost a century earlier. At that time, Oraibi had 700 inhabitants. (At its height it had over 1200 members but its population had been reduced by foreign diseases and tribal dissention.)

Before 1906, the United States government and the missionaries were attempting to destroy the traditional life of the Hopi. Before this time, the villagers - the Oraibis - always looked to themselves as the center of ceremonial life of the Hopi; however, soon the inherent tension created by the invading white culture began to undermine the ancient village. For years, there had been inner-tribal and inner-clan fighting between the "Hostiles," those that wanted to hold on to the ancient tribal life and were *hostile* to the bahanna's ways ("bahanna" or "pahanna" is the Hopi word for white people) and the "Friendlies," those that were *friendly* to the whites and eager to embrace the culture's conveniences, money, religion and values. (Similar dramas between embracing the new culture and upholding the ancient ways, had played out in every other Native American tribe and continue to do so to this day.)

Many Friendlies, mostly of the Bear Clan, felt that the bahannas, like other adopted clans, should be welcomed in because of the value of their knowledge, such as glass, guns and the windmills used to bring precious water from below the ground. Though they wanted to keep their ancient customs, religion and way of life, they also felt that the children needed to learn to read and write the white man's language to be able to success-fully negotiate with them.

The Hostiles, mostly of the Fire Clan, were lead by the indomitable Yukioma, who warned the tribe that adopting the white man's lifestyle and values would lead to the eventual destruction of the tribe; however, by then the seductive allure of the bahanna ways had captured the hearts and minds of many of the Hopi. Also, the United States government began to survey and reallocate tribal land and fields, disregarding ancient clan claims. This too created friction among the people. Soon the Hostiles and the Friendlies began to have separate kiva rituals, making them incomplete and impossible to be properly performed with a "good heart." The sacred hoop of the nation was weakening.

However, in many ways both sides were seeking to keep to their instructions. As John D. Loftin writes in his book, *Religion and Hopi Life,*

"Under pressure from the whites to become Christianized and Westernized, Hopi found keeping good thoughts a problem, and thus they began to worry about the possibility of drought . . . To resist the influence of a dominant society in itself evoked many bad thoughts that the Hopi felt might spoil the ceremonies . . . The friendlies felt they could preserve 'good hearts' only if they cooperated with the powerful whites by sending their children to school. The hostiles felt that 'good hearts' could not be maintained if many basic Hopi traditions were lost . . ."

As reinforcements to their positions, for several years the Friendlies encouraged clan members from Moencopi, a village fifty miles away, to move to Oraibi. The Hostiles encouraged their clan members from the nearby village of Shongopavi to move there. Tensions, with occasional fighting, increased. Finally, things came to a head. On September 8, 1906, the Friendlies, lead by their chief Tawakwaptewa, tried to forcibly remove the Shongopavi Hostiles from the village. Wanting to avoid bloodshed, the two groups decided to have a shoving match with the losers agreeing to leave the village permanently. What was even more important in this conflict was that unlike past inner-tribal conflicts of this intensity, this one was settled without violence - a huge step forward spiritually for the tribe.

The Hostiles lost (as prophesized) and left the village with nothing more than the clothes on their backs. They went about six miles further north on Third Mesa and established Hotevilla near a local spring. Families and clans were permanently split apart and main religious societies were shattered. Hotevilla then became one of the last lines of defense of the traditionalists. In a short time, they had built their stone houses, allocated farm lands, built the sacred kivas and the ancient Pattern of Life resumed.

After the Hostiles departed, Tawaquaptewa, the Friendlies' chief, said, "We can't live in the old ways any more. Now we must look to the white man's ways. Our rituals are gone, our clan system is gone. The clan land-holdings are finished." To symbolize this end, he displayed the secreted Soyalongw altar publicly in his home in the last years of his life. (However, he also felt that after a certain period, the full Oraibi Ceremonial Cycle might be revived.) Both sides were aware that the division of Oraibi and the cessation of the Oraibi Ceremonial Cycle were part of their prophecy.

To these defiant and proud traditionalists in Hotevilla, their new home was to be more than a village. It was to be a special holy place for "maintaining the balance and harmony with all life." They believed Hotevilla to be a true "microcosm of the world." How things went in Hotevilla reflected how things were progressing on the planet. However, despite their hopes for a unified group of traditionalists, a few years later even this group split up with many of the traditional leaders establishing yet another new village, Bakavi, across the road.

The Hostiles of the Fire Clan also took from Oraibi a sacred tablet, the Pathway Stone, and buried it in Hotevilla with a missing piece that prophecy said would one day be returned by "Our White Brother" - a bahanna that would one day come to complete their spiritual understanding. He would bring "friendship, harmony and good fortune to our people. When the time comes, he will appear. Let us watch for him." The traditionalists believed that if this tablet was harmed or destroyed, it would be the end of the village and can even bring "great misfortune which can extend to the whole of mankind." For this reason, in modern times they warned the Hopi Tribal Council not to bring in the underground utilities. (This tablet was disturbed when utilities were put in Hotevilla in 1996.) They also believed that it was the moving of this sacred object from Oraibi that resulted in Oraibi becoming only a ghost of its former self, while Hotevilla has thrived.

Julia and I walked with the children through the village towards the highway, about two hundred yards away. As we walked, the little girl pointed out an area where the shoving match line was cut into the surface stone. Next to it, also roughly cut into the stone, was this inscription of Yukioma's words: "Well it have to be done this way now that when you pass me over this LINE it will be DONE. Sept. 8, 1906."

"That's where my grandfather Stanley lives with his nephew Thomas," the young girl said pointing toward a small unpainted frame house with an outhouse in the barren front yard. With the children waiting in the front yard, we approached the house and knocked on the door. Thomas Numkena, a slim bespectacled man in his forties opened the door and after we told him we were there on a spiritual quest, he invited us in.

Thomas is a craftsman, specializing in repairing the famous Hopi kachina dolls. He seemed to be a kind, gentle soul. The house was one large L-shaped room, barren of all decoration, with a kitchen area and a living room. In one corner of the living room was a metal frame bed, with someone sleeping under the covers. The only other furniture was a second bed and an old kitchen table with three chairs. The house was neat but dusty, as is almost everything in this dry, semi-arid land. There was no electricity or plumbing. A small battery-operated radio was blaring a gospel station in the background.

We sat with Thomas and told him a little of our journeys to Jamaica, and now to his village in pursuit of any connection the Hopi might have to One Love.

"Our tribe is known as the 'Peaceful People,' " he said, "but now there are many problems here. My uncle, Stanley Bahnimptewa, is the last chief of Oraibi and he does not plan to appoint a new chief before he dies. He is ninety-two and he says that when he dies, all the secrets will go with him."

"Why is that?" I asked. "These secrets are almost a thousand years old. Shouldn't he pass them on to someone?"

"There is no one now to trust," Thomas continued. "He is in charge of Hopi money that we got from the government but he will not release it to the village. If he did, they would pave the road, bring in utilities and the spirit would die just as it has in other Hopi villages. He is a very powerful man. I have seen amazing, supernatural things happen to him. If he wants, he can split the ground. Many in the tribe are against him. Witches come some nights and throw rocks at the house. Next Tuesday they are forcing him to go to the Indian home for the elderly. He has many enemies and he is sick and blind. He cannot fight them much longer."

At this point Stanley, who was under the blankets, got up, picked up a red and white cane and walked over to turn the radio louder, moving slowly and weakly. In his blindness, he seemed unaware of our presence or perhaps just uninterested. After turning up the radio, he walked outside to the outhouse. When he returned, he sat in a chair and Thomas explained to him who we were.

"Well now, you have come to talk to me but I cannot say everything to you," he said. His voice sounded strong but somewhat confused. "The Tribal Council is not here so what I say is not as much. Many council members do not wish that I speak to outsiders. I do not want to speak to outsiders myself."

We learned that Stanley was Tawaquaptewa, the Friendlies' chief, adopted son. Stanley had lived most of his life in Southern California, where he was sent as a youth to the Riverside Indian School. He returned to Oraibi some years ago to take up his position as chief, claiming it was his father's promise to him. Many tribal members still considered him an outsider because of his long time away. In our talk, he said he knew nothing of reggae music and Bob Marley. He was a man besieged, with defenses now fully up.

"A white man is supposed to come but you are not that man," he said as we rose to leave.

"Here is some sacred cornmeal," Thomas said as we left, placing a small plastic bag of cornmeal in my hand. As Thomas searched for my hand, I realized that his eyesight was also very bad. "When you go to Supai Village, ask the Havasupai to pray for us."

We headed back down into the village with the children, who ran some distance ahead of us. As we passed one of the more modernized houses, a middle-aged woman came out with a stern look on her face.

"Where did those children take you?" she asked with a real attitude in her voice.

"Just on a tour around the village," I said, suspecting her concern that we had talked to Stanley.

"Did they ask you for money?" she barked. "They're not supposed to do that."

"No. They just showed as around," Julia said, as the woman retreated sullenly into her house.

Between the heat and the tense vibes at Oraibi, we both felt physically exhausted and emotionally drained. Powerful forces are at play in Hopiland and it is not always easy for outsiders to be there. Whatever spiritual force had once existed at Oraibi, now seemed totally gone. Only struggle and distrust remained. For over 850 years this village had lived a co-operative, communal peaceful life and now a wave of civilization had crushed it until it was all but dead.

After a few hours rest, we made the half-hour drive over to Keams Canyon to eat at one of the three cafes on the reservation. A few miles before Keams Canyon, we passed a brand new sub-division with modern-looking townhouses and a hospital, all built with tribal funds from the government - an "oasis" of modern suburbia in an otherwise barren landscape. Further down the road we passed the high school, tribal police station and the radio station, all new and modern.

We ate out on the restaurant deck and chatted with the waiter, a twenty-something Hopi man who had just returned to the reservation from Phoenix after a painful divorce. He wasn't particularly happy but he said it felt good to be back home. "I came home in the traditional Hopi way when a man divorces," he said, "with only the clothes I was wearing." (Hopi is a matri-linear society, the children belong to the mother's clan and the husband often moves into his wife's clan home.)

After dinner, we headed back to KUYI (which means water in Hopi) to find Karen. The evening was turning cooler - a break from the intense heat. The sunset was awesome, reminding us that though desolate, this land was also beautiful. Entering the station, we met Burt Poley, the station manager and a big reggae fan. We gave him a copy of *Rasta Heart* and told him what we were doing, which elicited an enthusiastic response from him. After a nice connection he brought us in the back to meet Karen, who was on the air broadcasting under her deejay name, Sister Parrot. (Karen is not Hopi but a Tewa Indian of the Kachina/Parrot Clan).

Karen is a vibrant intelligent woman in her thirties, with classic Native American beauty. Aside from being the local reggae deejay, avid softball player, runner and a wife and a devoted mother of her young daughter, Faye, Karen is a famous potter, whose pots often sell for thousands of dollars and are displayed at the Smithsonian Museum. She is known for using sacred red pigments from the Grand Canyon which she obtains from Havasupai friends. Gathering ancient shards of pottery she has found in nearby ruins, she often uses traditional designs on her pots.

"How did reggae get started out here?" I asked her between songs.

"Burt and I were part of a group called Culture Connection. We

promoted reggae concerts locally but it no longer exists. Everyone grew
up and went different ways but I still do some promotions and host this
show. It's funny that you have been working with Abijah in Jamaica. I just
met him a few days ago at a reggae festival in California, Reggae on the
River. I love him *and* his music."

It was fascinating to watch her play reggae songs, almost all from
Jamaican artists and then deliver news and information in the Hopi
language, a dialect of such richness and complexities that linguists believe
it reflects the high intelligence of its users. She played many reggae artists
including Luciano, Bushman, Morgan Heritage, Culture, Warrior King,
and many more, including of course, Bob Marley. It was all so strange -
a Tewa Indian in the middle of the Arizona desert playing Jamaican
reggae into the star-filled Hopi night. Yet somehow it was oddly familiar.

Not wanting to distract her from her show, we agreed to have lunch
together at the restaurant the next day, July 4. As we drove through the
clear desert night toward the motel, Julia and I started to reflect on the
day.

"You know, after leaving Oraibi I felt really depressed," I said. "It
seemed like the spirit of this tribe was withering, the ceremonies dying
out - at least in Oraibi. But after meeting Karen and Burt, I realized that
through the music, they are still teaching love to the tribe. I'm thinking
we may want to do a healing concert here like we've been doing in
Jamaica."

"We are trodding on the One Love path just like in Jamaica," Julia said
laughing, in complete agreement.

The next day, Julia, Karen and I had lunch at the restaurant in the
motel. We told her about our meeting with Stanley and how he was
being forced into an old-age home.

"That disturbs my heart," Karen said, "because that is exactly what
happened to my grandmother. She lived to be 92. Some of my family put
her in the rest home. I told them not to do that to her because to me you
are just sending her away to die. She took over as our mom after we lost
our parents. I loved her so much - her cooking, her love, her warmth,
her teachings."

"Is the spirit of the tribe still strong here?" I asked.

"With the Hopi and my people I think the strongest area is religion," Karen answered. "Our religion is the way we live. It's your friends. You just live it everyday. Religion, our original religion, is very important. There is always something. My brother is getting ready now for the Home Dance where we send the *kachinas* home to the San Francisco Peaks. You try to live and pass on what you have to the young children. There is always someone constantly in meditation for rain or peace. You have to respect everyone and anyone."

(The *kachinas*, or "katsinam," are Hopi spirit guides or messengers who send prayers for rain, bountiful harvests and a prosperous healthy life for all humanity. They are seen as friends and welcomed guests who bring food and gifts as well as lessons of appropriate behavior and consequences of unacceptable behavior.)

"Is the tribe experiencing the same problems as other tribes with alcoholism?" I asked.

"Alcoholism is a big problem here," she answered. "It's really sad. I have lost relatives that way. My father died of alcoholism and being a daddy's girl, the pain of watching my dad, the big ex-Marine, deteriorate in front of my sister and my two brothers, was a harsh reality. His love and happiness he gave us was all we cared about. And teenage suicide is getting worse. But you just have to believe in yourself and walk away from it."

"Is there a lot of inter-clan fighting?" I asked, wondering at how close they were coming to completing their ancient covenant to be the "Peaceful People."

"No, not really," she answered. "We can't have a lot of fighting because we depend on each other. Your father is from one clan and your mother from another. My father was from the Deer Clan, so all the Deer Clan are my relatives. But then we are all God's children, you know. God doesn't see children in color. The children are our future. I want my daughter to have what I had when I was growing up. It's just a whole world out there. But sometimes there is jealousy. If someone sees someone doing better they will try to pull them down. But usually there are good vibes. When our clan uncles' sons get married, we always go and mock their new wives but just in fun. We say that she is going to be lazy. She can't take care of our nephew but we can. We know how to do the cooking. No one takes offense. It's just in jest."

"That's really wise," I said, "because it defuses any possible jealousy by making light of it. It encourages everybody to kid with each other and be children again."

"Not only that," Karen said, "but it builds that woman's esteem where she thinks, *I'm an in-law now and I can do all that.* So the women have good relationships with each other."

"How are things between the Hopi and the Navajos?" I asked. I had read that since the arrival of the Navajos (or the "Dine Nation," as they refer to themselves) many years after the Hopi settled the area, there had been constant problems mostly with the Navajos grazing on Hopi land and stealing from their gardens. Many Navajos believed that aggressive action was the way to survive. Hopi believed it was through hard work and restrained behavior. In more recent times, the United States government had, in essence, promised areas of the reservation, called "Joint Use Land," to both Navajos and Hopi, resulting in a lawsuit, bitter arguments and painful forced relocations by members of both tribes. Now the Navajo, 170,000 strong with their huge reservation, surround and greatly outnumber the 12,000-member Hopi tribe.

"Relationships have never been better between the tribes here," Karen said, "I am Tewa and my husband is a Navajo."

"How are things between your tribe and the Hopi?" I asked. I had also read that some of the Hopi were asking the Tewas to abandon their ancient village, Tewa, which they had occupied since the 1700s. They had settled there after repeated requests by the Hopi, who were reluctant warriors, that the Tewa move there from their home near the Rio Grande to protect the Hopi from the Utes, Apaches and Paiutes. The Tewas still keep a strong tribal identity, tradition and language. Though all Tewas speak the Hopi language, only a few Hopi can speak the Tewa dialect.

"Things are going pretty well. There is much inter-marriage between the tribes so things are no longer clear-cut. A few think we should just up and leave but most people understand that this is our home too and that they should not do to us what the white culture has done to so many tribes when they forced them off their land."

"Are people moving back or leaving the reservation?" I asked.

"Well, you know, a lot of people leave saying they are going to make it better somewhere but they always come back. It's the culture and the religion that draws them back - the way of life. I went to school in Kansas and even there I knew what ceremonies were going on at home and I missed them. I could smell the stew and pudding."

"How did you start listening to reggae music?" Julia asked. "At the station you said you've been into it for 14 years."

"Well, I grew up on rock music. I was a big Rolling Stones fan. Then when I came back here I started going to some reggae concerts and listening to the words, the message, and I've just never stopped listening. Their message was so strong. I started giving my pottery to the artists as gifts for performing here."

"Is this One Love vibration being held by the Hopi and is that why many are listening to reggae?" I asked.

"Yes. I think this might be so because I'm just thinking of how we were brought up. The only male that was ever allowed to discipline a young girl is your mother's brothers or the male members of your clan. Your father cannot discipline you. He is from another clan. It's always been like that and it was a very good system. You look up to your uncles. They are always there to help you prepare for a dance or something. They are strict. You are not allowed to go to the dances with pants. Dresses are a must. We are ladies. I love them all so much. But you get close with your father and his clan, too. You depend on the women of your father's clan. They are always there to help you."

"The way we were brought up in our day-to-day life with our religion," she continued, "was that our prayers are not just for us individually or as a tribe but for the whole world. And when the men go into their ceremonies, the whole world is on their shoulders. They feel they are here to heal the planet. It's great here, but every year my daughter and I go to Jamaica in November for two weeks. I love it there. We stay in Negril. We just kick back. We go up to Mayfield Falls, lay on the beach - just relax."

"We were thinking that maybe we would come next year and do a concert here, perhaps with Abijah," I said, after telling her the story of our Jamaican journey. "Last night I was reading that part of the prophecies that states the Earth will not purify itself and settle its problems in the closing of the Fourth Cycle until the Hopi tribe purifies itself. The prophecies say that the Hopi must cure the ills of their own bloodlines so that everything will become peaceful naturally, by the will of the Creator. And we all know that One Love is the true purifier, that people must re-instill love and forgiveness in their hearts. Having this gathering here would help the tribe to purify itself. Mostly the youths would come. I've been getting the feeling we may be shifting a lot of our efforts from Jamaica to the United States. After all, who would be better to lead this country into forgiveness than the original people, the Native Americans. You have the moral authority to invite the rest of this country to join you. And having the healing ceremony on your ancient tribal land would be very symbolic."

"That would be great," Karen said enthusiastically, as we got in our car to head to the Havasupai reservation. "I would love to work with you on that. Let's stay in touch."

Chapter 2
The Havasupai

*"Everything that's negative will lead you away from the Creator.
Everything that's positive helps guide you on your path to the Creator."*
—Past Iroquois leader (Tadodaho) Leon Shenandoah

*"If you get down and quarrel everyday, you're saying prayers to the
devil, I say."* **—Bob Marley**

After leaving the Hopi reservation, Julia and I headed to Sedona, Arizona, a three-hour trip across the desert. There we met up with my childhood friend, Harley, and the three of us together planned to visit the Havasupai Reservation the following week. Julia and I were scheduled to speak at The Annual Bob Marley Reggae Festival. We would also set up a small booth to sell our books. These reggae festivals are held around the world every year. Many of these gatherings are held in the United States, mostly in Northern California where sunny weather is predictable and reggae is popular. They are also held throughout Europe, Africa, and South America. Some, like Reggae on the River, draw over ten thousand people for 3 days of camping, reggae music and generally good vibrations.

Sedona is considered the "New Age Capital" of the United States. Long known as a healing center for Native tribes, its "power vortexes" have recently been discovered by the modern-day locals. Psychics, astrologers, healers and channels abound in the area. A popular tour is a desert ride in pink jeeps to the best spiritual vortexes in the area. Recently the town has been "gentrified," complete with expensive homes, restaurants and shops.

None of this diminishes the natural beauty of the area. The small town is set in a wide valley with Oak Creek running through the middle. Surrounding the town on almost all sides are mammoth brilliant rust or yellow-colored canyon walls that dwarf the town. As soon as you enter the area, it becomes quite clear why the Indians knew this to be a power spot.

That night, Julia, Harley and I, went to dinner in Sedona and spent the evening driving up in the hills to overlook the town. The next day, Friday, we drove over to the Sedona Cultural Center where the festival was beginning later that day. Like the town, the Cultural Center is breathtaking. It is an open-air amphitheater with no seats, only terraced 8-foot wide strips of grass looking down onto a stage covered by an immense timber and canvas arched framework, with the huge rock formations silhouetted in the distant background.

We set up our booth and relaxed while watching the crowd stream by, a mixture of college and high school students and a few older hippies. Our booth was like a small reasoning oasis. Some people would stay a few minutes, some a half-hour or longer, joining us in the shade of our canopy. Around dusk, it was our time to speak. Our plan was to have Julia set the vibe by singing one of Abijah's songs, "When There's Peace Again, There Will Be Joy Again," followed by my talking to the crowd for a few minutes. Julia had never sung in front of others and I was very rusty in my public speaking. We were both a little nervous but looking forward to it. Actually I was more than a little nervous. Several times during the day I considered just calling it off, but the enthusiasm of the people coming through the booth kept me encouraged.

With a brief introduction by the emcee, we walked on stage. Neither of us really fit with the other performers who had been in front of the crowd that day, mostly young black or white full-dread reggae artists. Julia, with her long salt and pepper hair hanging naturally, her flowing dress and shawl, fit more than me. I looked like your basic fifty-something, bald-headed tourist on vacation heading for the golf course. I knew we needed to do something to grab the crowds quickly-wandering attention.

After the brief introduction from the emcee, Julia walked up to the mike barefoot, hesitated a few seconds, enough to create a slight tension and interest from the audience, and then, at the top of her lungs, let out with a long, loud, melodious JAHHHHHHHHHHHHH! that went on so long you could barely believe she could do it in one breath. (Jah is the Rastafarians' name for God.) It definitely got everyone's attention. After that, she began to sing - powerfully, beautifully, with all her heart. After a few stanzas, we melded in Abijah on his CD over the loudspeakers - a great transition. The vibes were set.

"Greetings, our brothers and sisters," I said, as I took over the mike. "For the last two years, we have made several journeys to Jamaica to search out the foundation of reggae's message of One Love - the music we have all come here to enjoy. We are here to bring you a message from the elder Rastas of Jamaica. Would you like to hear their message?!"

"YES!" the crowd roared back.

"Their message is simply this: they are asking all of us to claim our position in Creation to teach One Love to the world - as they have been doing for over 70 years. They are asking us to do what God sent us here to do - teach and learn One Love. They are asking us to join them in this. After the oppression they have been through, they have the moral authority to ask us. So claim your position and teach this One Love to everyone you meet. Give thanks."

As I finished, Abijah's "Revelation" played, as the crowd enthusiastically applauded. We both felt elated as we walked back through the crowd to our booth. Several people approached us with thanks and hugs. Others waved or said "thanks" with their eyes; however, as we walked through the crowd, I could also tell many people didn't know quite what to do with us and our message. Others I could sense were looking rather hostile, the message of love falling on a bitter - perhaps broken - heart. Then, there were a few who looked like they had been waiting all their lives to hear that message.

After our address, a woman in her thirties came up and introduced herself as Rebecca Reppert. She was an intense woman with Indian features and long black hair.

"Have you heard of the White Buffalo?" she asked.

"No. I haven't," I answered.

"Indian prophecy says that when the White Buffalo returns to Earth, it will be a time of great change," she said. "There have been many albino buffalos born with pink eyes. But several years ago, a real white buffalo was born. His return marks the beginning of this period of change that you just spoke about in your talk. I wanted to give you a little of his hair and a poem I just wrote after hearing Julia sing and you speak," she said giving me a tuft of white hair and a postcard with a picture of the white buffalo on the front and her poem on the back. It read:

> With One Love they are coming.
> Strong as the buffalo nations.
> Returning to their place on the continent.
> Withstanding great heat, withstanding strong winds,
> Withstanding hunger, they are.
> See them returning in numbers to their former hunting grounds.

> It was prophesied long ago
> the red, the yellow, the brown, and the white races
> would suffer like the buffalo.
> And then, enlightened, see peace as the good road
> for all nations and all beings.

> May it thus be under the sun:
> Enough rain for all.
> Enough food for all.
> Productive work for all.
> And visions of beauty
> stretching to the farthest horizons.

> May these blessings fill the eyes of the elders and the children,
> direct the middle wanderers,
> inspire in us a sense of Creation's higher purpose.

THE LEGEND OF THE WHITE BUFFALO

Perhaps the best known authority on the White Buffalo is Chief Arvol Looking Horse, the 19th Keeper of the Sacred White Buffalo Pipe of the Lakota, Dakota & Nakota Great Sioux Nation. In 1966, when he was 12, Chief Looking Horse was given the sacred pipe, called a C'anupa, by his grandmother, who had seen in a dream that he should be the next keeper. As he grew, his Spiritual Elders instilled the Sioux ancient prophecies in him. Much like the Hopi prophecies, the Sioux prophecies said that we are at a crossroads, indicated by the birth, in 1994, of the foretold White Buffalo, a sign of both warning and of deliverance. Named "Miracle," it was born in Janesville, Wisconsin. Eight more white buffalos have been born since then and are at the Spirit Mountain Ranch in nearby Flagstaff, Arizona.

The Lakota believe that over a thousand years ago they were visited by The White Buffalo Calf Woman - a Holy Woman, sent as an emissary from "Those Above." She gave them the White Buffalo Pipe, to be used as a peace pipe and for its smoke to carry their prayers to the Great Spirit. All Native American pipe ceremonies are based on this legend. During a ten-day period, she declared the laws and ethics upon which the Lakota people founded their society. Among other instructions, including the use of certain herbs and roots for healing, and rules for clean living, she gave them four most important moral commandments, which she shouted in a loud voice: "You shall not kill! You shall not lie! You shall not steal! You shall not commit adultery!"

Also, like Hopi prophecies, the Sioux prophecies noted certain signs. It is said that when hard glaciers become so soft that you can leave a hand print on them, this would be a sign that the Earth was in turmoil. That point has arrived at glaciers all over the planet.

Chief Looking Horse writes in his book, *White Buffalo Teachings*:

We are the watchers. We are the witnesses. We see what has gone before. We see what happens now, at this dangerous moment in human history. We see what's going to happen, what will surely happen unless we come together - we, the Peoples of all Nations - to restore peace, harmony and balance to the Earth, our Mother . . . We face chaos, disaster, and endless tears from our relatives' eyes, or we can unite spiritually in peace and harmony. It's time to bring the Message of the urgent need for Peace, of creating an energy shift throughout the world . . . The fate of future generations rests in *our* hands . . . You *must* decide. You can't avoid it. *Each* of us is put here in this time and this place to *personally* decide the future of humankind.

Chief Looking Horse goes on to explain that at this late hour we are just beginning to realize that there is a "great myth of progress and development." The myth, created by the sellers of technology, is that the more technological advancement, the better; however, it is now clear that technology has created toxic wastes for all and war, poverty and starvation for many.

In tribal times, Indian chiefs and elders planned for the care of their tribes seven generations in the future. Believing that their ancestors also were part of the tribe after their death, they also felt they were aiding tribal members seven generations in the past. Chief Looking Horse explains how it is now harder to pass wisdom to the younger generations. "These times move too fast for us to catch up," he writes in *White Buffalo Teachings*. "Babies are having babies. Today we have seven generations in a single century instead of over two or even three. We become grandfathers and grandmothers when we're not yet out of our thirties. When so many of our people die young, those who remain must become Elders. We go from being children to being elders. There's no in-between, no teaching ground."

The Sioux *Prophesies of the Ancestors* instructed people to honor the Summer Solstice at the Sacred Sites as it "will be the key to healing the destruction we have visited on our ailing Mother Earth." Since 1996, Chief Looking Horse has organized "World Peace and Prayer Day" on June 21, the summer solstice. The event encourages people worldwide to come together at their sacred sites and pray for peace.

Like the Hopi elders, Chief Looking Horse sees that inner work must be also done. As he states in his book, "We must move toward peace within ourselves, and learn to let go of anger, hatred, jealousy and everything that is holding us back from growing spiritually . . . Understand that the whole point of your own existence depends on becoming a Keeper of Mother Earth."

However, it was his last passage in his book that had the greatest impact on me.

We need a great healing.
And we need a Great Forgiving.
But healing can't begin without forgiveness.

We must forgive each other,
Forgive our loved ones,
Forgive our friends
Forgive our enemies,
Forgive ourselves.

We need to pray even for a person
who has done us wrong!
In our Tiospaye, our family,
when two people fight,
they are made brothers or sisters.

Forgiveness itself is a powerful medicine.
We need forgiveness to create Peace!

Mitakuye Oyasin!
(All our relations!)
In the Great Circle of Life.
Where there is no beginning
And no ending!

He-c'e-tu-yelo!

(So be it!)

On Monday, after the festival, Julia, Harley and I left Sedona and drove a hundred and fifty miles to Hualapai Hilltop at the remote southern rim of the Grand Canyon. From the hilltop, you leave your car and begin the eleven mile journey into the Grand Canyon to get to Supai Village, the ancestral home of the Havasupais.

The Havasupai Tribe, due to their extreme remoteness, is different from all other Native American tribes. Presently about 800 tribal members live in the village with a few hundred more living in the mesa above, mostly in Peach Springs. Many Havasupai also live in Hopiland. They consider the Hopi their "cousin" tribe. By the Creator's design, Cataract Canyon, the home of Supai Village and the Havasupai, is not only one of the most beautiful places in the country, it is also the most remote. It is the *only* town in the continental United States that you cannot drive to by car. In fact, you cannot even drive close to it. Until recently, you had to either walk five hours or three by horseback. In the seventies, helicopter service was begun several days a week. The helicopter trip takes about ten minutes. It is the only place in the country where the mail is still delivered by mule. Havasupais allow only a limited number of people to come to the village at any time. Once there, you can camp at the campground or stay in the small lodge. You've got to *really* want to go there and this keeps the casual tourists at bay.

Until recently, its remoteness kept it almost totally isolated from the society swirling above. We later talked to older tribal members who grew up in the village when there was almost no money in their world. Money came in the 1970s when electricity, plumbing, television and helicopters arrived. Before then, they hunted, fished, gathered and grew their own food and bartered for a few staples at the little trading post in Seligman, a two-day journey by horse and foot.

"Everything was free! There was trade," one man told us with joy in his eyes. Then with melancholy, he went on to say, "The elders told us not to change. They taught us everything we needed to know. We should have listened."

Now, with the helicopter service, modern utilities and satellite TV, the sense of remoteness of the village has been greatly affected; but, it is still very much removed from the intensity and vibrations of modern America. Even with modern utilities, it is a world apart - separate and isolated from the rest of the country, from the rest of the world.

The people that live there are Americans by law but Havasupai in reality. Their pace of life, their manner of relating to others, both tribal members and outsiders, and their worldview, is far different from their surrounding society. Even their language, which was only written in recent times, is different. They are the only Native American tribe in which *every* member still speaks the ancient tribal language. English is used only when speaking to tourists or government officials. Their physical environment, a small remote Indian village surrounded by the majestic walls of the Grand Canyon and home to four magnificent waterfalls, leaves an indelible imprint on all tribal members, as it does to a much lesser degree on all visitors. It is a truly magical, mystical place.

We hoped our visit there would unravel the mystery of why this ancient and isolated tribe of Native American Indians were Bob Marley and reggae fans. We had heard that in the 1970s someone in the tribe had brought Bob's music there to uplift the vibes in the village. Soon after, tribal members got battery-operated tape decks (there was no electricity in the village then) and started listening to his tapes. In a short time, Bob's music became the tribal drumbeat of many.

Bob had planned to visit the tribe but died before he could make it there. A year later, in 1982, Bob's mother, Cedella Booker, or Mama B as she is called, honored Bob's wishes by visiting the village, along with Tyrone Downey, a member of Bob's band. In front of Havasu Falls, their sacred waterfall, many of the tribe gathered as Mama B sang her son's songs. Many remember her visit as the highest moment in recent tribal history.

We arrived at Hualapai Hilltop around eight in the morning and it was already heading toward 100 degrees, with a forecast of a record-breaking 115. We had been warned to begin the trek before sunrise, but in our stupidity, Julia, Harley and I figured, *Hey, it's downhill and then flat. Let's sleep late. How tough can it be?* We sent our backpacks ahead by horse train - the best twenty dollars we spent on the entire trip.

We headed out with hats, sunscreen, and a few containers of water. The trail is eleven miles to the village and two more to the campground. The first couple of miles are sharp switchbacks going down a steep grade to the canyon floor 3000 feet below. Then it's nine miles through dry creek beds and red rock canyons to Supai Village in Cataract Canyon. There is no water until you get right outside the village, so you have to carry your own. Once you reach the village and campgrounds, there are four sacred waterfalls: Havasu, Mooney, Navajo and Beaver. These falls are not created by the Colorado River, which is six miles further down hill at the bottom of the Grand Canyon, but rather by Cataract Creek - its source a gushing spring, secret and sacred to the Havasupai.

We started on the steep switch-backed trail, spreading out so that we could descend in the privacy of our own thoughts. Though it was hot, the descent was easy. The trail is four or five feet wide and with no dangerous drop offs. Every twenty or thirty minutes you have to move over to allow a train of horses or mules to go by, carrying passengers and goods in or out of the village. The view as you descend is awesome, with the canyon over a mile wide at that point. You truly have the experience you are descending into the "Heart of Mother Earth," as the Havasupai call the Grand Canyon. As you go down, all concept of self seems to weaken. You are descending into a three billion-year old canyon that once was under an ocean and before that was a mountain range higher than the Himalayas.

About half way down, we passed a young couple coming up whom we had met a few days earlier at the Sedona festival. We chatted and as we parted he yelled over his shoulder, "It's amazing down there. It will change your life." *I'm always ready for that,* I thought.

By the time we hit the canyon floor, the beginning of the flat walk to the village, it was almost eleven, and the temperature had risen to its peak of 115 degrees. The trail now changed into dry riverbeds, around 50 to 100 feet across lined on either side with walls of the same height.

There was no shade anywhere - zippo, nada, none. Along the way, there are signs that say, "Caution! Beware of Flash Floods," which are unnerving because if a flash flood were to occur, you would be trapped in the riverbed by the walls. So what could you do?

Happily thinking we could cover the remaining distance in two hours, three max, we trudged along. However, the loose sand made for a much slower and exhausting travel than we had expected. After an hour, we were cooked! This was no trail. This was a furnace! A veritable oven! A walking rotisserie!

I am very heat-sensitive and hate getting hot. Julia and I have thermostat wars every winter. I am known for wearing sweatpants and a short sleeve shirt when everyone is bundled up. I love cool, even cold weather. Hot weather is just not my thing and now it's hotter here than any place I have ever been in my life. I mean this is not normal heat. This is grueling, baking, frying, miserable, draining, inhumane, unbelievable, "what-the-hell-are-we-doing-here" heat. I expected any minute to come across a bleached skeleton like in a bad western movie.

After two hours, I was asking God why we were assigned to work in two of the hottest places in the Northern Hemisphere - Jamaica and the Grand Canyon. If only we had taken the ten-minute helicopter ride! Or even the three-hour horseback trip! Or even if we had started at dawn like everybody said. But nooo! We've got to walk down like idiots in the middle of one of the hottest days of the year through the middle of the Grand Canyon! What the hell were we thinking? This is insane! No, it's past insane. It's dangerous! I feel like I'm borderline heatstroke.

Three hours in, I came upon Julia and Harl resting in one of the few shaded spots along the way. They were almost as uncomfortable as I was but not quite, given their slimmer, better-conditioned bodies. We were all in a daze - barely able to continue. We tried to estimate how far we were from the village.

"Well, we've been out almost three hours and back home Julia and I can easily walk three miles an hour so we must have walked nine miles, so the village must be right around one of the next bends," I said confidently.

Just then, a hiker came by heading out.

"How far to the village?" Julia asked.

"You're about half way," he said, without stopping. My jaw dropped. I looked at Julia and Harl, blinking, holding back tears. They looked the same.

"Let's kill him," I growled as he disappeared around the bend.

As we walked further, I wondered why anyone would choose to live in this desolate wasteland for hundreds of years. Not only why, but how? I knew the land looked like this for thousands of square miles in this area and that, except for the Havasupai, the Grand Canyon is uninhabited and uninhabitable. After another two and a half hours, near delirium and convinced I would soon die of sunstroke, we heard it. Water! A stream! Here in the middle of the desert. As we searched through some bushes, there it was! A beautiful turquoise blue two-foot deep, six-foot wide creek. Except for the first time I saw my wife and daughters, nothing has looked so good to me in my entire life.

Throwing our shoes off as quick as we could, we all jumped in, clothes and all. It was cold - delightfully, wonderfully, intoxicatingly cold! We were cold! - right here in the middle of the broiling desert at high noon in the middle of summer. Who could have believed it? We were now cold! Not cool but cold! One minute we were on fire, sweltering, and the next we were freezing - and loving it. We had made it! We knew that the village was now - finally! - right around the bend.

As we approached the village, the landscape changed dramatically. Trees, mostly willows and cottonwoods, and greenery started to appear everywhere. All of a sudden we were in Shangri-La, Arizona-style. We passed small frame houses with gardens full of corn and beans and shade trees dripping with peaches, plums and apricots. The canyon walls surrounding the village are hundreds of feet high, enclosing the tribe like huge protective sheltering arms.

The village center, where large shade trees offered some respite from the heat, includes the small tourist office, the tribal council building, the cafe, the lodge, the small grocery store, the post office, a modern-looking elementary school, a health clinic, and a church made from a metal Quonset hut. In addition, there are many small frame houses spread throughout the village, most with power and water, but many looking like they needed some repair. The streets are loose sand and the village has a rather roots feel to it. Now there is even Internet in the village, shortening the distance to the rest of the world.

There is a large open grass field next to the cafe where the helicopter lands. We were also passed by a tractor pulling a trailer with benches shaded by a canopy that could hold a few people. This, we learned, is the village bus system that is used for transportation by those too old or sick to walk to the store, post office or neighbors. The only other means of transportation in the canyon are a few golf carts and tractors and many horses, which is the main method.

We stopped at the tourist office to check in with Billie Jack, the tourist director whom I had talked with months earlier when I inquired whether his tribe did indeed still listen to Bob Marley. He assured me that most of the tribe were Marley fans, though some of the youths had started to also listen to hip-hop. I had sent him out 10 copies of *Rasta Heart* earlier in the spring and told him we were coming to investigate the link between the Havasupai and Marley. As we entered the office (air-conditioned!!!), I was pleased and surprised to see a copy on his desk.

As we wandered around the village center (tourists are not allowed in the "residential areas"), we quickly noticed the influence of Bob Marley was everywhere. Several tribal members were wearing Bob Marley tee-shirts and Bob's music was playing in the background at the cafe and the store. Almost everyone we talked to (most Havasupai would prefer to avoid the tourists coming through), no matter what age, was a big fan and would quickly tell us their favorite Marley songs. Many said they had been listening to his music since they were little children. There were even two youths named Denroy, after Denroy Morgan, the father of the reggae group Morgan Heritage.

After cooling down at the cafe, we started the two-mile, one-hour trek down to the campground. It was mostly downhill but at 115 degrees even that was a vision-quest. Finally, right before the campground, we came to Havasu Falls. These falls are considered one of the most outstanding in the world and rightfully so. Two massive streams of cobalt-blue, ice-cold water pours off these hundred-foot high falls, into a natural pool, almost the size of a football field, which overflows into a pristine string of travertine pools, perfect for quiet relaxation. We jumped right in, joining the other campers already at play. It was like the Garden of Eden in the otherwise inferno-like environment. Without it, I don't think we, or many of the other campers, could have lasted more than a few days.

Now revived, we walked a few hundred yards downstream to the campground, which stretches for a half-mile or so along the creek. Every campsite has its own private cold plunge. There were a hundred or so others campers stretched along the creek, mostly teenagers from church groups or scouts. A few longhaired college students completed the gathering. We chose a spot far downstream for privacy and the fact that it not only had a three-foot deep swimming hole but also an eight-foot diameter dammed-up natural whirlpool.

The canyon in this area is very high and very narrow, giving you only a sliver of the sky to observe. If a flashflood comes down, everyone in the campground can drown. Heavy rains miles away can dump water into the canyon and cause severe flooding. The tribe is warned in advance by the local weather service of any possible flooding and then quickly they ride their horses down to the campground to herd everyone up to the only high area where everyone must camp in very close quarters. Often this is done in the middle of the night and people must hurriedly pack up everything in the dark and reset up their camp.

After setting up our tents and making dinner, we explored the area and as soon as the night came and the temperature dropped to a still uncomfortable nineties, we all crawled *on top* of our sleeping bags exhausted. Our comfort was short-lived. Around two in the morning the wind shifted and started blowing upstream. As the wind passed over the sun-baked canyon walls it got superheated and immediately the temperature shot up 10 or 15 degrees. Within minutes all three of us were wide awake, soaking in the creek trying to cool down.

The next day we made a few inquiries in the village as to how Bob Marley's music was first introduced into the tribe. Many people said several people had brought it there in the 1970s, including Supai Waters, a tribal member now in his forties. When we asked how to find him many replied, "No one really knows where he lives. He doesn't have a house. He lives off the land. But he knows you are here and he will find you *if* he wants to." We did learn that in addition to being one of the people who introduced Bob's music, Supai Waters was the last tribal "Keeper of the Secrets." His grandfather, who raised him, was the last Havasupai medicine man and before he died, he passed the tribal secrets on to him. (Native American grandparents often raise their grandchildren. Their ancient knowledge and wisdom passes on not so much from parent to child but from grandparent to grandchild. That is why before their Sacred Hoop was broken, Native Americans always honored their elders and look forward to one day being an elder themselves. In "time long ago," old age was welcomed, not feared.)

After waiting several days for Supai Waters to find us, I was ready to give up and head out. The canyon was beautiful but just too hot. Finally, at dawn on the fourth day, he showed up at our camp spot. Supai Waters is an impressive person - about forty and a little over five feet tall and solidly built, with long jet black hair pulled into a dreadlock. His features are classic Indian, with a round intelligent face, animated and expressive. He moves gracefully and yet quickly with determination. You can tell he is wary until he has sized you up and decided whether you are worth his time or not. He seems very stoic and serious but his smile and laugh quickly creates a very human connection. We liked him immediately.

"I knew you were here and that I would find you," Supai Waters said. "I read your book and I know that we have work to do together."

"Yes. We felt that too," Julia said. "In fact, the nephew of the Oraibi Chief Stanley has given us some cornmeal and asked us to say a prayer for him and his uncle while we are here. But we wanted to wait until you were with us to do that."

"I know Chief Stanley and we can say a prayer together. Let's go down by the creek."

The three of us walked over to the creek. Supai Waters knelt and began saying a prayer in his native tongue and then in English. He held the cornmeal in his cupped hands, pressing them against his forehead, then his mouth, then his heart before throwing them in the creek. He and the prayer seemed ancient - sacred.

Supai Waters told us he heard Bob's music twenty five years ago and knew that it would help the spirit of the tribe. At that time, he was thirteen and going to high school in Mesa, Arizona.

"I see that you only have an elementary school here. What happens after eighth grade? Do the children have to leave?" I asked.

"Since the government has taken over, they have to go. It's the law. You have to go to high school in Phoenix or Mesa and live in a foster home. Or go to Oklahoma or California to an Indian boarding school. But most escape and come back within a year. They can't deal with the prejudice, the traffic, the frantic pace. If you don't send your child to school, social services can take them unless you home school and the families can't afford to do that. The correspondence courses are costly. I went to school in Mesa when I was eleven. The government will pay for the kids to go away, but they won't give the parents money to home school so they can stay here. Even if we had the correspondence courses, they have to be approved. The tribal government is still trying to destroy our tribal ways. The government that we have, the Tribal Council, is not Native Americans. Now it's all BIA-handpicked, by the government. The other reservations have their own self-determined government but here our government is all Anglo-influenced. We want to remove that and put in special people to guard and protect us. We want to vote in the right people. Now the decisions are made in closed meetings - not by the people."

"There are many resources around here they want, like high grade uranium. There are 99 claims. The government wants this - by the bible, the bullet or the ballot. Most of the people here do not understand what is going on. But I have been out in front of things - like the Global Peace March, indigenous forums, standoffs - to bring these things to the front. The government and business interests now know that this area of the country, the Four Corners, is one of the last untapped area of great resources - gold, uranium, coal, water. More than half the country's uranium and much of its petroleum and coal lie under Indian lands. The energy companies want our land. They will try to remove us - all the tribes in this area - to get it. The BIA will not help us. They are supposed to work for the native interests but they never have. They started as part of the War Department and it's been that way ever since - the BIA making war on the Indian. They are supervised by the Bureau of Land Management, the BLM, which is controlled by the energy interests."

"Is most of the tribe aware of this?" I asked.

"Here many are illiterate. We can read and write in our own language but not in English. That's how they control us. The government hired people from off the street and they committed crimes here and gave us bad press. The teachers were not certified. The children didn't get along with them. I want to change that. We need that love coming in here to sustain our survival."

"Maybe we can help in that area," I said. "Perhaps we can organize a One Love Concert here like we are doing in Jamaica. We thought about doing one in Hopiland."

"That is why you were sent," Supai Waters said. "It is written on the canyon walls."

"Written on the walls?" I asked.

"Yes. In petroglyphs that my grandfather showed me. It said that a man and woman would come from outside to help the tribe in time of need."

"We heard that your grandfather passed on the tribal secrets to you. Did he tell you anything about what might happen in the future?" I asked.

"We can disclose that at a different time, by the river. It is a sacrament," he answered.

Later that day, Supai Waters took us to meet Fidel, who is a tribal dancer with the Guardians of the Grand Canyon, the tribe's traditional dance group. As we talked, Fidel showed us pictures of the tribal dancers performing at various festivals both in the village and on the outside. Their costumes were magnificent, with brilliant colors, feathers and huge curved ram horns on their headdresses.

"Those headdresses are incredible," I said. "Were those from mountain sheep around here?"

"Yes," Fidel answered. "We only kill the sheep for food and then we use the horns for our ceremonies. Many years ago, white hunters came in and started to kill our mountain sheep for sport. They were killing many sheep. We did a ceremonial dance asking that this be stopped. Soon after that, the hunters couldn't find the sheep anymore so they stopped coming."

"Do you know all the ancient Havasupai dances?" Julia asked.

"No. I know many of the dances but some are now lost forever and that worries me and makes me sad," Fidel said. "Some died with our parents and grandparents before they could teach them to me. It was a time when the government was trying to stop the tribal dancing. Now I teach what I know to the children."

"Maybe this is the way it was supposed to be," Julia said. "Perhaps now you and Supai Waters and others will create new dances - dances that awaken the memory and the presence of the ancestors. Then people will remember with gratitude that the songs that they thought were lost will return."

"The loss of only some of the old dances will help people remember how the light almost died before it was rekindled," I said.

"The ancient wisdom is within everyone," Supai Waters said. "We will remember it when we most need it. It will emerge."

"That is a good way to look at it," Fidel said thoughtfully.

"Here is some hair from the white buffalo," I said to Supai Waters as we left Fidel. "We got it in Sedona from a woman there who told us about the legend. Her name was Rebecca."

"Thanks. I know her," he said. "It is good that you have given me this. It is a sign."

"A sign of what?" I asked.

"From the writings on the rocks," Supai Waters said. "Now is the time for our voices to be heard. Many leaders want to silence righteous voices - true voice, freedom voice, love voice, naturality, JAH himself, Earth voice, stars voice, creation voice, solidarity voice. That has been taken away but love is pulling us together like birds of a feather. We live by customs. You people are the right people, the right source. In the *Book of Books* we have a chapter to put back in and to tell the people. Like Bob Marley loved creation. I've been here with you people and I honor it because it is something very important here."

"Your connection with us?" I asked.

"Connection with you, connection with island people pon Jamaica," he said, surprising us by suddenly breaking into a melodious patois accent like a true native Jamaican. "Now dey take away de prophet, like de Calvary came and took away our leaders. Now we don't fight dem for freedom. Like de Rastas. Everyt'ing is taken away from mankind because mankind is short of glory, short in dere faith. De same as wit' de Indian people 'ere in America. Dey come an' take gold away from we. Dos rights, dat significance, has been taken away from de Grand Canyon. Dey try to destroy us here, slowly but quietly. But dere is a way. Dat door is Bob Marley - his voice, his message dat we relate to. Him say, 'dis is de door dat close becuz it cayn't take much more.' But him say anot'er door is open - reality is open. Through love, you must fight for freedom. Salvation is free. So we are 'ere today to put dis toget'er. Yes. I am honored to be a part of your work."

"And we are honored to be a part of your work," Julia said warmly, touched by his feelings.

"It is special to de source - to de Fat'er, de angels, to Abram, to Isaac, Jacob, Isaiah, all de prophets. An' from dat birth of a legend, I took Rasta way of life from de birth of a legend. To save my people, to save your people and to save all people."

"You became Rasta to serve that purpose?" I asked.

"Yes. To get love toget'er wit'out shedding another drop of blood," he replied. "My grandfat'er said in de old days our people could fly. Dey 'ad magic powers. One *kachina*, a Hopi medicine man, 'ad powers dat were so strong, 'e was banished from 'is village. He 'ad to live up in de peaks near Flagstaff. No one could get to 'im. De negative forces wanted to destroy 'im. He could grow apricots and corn in de middle of winter. My people rescued dis *kachina*. Dere is a peach tree here dat is from dis *kachina*. He taught us his way. It was an honor to be raised with my grandparents. They are in direct lineage to the original people of the Grand Canyon. They had the sacred red paint for our pottery."

"The same red clay Karen Abieta uses in her pottery?" I asked

"Yes." he said, lapsing back into perfect English. "This was a very beautiful canyon. The people had powers much greater than human concepts, so we had the exodus from certain canyons. The people developed to such a high state that they had to flee - the emergence."

"Why did they have to leave?" Julia asked.

"So that this power would not fall into the wrong hands. There was this one tribe that caused all the turmoil. No one knew where they came from. There are still more instructions embedded in the riverbed in pictographs important to us. That banishment stopped us from reading them. The head chief gave them oral traditions. My people are caretakers of the bowels of creation."

"How many people in your tribe now know this?" I asked.

"No one. Before they dispersed, the whole tribe knew it. I am the keeper of it. The people here give me that respect because of my grandparents. They don't question me but they know that there is something that is special. I don't disclose it but I emphasize it."

"What do you mean by that?" Julia asked.

"I sing about it, by teaching love. This is the love that is needed here so we can claim our moral rights. They can't hate us forever. We are the people of tomorrow. JAH give us talent. JAH give us gifts so we can live together in unity, not separation. When Bob's mother was here there was a different vibe. Babylon couldn't touch us. Before she arrived it was something - lightning flashed, floods, water pouring over the canyon walls. Then the helicopter came and people were out there joyous. Many Indian people pouring in the canyon all that day, all during the week. A lot of people were at the falls. They were all over. Now we are just blowing on the ember. The fire will come. I want to get this initiative through where I can go read the instructions, even those on private land."

"What instructions?" I asked. "The ones in the riverbeds?"

"Yes. The instructions for the natural course. I want to save a few of my people so we can capture our traditions and get some recognition. Now it is madness. I want to sing the natural course songs. Our mode of existence is still threatened because the United Nations is chartering new laws to overturn significant Native rights. They are abolishing our way of life, our dances, our beliefs, our songs. They are finding ways to get rid of our significance. If we don't maintain that significance, they're going to get at us and control everything. For more than 200 years the government did not provide education. People here have to understand that there's help around the corner."

"In what form?" I asked.

"Musically. And with dance. Now the government has stopped us from doing our dances. Doing it with the Hopi is good. We regard the Hopi as the sky people, the blue jay people, medicine people. They are the people that hold power to the sun, the moon, the stars. Those are those people. They are cloud clans, lightening clans, snow clans. We regard them highly, with much respect."

"How do they regard you?" Julia asked.

"As warriors, the arrow makers, the bow makers, all the warrior societies, the Guardians of the Canyon, the red paint and other relics that are there. Others didn't fit. They found my people and chose them and initiated us for that. They called us the 'goninas.' When the world started we were created to guard this canyon. The goninas are the guardians of the Grand Canyon. I'm from that clan. It is called Watahomigie, my clan. We're aiding this prophecy from the White Buffalo Calf to bring this love energy, this unification, this understanding from all races. That's part of the story that's written everywhere now in these prophecies."

"That and what's happening now - here, now with us three," Supai Waters continued. "I knew you were coming. It is written in the petrogylphs that my grandfather showed me in the dry riverbeds. I read in the petroglyphs that there would be visitors here, in this village. You are those people that I read about some time ago. You gave me the White Buffalo Calf hair from the woman. It is part of this prophecy that the visitors would do that - would bring the hair of the sacred white buffalo. You are here now. Your project is part of the fire that we are going to build and make it more. I really can't tell you much about this story but you are here. So I will give you some blue corn. This blue corn grows in the winter. So when the hard times come maybe you can grow a few next year and save a bunch. The blue corn is the one that is supposed to save the Indian people from this catastrophe that is about to happen. I will give it to you so that your grandchildren and their grandchildren will have this blue corn to survive. It's coming."

Supai Waters reached in a leather pouch and pulled out several kernels of dark blue corn and placed them gently in Julia's hand.

"We here heard that cry, that cry in the wilderness. Not just for one color, but for the children," Supai Waters said looking in her eyes.

"So you want to help your people with a safe haven if things get crazy up top?" I asked.

"Yeah. I'm doing that in my mind, in nature's course. It's love, full-ness. To me, love is the air, the water, the grass. Because when I sing to the Earth, it responds in a way I can understand. I feel the mothering power coming from the earth. Water is love. JAH is love. To me, love is natural. I want to build this love in the children, not the people of today, but the children so that they can find a way to Zion - in their minds, in reality. They can learn from our contribution."

"Our path seems to be heading more in this direction, working in our country as we did in Jamaica," I said. "We were thinking of doing a talk at the cafe Sunday night about what we think the connection might be between the Havasupai and Bob Marley and reggae. Maybe we can play some other conscious reggae artists like Luciano, Abijah and Morgan Heritage. We brought their CDs."

"There is a tribal meeting tomorrow, Saturday, at the Tribal Center and you can ask permission there. I will go with you."

By now it was starting to heat up so we all decided to head up to the cafe for breakfast and a cold drink (or two or three).

"Did you used to swim in Havasu Falls as a child?" I asked.

"No. The children were not allowed there. These waterfalls are sacred. They are for the *kachinas*, the Buffalo *kachinas*, the dancers. All the water-falls were sacred. The children could not go there but now with the tourists it's like a national park. We had swimming holes near the village. All this water gushes out of the ground about three miles from the village. It is like a geyser. It is a sacred spot. At night you can hear it, like it's breathing. People entered the planet in a nearby canyon at a time when large birds could eat people, when there were dinosaurs."

The next day, Saturday, we walked up to the village in mid-morning to talk with the tribal council. The meeting was supposed to be in the modern, air-conditioned tribal building but no one had the key, so the council met in the covered exterior walkway. Even with the shade it was easily over 100 degrees. Though we were not to address the council until late in the meeting, Supai Waters said we were welcome.

Privacy from outsiders was really not an issue anyway since the entire meeting was in the Havasupai language, except for a few English phrases like "BIA," "social services," "accountants," etc. Agnes, the tribal leader who did almost all the talking, led the seven-person council, mostly made up of women, with another 15 or so people sitting observing. The meeting seemed to mostly be about administrative business and the lack of funding for programs. Another issue was the need to hire a Hopi accountant since no Havasupai was trained in accounting. After a couple of hours, Supai Waters spoke and Julia and I asked permission to have a talk on the cafe deck. We gave them plenty of room to say "no," saying we would understand if they refused. This gave them more room to say "yes," which they did.

After the meeting we put up a few announcement signs around the store, cafe and post office. We knew with such short notice the gathering would be small. The next day, we walked with Harley from our campsite up to the cafe for a goodbye meal. He was leaving a day before us so he could spend a day in Sedona before heading back east. We walked him to the helicopter and hugged him goodbye. As always it had been great being with him, one of my main ties to my childhood - my past reality. Having watched a two-inch scorpion almost crawl in my sleeping bag the night before, Julia and I decided to spend our last night in the lodge and we wandered over and checked in. Air conditioning! I was in heaven.

Later that day, an hour before our presentation, ominous black clouds appeared over the canyon walls and the winds picked up heavily. Within 15 minutes, we were in a full-blown sandstorm, driving everyone inside. Soon the power went out leaving us without air-conditioning. I was glad we had a motel room for shelter. If the rains came, everyone in the campground would need to move to higher ground (which they later had to do after dark). It looked like our presentation would have to be canceled. As Julia and I looked out our motel window to watch the storm, a beautiful Native American woman came galloping by on her horse, her face determined, her hair almost straight back in the wind - a timeless vision.

A few minutes before our 7 o'clock meeting, the winds let up somewhat, the power came back on and we decided to head over to the cafe, though we knew the continuing winds and threat of rain would keep most people away. By a quarter after seven, there were 17 of us, a few other adult tribal members, six children around ten or twelve years old, and a couple from Denmark who were camping.

For an hour, as the wind quieted into a welcomed, cooling breeze, we talked about our journey through Jamaica and the connection between the Havasupai and Bob Marley, punctuated by playing Luciano, Abijah and Morgan Heritage. It was a small crowd but everyone enjoyed themselves, especially the kids, who loved the music and danced around.

After the talk, Julia, Supai Waters and I, walked back to the lodge room where we continued our reasoning.

"There are forces here that do not want your message to get out," he said as we walked over. "They brought the winds. They cannot stop it. It is the Father's work that we do."

The next day we left. We chose the ten-minute helicopter ride as opposed to the six-hour uphill hike.

"Things have changed since we brought the golden calves into the village," Supai Waters said as we walked toward the chopper.

"The golden calves?" I asked.

"Yeah. The computers and the TVs," he answered, laughing. "The youths watch MTV and they want to be like everyone up top."

"We understand the problem," I said. "The Rastas in Jamaica said the youths have been going astray since the satellite TV and videos showed them things they never knew existed."

"The vibes in the village since you two came have not been so good since Mama B was here almost exactly 20 years ago," he said as we walked towards the helicopter, looking Julia deeply in the eyes. "When you see the bald and the spotted eagles, tell them to send prayers to my tribe. Respect and love, my bredren and sistren."

He then turned and headed toward the village with no further explanation. *A very Indian thing to say*, I thought. *I'll watch the sky.*

The helicopter ride up was incredible - like a live Imax film on steroids. The view from the air of the reservation and surrounding areas was breathtaking. In ten minutes, we were at the Hilltop - which moments earlier had seemed a world, and a six-hour brutal hike, away. Now we were back in our familiar car with the magic of Cataract Canyon receding as we headed east toward our North Carolina home - and our rendezvous with the two eagles.

HAVASU 'BAAJA

Havasupai (pronounced "have a soup pie") means "People of the Blue Water" in English. Havasu 'Baaja is their name in their language. Though anthropologists say their tribe has inhabited Cataract Canyon since 1300 AD, their elders claim they have lived there much longer. In "times long ago," they spent the spring and summer in the canyon and the fall and winter on the plateau above, mostly hunting and gathering. They believe humans first appeared on Earth near here and consider all the Canyon sacred. They call the Grand Canyon the "Heart of Mother Earth" and their tribe is the "Guardian of our Mother's Heart."

Unlike their matriarchal Hopi, who are ancient friends and trading partners with the tribe, the Havasupais were patriarchal. Their tribe was really a collection of extended families of twenty to thirty people, with each family acting as an independent unit, in much the same way as the Hopi tribe was a collection of independent villages. They had no organized political structure or complex religious ceremonies; however, the family chiefs, or "talkers" as they were called, would meet occasionally to discuss issues related to the tribe.

Few missionaries or churches traveled into the canyon. Like all other Native American tribes, the Havasupai have always believed in one God. Again like all Native tribes, they believe the Earth was a gift from the Creator, *Tudjupa*. "Here is the land," He had told them, "where you will live. Go to the places where you find water. Mark off your land and live by the water. Name these places."

Though there were hardships, deprivation and isolation, the tribe lived a happy and peaceful existence, especially after the United States Army stopped the violent raids by the Apaches and Paiutes, which were described by one elder as, "We work, we make - they take." Like the Hopi, they were a peaceful people, never in serious conflict with the United States Army and only fighting in self-defense with their more aggressive neighbors. Their life before "civilization" reached into their ancient home is described in *The People of the Blue Water*, written in 1900 by a white school teacher, Flora Gregg:

Childhood days would be pleasant . . . There was no "nap time" nor "meal time" for Havasupai children. They played until they tumbled over in sleep, awakened when they felt like it . . . Children and grownups played together, and the stream was their playground. The little folks darted through the water . . . The women frolicked, laughing and screaming . . . while the men, enjoying more freedom in this sport as in other activities, wore only loincloths . . . The intelligence used by the parents in training their children would set a worthy example for any race. A mother did not scold. Instead she taught her small daughter to play grownup, to weave baskets, to sweep the floor, carry water and make fiber brooms . . . But wisely, instruction went beyond material things, for the little girl was also taught to be kind to her husband's people . . . This early training was responsible, I think, for the harmony with which those related by marriage worked and played together . . . Most beautiful of all, to me, was the instruction to children regarding the care of the aged. "When your grandparents are old and blind, lead them gently where they want to go . . . If they have no teeth, feed them warm corn mush." Contentment, even happiness, permeated the village. Secure in their homes, crop failures unknown, storehouses filled . . . a kindly, trusting people lived there - a people gifted with native wisdom, warm with laughter and carefree play.

The tribal disintegration hit full force when the children were taken away and placed in Indian schools. The full impact of this was outlined in a warning by the Chemehuevi Indian who had come to them as an evangelist, reminding them of the old ways and warning them of the penalties of forgetting the customs of "Those Long Ago." He prophetically warned:

Don't send your children to the school of the white man. If you do, they will grow up with the heart of the white man, and the place of the Havasupai will know them no more. Your tribe will be broken up . . . He thinks if he cannot drive you out he will seduce you out, and this school is the offer he makes to you, so that he can get your children into his hands. There he will teach them to make fun of you; to despise your method of living; your houses, your food, your dress, your customs, your dances will be ridiculed by him, and so you will lose favor of Those Above.

By the mid-1800s miners, settlers and ranchers had seized much of their territory, destroying their livelihood of hunting and grazing. Before the destructive influence of the white "civilization," the Havasupai lived in peace except for occasional skirmishes with small marauding bands. There was food at every house and everyone lived as one large extended family, which they were. The tribe grew and stored food in caves in the canyon walls, not only for the immediate future but for years ahead. Powerful floods, with rainwater pouring over the canyon walls in vast sheets, would occasionally threaten the village. Houses lost were easily and patiently rebuilt by everyone in a cheerful and unhurried manner.

In the *Annual Report* of the Department of the Interior for 1901, the tribal life was described:

The Havasupai is entirely self-supporting. He depends on the products of his farm for his livelihood. He is proud of his gardens and his orchards, but prouder still of the fact that he labors. Living on the banks of a clear, sparkling stream, he is never troubled by crop failure. He utilizes the water of the stream for irrigation purposes and an abundant crop is assured him. The almost perpendicular walls of the canyon, which he has made his home, are lined with storehouses which in the autumn he fills with corn, beans and other products of his labor.

When the United States government established the Grand Canyon National Park in 1919, they reduced the Havasupai reservation, established in 1880, to a mere 518 acres, a fraction of their ancestral tribal lands which consisted of millions of acres. By denying them access to their traditional hunting grounds, the government reduced them to a near starvation subsistence. In the 1890s, the Anglo schoolteachers arrived with the intent of not only teaching reading and writing, but destroying the Havasupais' ancient religion and supplanting it with Christianity. In this area, they were not so successful. Missionaries were few and no formal church was established there until 1948 when the Quonset hut was helicoptered in to serve as an Episcopal church.

In the 1890s, the Havasupai, like many other tribes in the Southwest, adopted a native movement, a "peace and prosperity ritual" known as the Ghost Dance. It was begun by a Paiute holy man named Wovoka, a self-proclaimed messiah, claiming to have visited the Great Spirit in a vision. He told the tribes that by dancing the Ghost Dance for five days at a time, the Great Spirit would return their dead ancestors to life, bring back the buffalo and dwindling game, and allow a return to the old ways and their previous happy condition. His was a vision of universal peace. The Earth, which had grown old and tired, would be regenerated and the entire Indian race, living and dead, would be united and live forever free of death, disease, and misery.

Wovoka told the people to discard all things warlike and to, "Do no harm to anyone. Do not tell lies. When your friends die, you must not cry." Though Wovoka had envisioned Indians and whites living in peace, some tribes reinterpreted Wovoka's vision to include punishment for the whites that included their total annihilation. This frenzied Ghost Dance movement was embraced by many chiefs and swept through the tribes with intensity. As the tribes spent all day dancing and chanting, normal life, including school attendance, stopped on the reservations.

This frightened the government authorities, who quickly banned it, to the point of killing some who insisted on participating. Many braves mistakenly believed that wearing their Ghost Dance shirts into battle would protect them from the white man's bullets. The government's fearful reaction lead to the death of Sitting Bull and the massacre at Wounded Knee in 1890, where 500 troopers of the 7th Cavalry surrounded an encampment of Sioux, many wearing their Ghost Dance shirts. Supposedly there to protect them, the soldiers, armed with four Hotchkiss guns, opened fire on the camp. When it was over, hundreds of Sioux men, women and children were dead, left to freeze into grotesque forms as a blizzard set in.

This unjustified slaughter of men, women and children, along with the failure of predictions on appointed dates, convinced the Native People that their efforts were in vain and the Ghost Dance was abandoned. However, it was responsible for bringing a spirit of brotherly love among warring tribes such as the Ute, Cheyenne and Pawnee. Over also was the Indians' armed resistance, fought by what the United States Army later begrudgingly described as the "greatest warriors on the face of the planet." Though a few individuals and small groups fought into the twentieth century, Wounded Knee was the last military confrontation in the centuries-long Indian wars. However, as we shall soon see, Wounded Knee was not over as a symbol of Native American resistance.

By the 1960s, the existence of the Havasupais was threatened. Many had died from diseases such as tuberculosis and syphilis brought in by the whites. Most federal services were withdrawn, the school was closed, the population was decreasing and only eight acres were under cultivation. The government attempted to relocate the tribe, probably to have easier access to their land and resources; however, the tribe persisted and has been thriving ever since. The reservation was enlarged in 1974 when the tribe was granted 185,000 acres, the largest amount ever returned to a single tribe. Their reservation consists not only of their 3000-foot deep canyon home, but land on the surrounding plateaus.

The encroachment on their land continues. In 1974, uranium was discovered on the reservation. Though the tribe tried to stop its mining, the Supreme Court ruled against them and mining was permitted. In fact, 65 percent of all the uranium reserves in the country are located on Indian reservations or treaty lands, as is over 35 percent of the strippable coal. Uranium is very dangerous to mine from the Earth, creating a trail of death in its wake. Indigenous people are usually the victims of uranium's carcinogenic trailings. Radioactive dust contaminates their food, gardens, drinking water, and their air. Native people believe it should stay underground.

Abandoning their practice of no central organized political structure, the U.S. government-supported, seven-member Havasupai Tribal Council adopted the Havasupai Tribal Constitution in 1939. In most ways, however, the Bureau of Indian Affairs was, and is, the real governing force, especially since they control the purse strings. Today, the Havasupai Tribal Council is the democratic representative of the tribe and allows it a greater sense of independence and self-determination; however, without continued government funding the tribal economy would collapse, and the Council's influence and power would be greatly reduced. Since most tribal members have lived their entire lives in the village, many are not sophisticated in the workings of the modern world. They have at times been manipulated by the government and mining interests.

With around 12,000 people a year visiting Havasu Canyon, tourism is the largest, and one of the few, employers. The tribe has a very young population (median age is 24) and much to our surprise we were told few elders are living there. Many have died from mounting health problems such as obesity, diabetes and kidney failure. Many more live on the plateau above in Peach Springs so they can be near the clinic, especially the kidney dialysis center.

The current goals, as stated by the tribe, are as follows:

- Our strength comes from the land, which is sacred. The following are the principles which guide our development as a people:
- To preserve the magnificence of our homeland. The Havasupai people and our homeland are inseparable. Preserving the land is a sacred responsibility.
- To protect our natural resources, both animal and plant life, that contribute to our healing and spiritual direction.
- To preserve our cultural identity in every way possible. The land that gave us birth defines our identity. The land helps to preserve our cultural identity by separating and insulating us from those influences we do not wish to incorporate into Havasupai life.
- To use our homeland to provide sustenance for ourselves and to return to a self-sustaining life.
- To provide our children with more alternatives than our parents had. Such alternatives can come only with better education and increased employment opportunities on the reservation.

- To provide the people with the best possible health and sanitation facilities.
- To provide housing for all the Havasupai people; housing that will utilize as much as possible the natural materials of the land and have the feeling of the outdoors, yet protect and give warmth to the inhabitants.
- To make the most efficient use of the water available to us.
- To make the least wasteful use of the energy resources available to us.
- To carefully control the influences that could destroy our privacy and sense of tribal community.

Chapter 3
The Valley of the Vapors

"There's no need to worry. The Creator's upset when we worry because He's able to take care of everything. If we worry then He knows we're not relying on Him. Whatever concerns you have doesn't matter because it will work out the way it's supposed to be. Your worry doesn't change anything; it just delays things from working out the way the Creator planned all along. There are things that worry can do. It can make you take your mind off your path. It can make you sad while you're waiting to see what's going to happen. And it can make you have illnesses, sometimes that can shorten your life. All those things displease the Creator. You could be about more important matters for the benefit of the people."
—**Past Iroquois leader Leon Shenandoah**

"Don't worry 'bout a thing cuz every little thing gonna be all right."
—**Bob Marley**

J ulia and I left Supai Waters and the Grand Canyon and started our three-day drive home. Driving across Arizona and New Mexico was pleasant and peaceful - little traffic and awe-inspiring views. As we approached the East, the traffic increased and the views were interrupted by shopping centers, housing tracks and other manmade structures. We were in great spirits. The entire trip had been amazing - more than we could have ever anticipated. We both realized that we had been guided to another rich vein of One Love. Julia kept watching the sky for the two eagles, more convinced than me that Supai Waters' parting comment was more than a metaphor.

"You know, my father was raised near Hot Springs," Julia said as we passed an interstate exit for the Arkansas town on our second day of driving. "I've always wanted to go there. My mother and my sisters went there and said there is a really nice old hotel where you can bathe in the hot springs."

"Well, let's go," I said, turning off the Interstate. "It's just an hour off the highway and it's our last night on the road. A classy old hotel and a hot soak sounds a lot more appealing than a motel on Interstate 40."

We drove on back roads through the Ouachita Mountains, or Zig Zag Mountains, as they are known locally because of the way they fold back on each other in abrupt hairpin turns. Around dusk, we entered Hot Springs. The town, nestled in a valley, looks pretty much the way in did in the 1920s. The valley is tight and small, perhaps 600 yards long by 200 yards wide. There is one main street running through the small downtown area with two- and three-story brick shops, restaurants and bars and classic hotels. Running through the middle of town is Bathhouse Row with its garishly ornate 1920s bathhouses, all perfectly restored. Only one, The Buckstaff Bathhouse, is open to the public. The ambiance of the town transports you back to a simpler time when Hot Springs literally "Bathed the World."

We checked into the crown jewel of the town, The Arlington Hotel, a huge old hotel that reflects the opulence of the pre-depression era. After settling into our room, we soaked in their large hillside open-air hot bath that overlooks the mountains and the town. At sunset, we headed across the street to a local restaurant for dinner where we got into a conversation with a very open-hearted African-American waiter. He was a big Bob Marley fan so I went out to the car and got him a copy of *Rasta Heart* while Julia told him a little about our visits to the Hopi and the Havasupais.

"You know, if you're interested in Native Americans, there's an Indian craft co-op down the street," he said as I rejoined them. "I work there as a volunteer sometimes. It's run by two Cherokees. You ought to go see them. They open every day around ten. Their names are Chief White Eagle and Chief Red Eagle." Julia and I looked at each other and smiled broadly.

The next morning we went to their Native American craft shop, Ish'Na, promptly at ten. The store was right on the main street, at the foot of the row of bathhouses. There was no sign to let you know it was a store, just a lot of crafts in the windows. We walked in and were greeted by a tall, heavyset man in his forties with a beautiful black long ponytail and a big smile. He introduced himself as Chief Red Eagle and when he heard a little of our story, he instantly called Chief White Eagle on the phone to come over. (My research at the Smithsonian's National Museum of the American Indian turned up no references to these "chiefs." Their titles may be self-appointed or symbolic. Every Cherokee village had a peace chief called White Eagle and a war chief called Red Eagle.)

As Red Eagle showed us around, we realized that this was not your ordinary Indian craft store. The store sold crafts not just from the local Native American craftspeople, but from tribes all over. The store seemed to ramble on forever. A large circular stairway, made entirely of rough cut local timber, took you down to a lower level, about the size of an average living room, which they had been excavating - right in the middle of the store. It looked like a gem mine, complete with the natural stone walls and an area set up where a local volunteer did gem work.

"Is this Cherokee land?" I asked. "I thought they lived in Oklahoma."

"This land was for many tribes," Red Eagle said as we settled into some comfortable over-stuffed arm chairs. He put some native tobacco in a beautiful deer antler pipe, decorated with bound leather straps and large feathers and passed it around. "To the original people, this valley was called 'Nowasalon,' which meant the 'Land of Healing Waters' or 'Breath of Healing.' Indigenous people from the Yucatan to Alaska would come here for healing. The springs had curative properties. They would bathe in the pools and drink the water. Each tribe had their own area but no one tribe ruled the valley. The Caddo Indians lived in the area but this valley, the Valley of the Vapors, was no tribe's territory. It was considered a gift of the Great Spirit to *all* people. No weapons were allowed in the valley. It was neutral ground, especially for warring tribes. No bad vibes. No tribal animosity. If we were at war with each other and you came here for healing and I came here for healing, we couldn't fight or argue with each other. If we did, our own people took us out of the valley. You had to be peaceful while you were here. All the springs flowed freely before they blocked them up. President Andrew Jackson saw this as a profit-making thing and declared it national land. Speculators blocked most of the springs and built the bathhouses."

A few minutes later, Chief White Eagle came in with his wife and their newborn daughter. As we settled in, I told him a little about our journeys through Jamaica, Supai and Hopiland and of Supai Water's request that the two eagles send blessings to his tribe.

"Your approach was announced," Chief White Eagle said. "I know you people and I have been waiting for you."

"I don't know how that could be," I responded incredulously. "We just decided last night to come here and no one even knows we're here, not even our daughters."

"Last week this Rastafarian man and his family came here. He wanted to sell me his flutes and drums. His name was Ras Miguel Medina. He is from Southern California. Here is his flyer," he said handing me a flyer that was sitting nearby on his desk. It showed beautiful African drums and flutes. "I didn't buy any because we only sell Native American crafts but we had a good connection. The last thing he said before he left was, 'Our messengers are coming to see you. They will be here soon.' So when Red Eagle called me and said you were here and you had written a book called *Rasta Heart*, I knew you were the messengers he spoke of. And I know the nephew of the Oraibi chief Stanley and Supai Waters. I was with him at an Indian gathering in Alaska."

"That's amazing," I said.

"You are on the Beauty Path," his wife said as we passed the pipe saying a blessing for the Havasupai. "It has guided you here."

We spent several hours together learning of the history and legends of the area. Very little is known about this valley in pre-colonial times and my research through the Smithsonian National Museum of the American Indian in Washington turned up no Native American references to it. Like so many "Indian legends" it could be completely true, exaggerated or a total prefabrication. All the information below is from the only book available on the valley, *Indian Folklore Atlas of Hot Springs National Park* by Marcus Phillips and Sandra Long. Though well researched and academically reviewed, its main source of information was unwritten local legends.

According to their research, Native Americans have been in the valley for at least 10,000 years. It was also called "Manataka" or "Valley of Peace" or "Place of Peace." The nearby Caddo Indians considered it the "Garden of Eden." There were no permanent settlements or residents in the valley. That's why archeologists cannot find many artifacts in the valley; however, the novaculite flint from this area has been found in artifacts of tribes all over North America. The quality of the local crystal is considered by both gemologists and collectors as the purest in the country, perhaps the world, with some growing to boulder-sized formations. Two large crystal formations have been located miles apart in the area. Scientist believe they are connected deep underground making them in reality one huge crystal formation. Nowasalon is in the exact middle of these two mammoth crystals.

The book says that the hot spring water began as rainwater and then it slowly seeped into the Earth. Thousands of feet down it is superheated and shoots into these 47 springs through faults and crevices, picking up curative minerals on its journey to the surface. This process takes over three thousand years so the water, which is completely free of bacteria and slightly radioactive, is very old and very pure. Different springs are curative for different ailments.

In pre-contact times, there were trails coming into the valley from all directions. Tribes from all over the continent would journey here. These trails linked with major trading trails that traversed the whole country. Native tribes in both North and South America were linked in a vast network of trade. During times of famine, trade partners sent food. Guatemalan macaw feathers were used by Taos Indians of New Mexico and indigenous people in Honduras made pipes from Minnesota pipestone. According to the book, this ancient trail system was like a giant wheel and Nowasalon was the hub of inter-tribal activity and diplomacy. It was not only neutral ground, it was sacred ground.

Legends say a beautiful Indian princess would appear and drop an eagle feather at the feet of the angry parties reminding them to let their anger fly out of the valley. Great councils for all tribes, some so large that they encircled the entire valley, would be held with singing and dancing around great campfires. Medicine lodges were erected. It was said that rare healing plants grew in a great circle around the valley. They were gathered by the women of the tribes while the men gathered precious healing crystals and clay, along with flint, gold, silver, pyrite, and whetstones. The local novaculite rock was highly valued for its fine flint for making tools and weapons. Gifts were exchanged among individuals and tribes to foster friendship and diplomacy. Friends and relatives separated by marriage would reunion here. Legends also say that the elders and chiefs of warring tribes would meet here to resolve their differences. Many tribes met here and exchanged stories and shared their simplistic technology, their ceremonies and rituals.

People from different tribes would sit in the pools or gather flint together or sit around campfires at night and exchange stories. It was a festive atmosphere, like being at a huge family gathering. They learned from each other. The medicine men and shamans shared their knowledge of medicinal plants. The women exchanged recipes, techniques for basketry and pottery and fashion designs. Though they learned each other's tribal languages, there was a universal sign language that everyone understood - a common all-tribe language that is now lost, perhaps forever.

There were tribal and intertribal dances and drumming circles in a central plaza and just outside the valley, blankets were spread out with items for trade. People would share their campfires at night with people from other tribes. Those who were familiar with the springs and plants would share their knowledge with the newcomers.

The tranquility of the Valley of the Vapors came to an end in 1832 by order of President Andrew Jackson, who considered Indians "savage dogs," and was the mastermind of many racial atrocities, including the

infamous Trail of Tears. Jackson pushed Congress to take an unprece-
dented action in the nation's history, and one that was unconstitutional,
by confiscating Nowasalon. Jackson was warned by the United States
Supreme Court the government was prohibited by the Constitution to
own land but he proceeded anyway.

Despite these warnings, the valley was declared national land and
the springs were dammed up. Soon settlers were building bathhouses
and homes in the sacred valley. In 1875, they too were given the boot so
that the federal government could sell choice property to selected busi-
nessmen. What was left of the Hot Springs Federal Reservation in 1921
was turned over to the newly created National Park System and became
the second national park after Yellowstone. Today, it is known as Hot
Springs National Park. In the name of "protecting visitors and the environment," the government covered all but two of the forty-seven springs.
Today you cannot access these two springs without paying. No plaque or
statue has even been erected honoring Nowasalon as a sacred Native
American site.

After trading more stories and gifts, including Red Eagle's gift to us of
the beautiful deer antler pipe, Julia and I headed out to our home, not
far from the Cherokee Boundary area that is home to the Eastern Band
of the Cherokee Nation. This area was their original tribal land before
most of the tribe was forcibly removed during the Trail of Tears. Before
this removal, some Cherokees fled into the mountains near our home and
hid for decades until a small piece of their original land was restored to
them.

Our area too is sacred ground. We live on the eastern slope of
Grandfather Mountain - the oldest mountain, and the only quartzite
mountain, on Earth. Because of its cold winters, no Indians lived permanently on our mountaintop but many tribes came in the warm months
to gather food and medicinal herbs and to enjoy the many waterfalls.
This area of the Blue Ridge is one of the most bio-diverse areas for vegetation of any place in the world. The headwaters (the highest spot) of the
New River, the second oldest river in the world, begins in a large, clear
pond in our backyard. Julia once found a crystal arrowhead next to the
pond. Our journey had been full and it was good to be home.

THE U.S. GOVERNMENT'S ATTEMPT
TO BREAK THE SACRED HOOP

Jackson and the new government understood that if they were going to continue taking the tribal lands and destroying native societies, they needed to stop all inter-tribal gatherings that might lead to a united resistance. His intention was always clear as he stated in 1832, "These tribes cannot exist surrounded by our settlements . . . They must necessarily yield to force of circumstance and, ere long, disappear."

In 1830, with President Jackson's enthusiastic support, the Congress of the United States passed the "Indian Removal Act," which allowed the government to remove millions of Native Americans from their tribal land. Though controversial, President Jackson quickly signed the bill into law. The Cherokees attempted to fight removal legally by challenging the removal laws in the Supreme Court and by establishing an independent Cherokee Nation. In 1832, the United States Supreme Court ruled in favor of the Cherokee. Now it would take agreement by the tribe and a treaty to remove them; Jackson held the court's ruling in disdain and illegally ignored it saying "[Supreme Court Justice] John Marshall has rendered his decision, now let him enforce it."

Through bribery, intense coercion, intimidation and by splintering their leadership, the government soon got some of the tribal leaders to agree to resettle. Soon the Choctaws, the Chickasaws and the Creeks were forcibly removed, wailing in pain as they touched their beloved streams, trees and rocks farewell. As they marched westward, 10,000 of the 22,000 Creeks died in route.

Though dispirited, many Cherokees adamantly wanted to stay on the original lands. Only, a minority, less than 500 out of 17,000 Cherokee in North Georgia, agreed with removal, believing that living in a strange land that was all theirs was better than living on their ancient tribal land under constant assault and attack by the government, settlers, miners and land speculators. They signed a treaty that gave Jackson the legal document he needed. Ratification of the treaty by the United States Senate sealed the fate of the Cherokee.

Men, women, and children were taken from their land, often by force, herded into makeshift forts with minimal facilities and food, and then forced to march, in the middle of winter, a thousand miles from their tribal home in the southeast to their new home in Oklahoma. This was particularly devastating for the Cherokees, who had never been a nomadic people and had assimilated the white man's ways to a large degree. Under the generally indifferent army commanders, human losses for the first group of Cherokee removed were extremely high. Between 4000 to 6000 died en route.

As with the Hopi, much of this was foretold in their tribal legends and prophecies. Cherokee legend reveals that some 3500 years ago, God revealed Himself to a people in their ancient tribal land. The Creator gave the people a mother town called "Kituhwa" and the people a new name, "Keetoowah." (the word "Cherokee" has no meaning to the tribe). The town was near present day Bryson City, North Carolina, near the Cherokee reservation. It was from Kituhwa that the Creator revealed His true name to the Cherokee people. He said His name was "Yowah" (similar to the Hebrew word "Yahweh") and the people would be "kit-Yowah" or "from God." As with all peoples, He had called them to be His people, to become "a light to the nations."

There is an ancient Cherokee prophecy that states, "The Cherokees will lead all the other tribes back to the Great Spirit." Cherokee prophecy has some remarkable similarities to that of the Hopi. Handed down as a traditional Cherokee story from grandmother to grandchild, the story-teller cautions that long ago before the Europeans discovered Turtle Island (North America) and her indigenous people, the elders warned of the monsters with white eyes yet to come. The spirits foretold that this monster would cross the great eastern water (similar stories are to be found among the Aztecs and indigenous Mexican people).

"There is a white ball from way east," the prophecy says, "who is your enemy, coming and your grandchildren's feet are directed west. They shall have great trials on the edge of the prairie. They shall be divided into different factions and their blood shall be about only half. Families shall be divided against each other and they shall disregard their chiefs, leaders, and medicine men. But if these younger generation should endeavor to follow the Creator's instruction there is a chance to turn back east and if not, the next move shall be west, on to the coast and from there on to the boat and this shall be the last. If the Keetoowah people are destroyed or become extinct, then the end of the world will follow."

The Trail of Tears, or "the trail where they cried" as the Cherokee call it, that moved the tribe westward, to the "edge of the prairie," proved this prophecy correct. Fortunately, the Cherokee were forcibly resettled in Oklahoma not the West Coast, thereby preventing the total destruction of the tribe. Some later "turned back east" and a Cherokee reservation was later established in Cherokee, North Carolina, in the Smoky Mountains, near our home.

In another tragic example, the Cherokee treaty of 1791 states: "The United States solemnly guarantee to the Cherokee nation all their lands not hereby ceded." Then in 1832, they forcibly uprooted the entire nation from this *guaranteed* land and marched them over a thousand miles on the "Trail of Tears" to Oklahoma.

When the tribes attempted to use the United States court system to force the government to honor the legal treaties the government had initiated, written, agreed to and signed, they were thwarted by whatever means was most effective, legal or illegal, ethical or unethical. The degree to which the United States court system failed the Native Americans was noted by Governor Horatio Seymour, the unsuccessful contender to President Ulysses S. Grant. Seymour stated:

> Every human being born upon our continent, or who comes here from any quarter of the world, whether savage or civilized, can go to our courts for protection - except for those who belong to the tribes who once owned this country . . . The worst criminals from Europe, Asia, or Africa can appeal to the law and courts for their rights of person and property - all save our native Indians, who, above all, should be protected from wrong.

Jackson's illegal actions were just part of a long series of broken treaties, lies, illegalities and deceptions designed to steal Native American lands by the United States government and private interests. Several pieces of legislation reveal the United States government's switch from seizing tribal lands by force and violence to using "legal" manipulations instead.

In 1887, the General Allotment Act (also called the Dawes Act) was passed that provided that individual Indians could now own their individual plots of land that were formerly part of the communally owned tribal land. The Indian land had already been reduced by ninety-five percent due to the government policy of "Manifest Destiny" and "eminent domain" laws, the concept that it was God's will for white European descendents to take over and own Indian lands. The Dawes Act broke the communal-tribal ownership of their remaining land and placed it in hands of individual tribal members who could sell it at will. Almost immediately, millions of acres of land went from Indian to white ownership, just as the government had planned.

Senator Dawes, the architect of the Dawes Act, is quoted as saying, "The head [of the Cherokees] told us that there is not a family in that whole nation that had not a home of its own. There was not a pauper in the nation, and the nation did not owe a dollar . . . Yet the defect of the system was apparent . . . There is no selfishness, which is at the bottom of civilization."

The Dawes Act was one of the greatest land steals in history. It rolled from reservation to reservation, slicing up tribal lands. When it was over, 50 million acres of the 90 million acres "guaranteed by treaty" was plundered from Native tribes - over sixty percent of their lands. It had accomplished just what it was intended to do when President Theodore Roosevelt hailed it as a "mighty pulverizing engine to break up tribal mass." With much of their land gone, the tribes had few sanctuaries to maintain their ceremonies and traditional ways.

In 1934, ten years after Native Americans were finally given United States citizenship status, The Indian Reorganization Act, considered another "liberal reform" to help the Indians, offered United States government assistance in converting the ancient tribal governing systems into modern democracies. Actually, the true intent of this legislation was to break the hold of the slow-moving, consensus-based governance of the tribes which almost always decided against the sale of land and leases for oil, coal and gas. The new American-style government imposed on the tribes destroyed all this and further opened up Indian land to development, especially since Indians vote "no" by refraining from voting at all, thereby giving the minority "yes" vote the advantage.

The third blow to Native American rights and sovereignty was the Indian Claims Commission Act. It was created in 1946 and again considered another "liberal reform" to help the Indians. Its stated purpose was to "settle finally any and all legal, equitable, and moral obligations that the United States might owe to the Indians." However, it was a fraud in both concept and execution. Its real purpose was to finally settle all Native American claims to their land so that rights for resources could be sold to gas, coal, uranium, oil and other corporate interests.

The Act's intent was *never* to give any land back to the Indians, but rather to pay them money for any land they could prove they had lost as the government broke treaty after treaty. Cash payments for lost lands, at century-old prices, was the only method allowed to resolve Indian grievances. All requests to grant land titles to the Indians were refused. Once this money was awarded, the tribe's land title was permanently lost and they were barred from seeking further compensation. In essence, it was a legal mechanism to once and for all sever Indians from much of their tribal land. To assist in this unstated goal, the Act allowed *any* tribal member to sue, and settle, on behalf of the entire tribe. So even if most of the tribe wanted to continue to fight to get their land back, *one* solitary member, usually assisted by a white lawyer eager for a percent of the settlement, could permanently give up title to their tribe's land. Once their land was lost, tribal members could be scattered in relocation programs in the cities.

During the Eisenhower administration of the 1950s, Congress passed a resolution to "terminate" all Indian reservations and to "relocate" Original People from their lands and into the cities. Its aim was to give "independence" to a people who had been totally dependent on the government for over a century. "Terminate" and "relocate" soon became two of the most feared words to Native Americans. Meager food and commodity supplies to the reservations were cut off. They were given two options: relocate or starve. They pleaded with the BIA, once part of the Department of War, and the agency supposedly designed to help native peoples, but got only a deaf ear and a cold shoulder. After several years of renewed atrocities, the government abandoned this program as unworkable.

More recently, in the 1989 Gasket-Orleans Supreme Court decision, three northern California tribes lost their attempt to block construction of a United States forest road through their sacred sites in the Six Rivers National Forest. This decision was a devastating blow to Indians trying desperately to preserve what little was left of their culture. As Steven Moore, a lawyer of the Native American Rights Fund, said of the decision, it is "a life-threatening blow to Indian religion . . . in such a way as to unilaterally subordinate Indian religious values to the economic interests of timber, mineral and water-power developments."

Today, Native Americans fight, not on the battlefield but in the courts, to recover and protect their tribal lands. The battle is an uphill one, with occasional victories of recovered land but more often with financial settlements or legal setbacks. As Iroquois Tadodaho Sidney Hill said in 2005, "We're going into your courts for what's supposed to be best and right. Can you see our side? Is it possible for you to see the emotion and how it feels with what we've lost? Our health? The treatment of our people? Does that mean anything to a judge? To homeowners? To anybody?"

Even institutionalized oppression of the Native Americans is not a issue of the past. It continues to this day. As Leonard Peltier, the American Indian Movement (AIM) activist falsely accused and imprisoned for over three decades, writes in *Prison Writings: My Life Is My Sundance*:

> Yes. We have wounds. And these atrocities against my people continue to this day, only now they are carried out with more sophisticated means than the Gatling guns and cannons and sabers. There are subtler ways of killing. Call it death by statistics.

Today, white men lets his statistics do his killing for him. Indian reservations in South Dakota have the highest rates of poverty and unemployment and the highest rates of infant mortality and teenage suicide, along with the lowest life expectancy - barely forty years! - in the country. Those statistics amount to genocide. Genocide that disguises itself in the form of poor health facilities and wretched housing and inadequate schooling and rampant corruption. Our remaining lands, eyed by a thousand local schemers only to eager to stir up trouble and division on the reservation, continue to be sold off acre by acre to pay off tribal and individual debts. No square inch of our ever-shrinking territory seems beyond the greedy designs of those who would drive us into non-existence.

So in the end, all this was the Anglo culture's approach to their "Indian Problem" - first *genocide*, and when that didn't work, *reservations*, and when that didn't work, kill the culture through *"acculturation."* Or as Navajo Ginger Hills say, "They came with the Bible in one hand and the gun in the other. First they stole gold. Then they stole the land. Then they stole souls." However, their souls were not really stolen. They have survived it *all* and are now thriving and remain a vital repository for the wisdom we all need.

*Hopiland - the home of the Hopi- Second Mesa villages
of Mishongnovi and Sipaulovi on hills in distance*

The home of Bob Marley in Kingston, Jamaica

Julia near Prophecy Rock in Hopiland

Supai Village - Home of the Havasupai

Julia at Supai Village at the end of our hike

The sacred Havasu Falls in Cataract Canyon, two miles from Supai Village

The daily delivery of mail and supplies to Supai

Supai Waters (standing) with other Havasupai friends

*Supai Waters tells Julia to watch for the two eagles
as we wait for the helicopter out*

The Arlington Hotel and bathhouses in the Valley of the Vapors

Alicia addresses a school in the Jamaican mountains

Mackie Conscious and Abijah sing to students at
Spanish Town High with Julia and the mayor

Abijah with children in Kingston inner-city school

Julia talks with the students about forgiveness

Abijah transforms bullies into teachers of love

Grammy-nominated artist Luciano performs at our Bob Marley 58th

Julia with reggae artists Swade, Ernie Smith, Luciano and Mackie Conscious at Bob's 58th birthday at the University of the West Indies in Jamaica

Our family addressing live and television audience at Bob's 59th in downtown Kingston

Reggae legends Mystic Revelation of Rastafari at Bob's 59th

Candidate for Jamaican Prime Minister, lawyer and talk show host Antonnette Haughton addresses her fellow leaders at our One Love Leadership Event

Jamaican "chiefs" at our "One Love Leadership Concert" in Kingston

Scram (in background) putting up "Fires of Forgiveness" posters

Scram and Alicia after the "Fires of Forgiveness"

The crew preparing to build the stage at the "Fires of Forgiveness"
- Scram, Chris, and Bongo Roach

Abijah sings and speaks to the kids at Keam's Canyon School in Hopiland

*Hopiland reggae deejay Karen Abieta (Sister Parrot)
interviews Abijah at KUYI*

Julia with banner we used at all Hopi concerts

Abijah with Hopi students at Second Mesa School

Our concert at Second Mesa School

Our concert at Hopiland Junior and Senior High School
with Abijah, Zema and Joseph Israel and his band

Damon in our van at the Sierra Nevada World Music Festival

Radford, Lorna and Rad Quamahongnewa preparing to helicopter into Supai

Preparing to helicopter Uproot's equipment into the Canyon

Author addressing Havasupai at the "Reclaim the Grand Canyon Concert"

*George and Roberto Flores of Uproot speak and perform
at the Havasupai concert*

Duane and Rad enjoy the travertine pools at Havasu Falls

Chapter 4
The Wisdom of
the Ancients

"If any man does anything, sincerely believing that thereby he is worshipping the Great Spirit, he is worshipping the Great Spirit, and his worship must be treated with respect, so long as he is not trespassing the rights of others."
—Wabasha, a Lakota Chief in the 18th century

"Emancipate yourself from mental slavery. None but ourselves can free our minds." **—Bob Marley**

After returning from our journeys to Hopiland, Supai Village and the Valley of the Vapors, we both realized that we had been guided to our next assignment, that of bringing forward the drumbeat of One Love emanating from these Native American tribes. In addition to our continuing travels to the tribes, I began to research the *reality* of who were, and are, the Native Americans.

Soon it became apparent, that it is in the remembrance of who we *all* truly are, that the wisdom of America's First People can be helpful. Many Native Americans of today have lost contact with this ancient wisdom and have been assimilated into the dominant culture and adopted its worldview. Many of the old ways have been shunned or forgotten. Today's society does not easily lend itself to follow these old ways, even on remote Indian reservations. However, Native Americans are still the guardians of a legacy from a time when their ancient tribes walked this planet in peace, certainty and dignity. Even today, with many tribal members, this wisdom and worldview is alive and vital.

These ancient cultures were not perfect, nor were their lives idyllic. After all, human nature is the same everywhere. However, their societies were designed to bring out the best in humans - to create the most happiness, freedom, and health. For the most part, pre-contact Native Americans lived in harmony with their environment and their neighbors, with good health, cradle-to-grave security, meaningful and satisfying human relationships and lots of free time to enjoy their lives. If it wasn't the Garden of Eden, it may have been close. It is what many of us are seeking now.

In past Cherokee chief Wilma Mankiller's book, *Every Day is a Good Day*, Onondaga Clan Mother Audrey Shenandoah recently described the difference between her traditional culture and the larger culture, "Our people know more about acceptance and contentment than our white brothers and sisters who seem to think they have to be deliriously happy all the time. They are looking for something that their world doesn't offer them. It makes them unhappy if things are not the way they think they should be. They spend a lot of time trying to find happiness rather than peace of mind. Our seasonal cycle of ceremonies are to bring peace of mind. Healing is left to the Creator."

It needs to be noted that it is often difficult to get an exact picture of indigenous tribes before the colonists came. They did not record their history in books and as soon as the early European writers started to record it, their tribal cultures were already contaminated by the invasion. Also there were different levels of culture within the 600 tribes, different levels of development. They span from the organized populated villages and social structure of the Anasazi of the Southwest to the small independent family structure of their neighbors in the Grand Canyon, the Havasupai. However, from the history and information that has been revealed, it can be concluded that their system of tribal life offered greater true human happiness than our present one. And in the end, if all our civilized development has not lead to greater happiness, what has been its value?

IT'S NOT A RACIAL THING

As we examine both the elegance of pre-Columbus Native American life and the brutality of the invading European culture, we need to realize that as easy as it is to condemn the white race for all these atrocities, this is really not a race issue. It is a human issue, or as the Native Americans would say "a two-legged thing." It is easy to fall into the trap of blaming entire societies or countries, or even entire races, for the deeds of a few individuals.

For the last few thousand years, whomever has had the greater power, physically, politically and/or financially, exploited those with lesser power (which is why women are exploited in *all* cultures). Unconscious people will exploit those with their *same* skin color, religion, and nationality as easily as they will exploit those different from them. It continues to this day. The color of the indigenous people living on the North America arrived could have been white and the skin of the invaders could have been red, if the Creator had planned it that way. We need to move beyond race condemnation. Past Iroquois leader Leon Shenandoah gave us the instructions of the "Good Mind" when he said, "It's hard to do the ceremonies when you are angry or fighting with other people. It is better to forgive because how can you give thanks when you are filled with anger." His sentiments reflect the words of another Native American chief who said, "The elders have forgiven the atrocities."

Whites have enslaved whites and blacks have enslaved blacks. Even Native Americans and freed slaves eventually became slave holders, even slave traders. As early as 1540, one thousand Indians joined the forces of Spanish conquistador Vasquez de Coronado to help him conquer other indigenous peoples. Native American tribes fought in the forces of the United States Army to destroy their neighboring tribes. As Jamaican dub poet Cherry Natural says in one of her poems, "Give the oppressed a little power and they become the oppressor."

Continuing to blame a race or a society of people, keeps us stuck in a victim consciousness. As LaDonna Harris, a Comanche and Indian rights activists, recently said, "I think some of our people have been trapped in a victimization mentality for generations, and they then unwittingly become victims of their own victimization and can't stop the behavior. We are capable people who can do anything we set our minds to do."

Forgiveness is the key to healing this ancient wound. The most sacred sites on Earth are not religious shrines or cathedrals of worship, but rather any place where an *ancient* hatred has become a *present* love. As Native American activists Leonard Peltier writes in his book, *Prison Writings: My Life Is My Sun Dance*:

> There I go, being vindictive and vengeful myself, wishing harm on others as they have wished it on me. I have to watch that in myself. I have to step on the head of that snake every time it rises. There's always someone to hate. The list of those who have earned our hatred - and spurned our hatred - is endless. Shall we draw up lists of each other's crimes? Must we hate each other all the time?

If it is not race that created such different societies, what was it? As you will soon see, it was really different worldviews; it was the different cultural stories we told ourselves about who we are. It is the stories and the storytelling, whether told around a campfire, in front of a tipi, in a classroom, or on television in front of a gas fireplace, that molds a culture's citizens and forms their self-concepts. They either appeal to our higher or lower sentiments. The stories the ancient cultures told themselves - stories that addressed the spiritual, psychological, social and political needs of the tribe - often brought out the best in people, just as our modern stories often bring out the worst. As the ancient First People knew, there is sacred power in tribal stories - power that guided the people Home. And as we shall see, these stories are often communicated through songs and dances. As Oglala Sioux Chief Luther Standing Bear writes in his book, *Land of the Spotted Eagle*, "These stories were the libraries of our people."

In order to truly understand who the indigenous people of North America were, we must first understand who they were *not*. Though it has been somewhat corrected, much of what we know of them has been filtered through an educational system and a modern media that either intentionally, or through ignorance, misinterpreted what was going on here before the explorers arrived. History is always written by the victors, never by the vanquished. As Howard Zinn wrote in *The People's History of the United States*, in referring to the accepted historical accounts of the founding of this country, " . . . the quiet acceptance of conquest and murder in the name of progress - is only one aspect of a certain approach to history, in which the past is told from the point of view of governments, conquerors, diplomats, leaders." As Benjamin Franklin noted, "Historians relate, not so much what is done, as what they would have believed."

The original Native Americans were neither unsophisticated, disorganized, nor heathens. They were not barbaric and were *not* living in the Stone Age. They also were not "noble savages" or "mystical children of nature." They were rather human beings who were living under a vastly different social, political and economic system - a system that emphasized different elements of our universally shared human nature. It is estimated that there were between 2 to 18 million people in over 600 tribes living in what was to become the United States and Canada when the first European explorers landed. They had been here for tens of thousands of years. The "New World" that the explorers claimed they discovered was anything but "new."

Though their customs and legends differed greatly, every tribe shared two beliefs in common - that there was one God, one "Great Spirit," one "Great Mystery," and this Divine Being had given the Earth to *all* people as a gift. More than anything else, all Native Americans are known for their deep spiritual connection with the land and nature, which will be key to saving the planet.

It is understandable how the early colonists were unable to truly comprehend the Native Americans they encountered. Europe in the 1500s was technologically advanced for its time. They had large cities with organized governments with clearly defined absolute rulers. Great cathedrals and palaces dazzled the population with man's achievements. People were enjoying modern inventions like the printing press, clocks, coal heat, oil lamps, the wheel, sailing ships and horse-drawn carriages.

Along with these modern wonders, these societies also had the corrupted rule of the aristocracy, unhealthy living conditions, exploitive labor practices, crime and jails, the Crusades and legalized human slavery. The Native Americans had none of these. Unlike almost all other people on the planet, there was one thing more the pre-contact tribes lacked - alcohol (which Indians came to call "mind twister" or "mind change.") This lack may have allowed them to reach a higher state of spiritual and social understanding.

Native Americans, though living simple lives close to nature, were deep philosophical thinkers - pondering man, nature and the supernatural. As we will see, the complexity and elegance of their legends, customs and ceremonies rivaled, and often surpassed, those of Europeans. To the early settlers, any people living in small tribes close to the land, as their ancestors had for thousands of years, were primitive, ignorant savages in severe need of civililizing.

The colonists encountered a civilization with a just and harmonious social structure and a highly civilized state compared to what they were accustomed to in Europe, where the people were oppressed by the divine right of kings, the nobility, the self-serving clergy, and religious persecution. In pre-contact America, there was no aristocracy that controlled the land and made the masses into indentured servants and serfs.

The Europeans found a people that greeted them with unsuspecting kindness, who were uniformly patient and reasonable, who were healthier and led more leisurely lives, had few degenerative diseases, little crime, no police or jails. They were a people who valued cooperation rather than competition, mutual respect over domination, equality rather than exploitation of women, and a sustainable use of resources. The settlers somehow deduced that these "primitive" people were in great need of being shown the proper way to live by the newcomers.

As Howard Zinn writes in *The People's History of the United States*:

So, Columbus and his successors were not coming into an empty wilderness, but into a world which in some places was as densely populated as Europe itself, where the culture was complex, where human relations were more egalitarian than in Europe, and where the relations among men, women, children and nature were more beautifully worked out than perhaps any place on earth.

Oglala Sioux Chief Luther Standing Bear expressed his views on this contradiction in 1933:

> It is not a question of the white man "bringing the Indian up to his plane of thought and action." It is rather the case where the white man had better grasp some of the Indian's spiritual strength. I protest against calling my people savages. How can the Indian, sharing all the virtues of the white man, be justly called a savage? The white race today is but half civilized and unable to order his life into ways of peace and righteousness.

What the colonists did not understand then, and most people still do not understand, was that these differences in the growth of technology were not due to the Europeans superiority or greater intelligence or industriousness. It was due rather to two very different worldviews. It was due to different stories. After examining these two different perceptions of the universe, perhaps it will become clear which was the more enlightened race.

TWO DIFFERENT STORIES
TWO DIFFERENT WORLDVIEWS

Let us begin by looking at the Native American view of the Divinity. An excellent description is offered by Ohiyesa, a Santee Sioux. Born in 1858, Ohiyesa lived the traditional nomadic life of the Sioux (Lakota/Dakota/Nakota tribes) in Canada and Minnesota until the age of 15. In 1873, he entered the white world that had been embraced by his missing father, who suddenly reappeared. He became Charles Eastman and eventually received an undergraduate degree from Dartmouth and a medical degree at Boston College before returning to the Pine Ridge Sioux reservation in South Dakota as their government physician (including tending to casualties at the Wounded Knee massacre).

In his book, *The Soul of an Indian*, Ohiyesa writes:

The original attitude of the American Indian toward the Eternal,
the 'Great Mystery' that surrounds and embraces us, was as simple
as it was exalted. To him it was the supreme conception, bringing
with it the fullest measure of joy and satisfaction possible in life.
The worship of the Great Mystery was silent, solitary, free from all
self-seeking. It was silent because all speech is of necessity feeble
and imperfect: therefore the souls of my ancestors ascended to
God in wordless adoration. It was solitary, because they believed
that He is nearer to us in solitude, and there are no priests author-
ized to come between a man and his Maker. None might exhort
or confess or in any way meddle with the religious experience of
another. Among us, all men were created sons of God and stood
erect, as conscious of their own divinity. Our faith might not be
formulated in creeds, nor forced upon any that were unwilling to
receive it: hence there was no preaching, proselytizing, nor persecution, neither were there any scoffers or atheists.
There were no temples or shrines among us save those of nature.
Being a natural man, the Indian was intensely poetical. He would
deem it a sacrilege to build a house for Him who may be met
face to face in the mysterious, shadowy aisles of the primeval
forest, or on the sunlight bosom of virgin prairies. . . Knowing that
God sets no value on material things, he took with him no offerings or sacrifices other than symbolic objects, such as paints and
tobacco. . . I believe. . . that the spirit of Christianity and of our
ancient religion is essentially the same.

A few enlightened missionaries and colonists quickly realized that the
Native Americans were living more Christ-like lives than any people in
recorded history, a people who lived with few possessions and complete
trust in the Creator to provide. Lewis Henry Morgan, an early ethnologist
and writer on Native cultures, noted in his *League of the Iroquois*:

Eminently pure and spiritual, and internally consistent with each other, the beliefs and the religious ceremonies of the Iroquois are worthy of respectful consideration. A people in the wilderness, shut off from revelation, with no tablet on which to write the history of passing generations, save the heart of man, yet possessed the knowledge of one Supreme Being, and striving, with all ardor of devotion, to commune with Him in the language of thankfulness and supplication, is, to say the least, a most extraordinary spectacle . . . The Indian had no Sabbath, no sacred writings to furnish him an inexhaustible fountain of instruction; but his gratitude was awakened by every returning manifestation of divine goodness . . . Seizing upon the moment when the conspicuous evidences of the protecting care of the Deity were before him, he acknowledged both His existence, and His beneficence, and manifested, at the same time, his gratitude, and devotion, by those simple rites which the piety of his heart suggested.

However, to most Europeans, this manner of worship looked to the settlers like paganism and blasphemy. Where were the churches, the savior, the paid clergy, the holy books, the struggle to find the "one true way?" Surely no God-fearing people could understand the Divinity without these. "These people are heathens that God has sent to us to bring to His true religion and save their lost souls," the missionaries reasoned.

The Native Americans were bewildered by the white man's religion, which focused on worshipping one day a week. They viewed tithing to the church as little more than trying "to bribe the Creator," a concept they found ludicrous. They did not understand the white culture's view of a punitive, vengeful God, who gave man one life to get it right in spite of so many temptations. God in the Euro-Christian tradition is often seen, as Joy Harjo of the Muscogee Creek Nation describes, "as a judgmental old white man without a sense of humor, presiding over heaven and hell."

Pre-contact Native Americans believed in the immortality of the soul and that bad deeds could be atoned for by doing good deeds. They resisted the concepts of heaven and hell preached by the early missionaries. If being in heaven meant being with the Christian colonists who robbed, cheated and killed them, they preferred the company of generations of their unsaved relatives in hell.

Native Americans did not attach a moral stigma to wrong actions. Without guilt, they simply believed that they would pay the price for the wrong action. Nor did they embrace the view that humanity is born in sin and are sinners by nature whose only possible salvation was through accepting one particular religion and savior. Native Americans did not believe people were born sinful because this concept did not reflect the way most of their tribal people were behaving (though it was soon clear that it *did* reflect the way many white people were behaving). They saw every human being as part of a good and beneficent Creation. They did not perceive their Creator as separate from them and that they needed to earn their way back to Him. They believed they walked *with* the Creator always and that Divinity was *within* each person. They did not believe that they needed to win his favor because they did not believe they had ever lost it.

As Luther Standing Bear said in 1905, the Great Spirit:

> . . . was not aloof, apart, and ever seeking to quell evil forces. He did not punish the animals and the birds, and likewise. He did not punish man. He was not a punishing God. For there was never a question as to the supremacy of an evil power over and above the power of Good. There was but one ruling power, and that was Good.

Native Americans did not teach their children that they were born in sin, but rather that they were born inherently good and in harmony with the Great Spirit. They intuitively understood that freeing people from spirit-crushing guilt and fear builds self-esteem, the basis of individual happiness. Christian philosophers either never understood this or believed, no matter how emotionally damaging, congregants should be ashamed of their sins and fear God.

Native Americans had no fear of death or eternal damnation. Nor were they fearers of a devil nor did they believe in the supremacy of an evil power over and above the power of Good. They saw no punishment from a judgmental and vengeful God. They lived the Ten Commandments, especially the first, which instructed us to put no other gods before Him. We were given this instruction *first* not because we are to fear His jealous wrath, as many Christians believe, but rather to put anything but the Creator first - possessions, power, pleasuring, achievements, even loved ones - would only bring us unhappiness, which a loving Creator did not will for his children. Hence the Creator made it His *first* Commandment.

Even the concept that Adam and Eve were punished for falling from grace, and condemned to hard labor and painful childbirths, did not ring true to them. They enjoyed their activities to secure food for the tribe and the women had no fear of birth-pain which they viewed as a holy moment in their lives, one usually experienced alone and in nature. Indeed all activities needed to sustain life in tribal times - hunting, fishing, gathering, drying and preparation of food, shelter building, farming, water and wood gathering, fire building, clothes making - were inherently uplifting, enjoyable and good for the body, mind and soul. Theirs was a life of pleasant routines. They felt no need to change it. Why invent a labor-saving device when you enjoyed the "labor?" Why build a big dwelling full of possessions when you relished living simply in the Creator's world?

There was no one holy day a week. To Native Americans every day was holy and all things - humans, animals, plants, rocks, the Earth - were innately spiritual. They were troubled by the new white man's theology, with its emphasis not on thanking, but rather on pleading for blessings every Sunday and on a few holidays. To them, there were no special days to thank the Creator. They never argued about beliefs but believed that the spiritual paths of *all* people were valid. There were no beliefs or spiritual paths that were held above others as more complete or more truthful for they knew the Great Spirit was called by many names and had many faces and many stories.

The settlers' religious arguments also mystified the Native Americans. As Chief Seattle of the Nez Pierce noted, "We do not want churches because they will teach us to quarrel about God, as the Catholics and Protestants do. We do not want that. We may quarrel with men about things on earth, but we never quarrel about the Great Spirit."

To the Christian settlers, these "pagans" just did not get it. As an early missionary Rev. David Brainerd wrote in his diary in 1822, "It is next to impossible to bring [the Indians] to a rational conviction that they are sinners by nature, and that their hearts are corrupt and sinful. . . . I observe to them that this may be the case and they may not be [aware] of it [because of] the blindness of their minds." Another famous Puritan theologian, Dr. Cotton Mather, bragged after a bloody massacre of the Pequots, "no less than 600 souls were brought down to hell that day."

As one Native American Elder noted, "Fear, guilt and greed are demanding Gods." And as Luther Standing Bear wrote, "For one man the world was full of beauty; for the other it was a place of sin and ugliness to be endured until he went to another world."

The settlers believed they must stop these native satanic practices even if it meant killing the "savages" to save their souls. Of course killing them was also an expedient and inexpensive way of stealing their tribal lands. To the Europeans, coming from a city/state culture based on developed commerce and agriculture, the native land appeared as foreboding wilderness. Like most city dwellers, to them land was just another commodity, like a horse or a loom, to be bought and sold. By the settlers' way of thinking, the Indians had not even developed land as any intelligent, industrious people would. They weren't really even using it. It was still "wild," theirs for the taking to develop for God, in Genesis, had given them dominion over it.

As recorded by one senator in the 1880 United States *Congressional Record*:

> An idle and thriftless race of savages cannot be permitted to stand guard at the treasure vaults of the nation which hold our gold and silver . . . The prospector and miner may enter and by enriching himself enrich the nation and bless the world by the results of his toil.

The Native Americans' view was quite different. The white race was striving for the "conquest of nature." The red race was at home on "Mother

Earth." Land was not wild, but existed as the Great Spirit had created it. The land was home - pristine and beautiful, to be protected for "seven generations into the future." Except for brief periods in their tipis or lodges, they spent most of their day in nature, enjoying its beauty and bounty. They sat and reclined on the ground with a feeling of being close to a mothering power. No matter where they traveled, they were with Mother Earth - always safe with her. The same spiritual force that had breathed life into them, had breathed life into the flowers, the rocks, the trees, the wind, the animals. No other culture has ever surpassed the Native American reverence for nature. They did not see the earth as so many resources that had to be wisely managed, but as a Mother - a cherished relative that should be respected and gently cared for. They practiced spiritual ecology, the highest level of environmental awareness.

As Chief Luther Standing Bear noted:

We did not think of the great open plains, the beautiful rolling hills, and winding streams with tangled growth, as "wild." Only to the white man was nature a "wilderness" and only to him was the land "infested' with wild animals and savage people." To us it was tame. Earth was bountiful and we were surrounded with the blessings of the Great Mystery. Not until the hairy man from the east came and with brutal frenzy heaped injustices upon us and the families we loved was it "wild" for us. When the very animals of the forest began fleeing from his approach, then it was that for us the "Wild West" began.

What the settlers failed to understand, what they culturally *could not* understand, was that these indigenous people lacked the ambition to create a more technically advanced world because they were quite happy and content with their existing ways. Technological development is driven for the most part by the desire for money, comfort, protection, and domination. Native Americans sought none of these. Their lives were peaceful, secure and dignified. Most tribes only devoted a few hours a day to survival issues. The rest of their time was free for exploring, artistic endeavors, devotion and enjoying the satisfying relationships of tribal life.

They already had what most people are looking for.

These ancient tribes, many known for their "Give-away-dances," were not materialistic as were these new white settlers who had "the sickness only the yellow metal would cure."

As Ohiyesa wrote:

> The Native American was generally despised by his white conquerors for his poverty and simplicity. They forget, perhaps, that his religion forbade the accumulation of wealth and the enjoyment of luxury. To him . . . the love of possessions has appeared a snare, and the burdens of a complex society a source of needless peril and temptation. Furthermore, it was the rule of his life to share the fruits of his skill and success with his less fortunate brothers. Thus he kept his spirit free of the clog of pride, cupidity, or envy . . . [The Indian] would not be forced to accept materialism as the basic principle of his life, but preferred to reduce existence to its simplest terms . . . It is our belief that the love of possessions is a weakness to be overcome . . . it will in time disturb the spiritual balance of man . . . Not 'to have' but 'to be' was our national motto.

Even Christopher Columbus, whose explorations were in reality searches wealth, noted the Indians' non-materialistic, generous nature. He wrote to his Spanish sponsors about the Arawak Indians: "These are the friendliest people . . . There cannot be a better or more gentle people than these anywhere in the world . . . [their] houses are the most beautiful I've ever seen . . . They are free with all they possess . . . Of anything they have, if you ask them for it, they never say no: rather they invite the person to share it, and show as much love as if they were giving with their hearts."

This was the same man who later became rich as a slave-trader of the Indians he so respected. He later wrote to the Spanish monarchs in 1493: "It is possible, with the name of the Holy Trinity, to sell all the slaves . . . Here are so many of these slaves . . . that although they are living things they are as good as gold . . . Let us in the name of the Holy Trinity go on sending all the slaves that can be sold."

Within forty years of Columbus' landing in Hispaniola (now Haiti and the Dominican Republic) *none* of the estimated eight million indigenous Carib-Indians were alive. As Bartolome` de las Casas, a priest who transcribed Columbus's journal and participated in the conquest of Cuba, wrote in his *History of the Indies*, ". . . in a short time this land which was so great, so powerful and fertile . . . was depopulated . . . My eyes have seen acts so foreign to human nature, and now I tremble as I write . . . from 1494 to 1508, over three million people have perished from war, slavery, and the mines. Who in future generations will believe this? I myself writing it as a knowledgeable eyewitness can hardly believe it."

The English were no different from the Spanish. Once they began to settle the colonies, they soon found that the freedom-loving Indians could not be enslaved, and not being able to live with them, they decided to systematically exterminate them. Just as they viewed humans as a profitable resource to be tapped, these early explorers viewed the land the same way. As Howard Zinn wrote in *The People's History of the United States*, "Behind the English invasion of North America, behind their massacre of the Indians, their deception, their brutality, was that special powerful drive born in civilizations based on private property."

The settlers looked out on this "wilderness" and thought that it was not only their right but their duty to tame and use as they saw fit. Since the Indian did not believe he owned it, it was unclaimed, theirs for the taking. When the settlers looked at the small Indian villages occupied by 50 to 1000 people, they were assured that their European culture must be superior. After all, their ancestors had also once lived like this throughout Europe; however, they had developed from the small communal tribes to the large city/state societies. Surely this was an advancement that these natives had been unable or unwilling to manifest.

What they failed to understand was that these ancient people in their wisdom *intentionally* decided not only against the accumulation of possessions and wealth (the basis of capitalism), but against large concentrated population centers.

As Ohiyesa writes:

It was not then, wholly from ignorance or improvidence that he [the Indians] failed to establish permanent towns or to develop a material culture. To the untutored sage, the concentration of population was a prolific mother of all evils, moral no less than physical . . . and not less dreaded than the pestilence following upon a crowded and unsanitary dwellings was the loss of spiritual power inseparable from too close contact with one's fellow-men . . . It is simple truth that the Indian did not, so long as his native philosophy held sway over his mind, either envy or desire to imitate the splendid achievements of the white man.

There was no commerce except bartering with neighboring tribes. It was not their custom to store things for later resale, to fence land and domesticate wild animals, or to gather things for the sake of mere possessions. These cooperative cultures were for the most part hunting and gathering tribes who lived off the available land and its naturally-available resources. Their worldview allowed *total* trust in this as they, perhaps more than the Christian newcomers, believed that the Creator would provide for them as He did for "the lilies of the field." They believed the Creator created *and* preserved them. It was this complete trust in a loving - not punitive - God that created a tribal society that maintained its millions of members in health, happiness and freedom for thousands of years. It seems so simple. They strove to love as they believed God loves.

As an Iroquois prayer stated, "We return thanks to the Great Spirit, in Whom is embodied all goodness and Who directs all things for the good of his children." And as Leon Shenandoah says, "There is no reason to ask [God]. He has given us everything for us to enjoy. That's why our greetings is 'thanks.' "

This "knowing" was pervasive among the hundreds of tribes, past and, for many, present. As Navajo and environmentalist Ella Mulford says, "I go through life knowing there is a Creator who is all knowing, all good, and a protector. I can't imagine not having this knowing. Spirituality has helped indigenous people survive."

Never wanting to enslave their friends in the animal kingdom, the Native Americans domesticated no animals, used no diary products and ate little meat, unless the environment demanded otherwise. When they did kill animals, they prayed before and after, thanking them for their contribution to the tribes survival. Many said that the animals were never afraid of humans until after the white man came. They employed sophisticated methods of food preservation, even freeze-drying. To provide for the tribe, some used limited agriculture, often developing very high-yield strains through generations of natural genetic engineering by selective cuttings, grafting and seed selection. This plant development was done almost exclusively by the women who retained all the biological information. Modern botanists have noted that these First People, using simple but intelligent trial and error, may have been the best plant breeders in the world.

There were no pre-contact Native American police or jails. Personal behavior was regulated by an enlightened series of moral codes and mores. The Lakota word for this governing power of custom was "wouncage," literally, "our way of doing." As Luther Standing Bear explains:

> Wouncage constituted, for the Lakota people, the only authority . . . therefore it was hard for a person to get away from Wouncage. In other words, it was harder to break the laws than to keep them. Consequently, there were few law-breakers . . . Written laws were not a part of the tribal consciousness . . . The Lakotas were, in fact, bound by the only codes that endure - those written into the essence of living . . . The way of the tribe in dealing with an offender was simple and dignified . . . There was no violence such as whipping, no taking away of personal effects nor personal liberties . . . When it became necessary for the band to protect itself it did so by merely ignoring and ostracizing the violator . . . . This sort of punishment was usually sufficient to make the offender change his habits. . . A Lakota may lie once, but after that no one will believe him . . . if a man's offense was serious, say if he were a murderer, his exclusion from the band would be permanent. He would suffer neither for food or clothing, but he would not be welcome at the tipis of others and no one would visit his

tipi. In time of sickness he would be cared for by near relatives, but he was never again accepted as a creditable member of his band . . . There was domination, but it was self-domination, the mother, father, sister, brother, and all, voluntarily placing their person in secondary importance to the needs of the band and the nation . . . And by thus they themselves were never neglected.

This concept, that each individual lived for the tribe, can be seen as personally limiting to the modern Western world, where individuality is held as the benchmark of human freedom. Though personal freedom was cherished by the tribes, personal ambition and aspirations were redirected toward the greater good of the tribe. Everyone lived for everyone else - for the family, the clan or band, the village, the tribe. No one broke away and pursued their own individual goals without considering how these might serve their responsibilities to the tribe. In our present day societies, with no sense of tribe or land, the power of this system to create human happiness and security is often loss in what seems to be personal sacrifice.

Their tribal size remained stable without the problems of overpopulation (though very ancient tribes in the Hopewell Mississippi Delta and South America grew to large city-states). For the most part, they managed to live within the resources available. Their societies were observed to be more just, equitable and egalitarian than those of their conquerors, with no social classes or power based on owning land and means of production. Their health care, through the use of sweat lodges (the "Indian hospital"), healthy eating, exercise and medicinal roots and herbs, was superior to that of the colonists. They believed that the Creator had given a plant to cure every illness. They were able to sustain their way of life without major warfare or damage to the environment for millennia.

These two vastly different worldviews had been developing for thousands of years before the Europeans had even set foot on the North American continent. For millennia, before the advent of the first city/state, almost all of humanity lived in cooperative tribal cultures very similar to the ones found in North America by the early settlers. In his excellent book, *The Last Hours of Ancient Sunlight*, Thom Hartman referred to these ancient tribal societies as "Older Cultures." They were older because they have lasted for 200,000 years of known human history. Their lives were elegant in their simplicity.

The city/states, which began in Sumeria 7000 years ago, with their competitive economic and political structures, are still a relatively new human experiment. Hence, Hartman calls these the "Younger Cultures," not referring to the age of individuals but rather the age the system or worldview has been around. (For purposes of clarity, I will refer to the "Older Cultures" as "Cooperative Cultures" and the "Younger Cultures" as "Competitive Cultures.")

The major difference between these two types of culture is their world-views, especially in how they regard the planet. Each has different, and conflicting, stories they tell themselves. The domination-driven Competitive Cultures felt that the Earth was theirs to conquer and control, to plunder and own. They desired to subdue and rule the planet and other tribes, to seize as much as they could by whatever means necessary. Man was at the top of an hierarchical universe - the top of the food chain. And all this led to the single most corrupting factor - money - the love of which the Bible tells us is the root of *all* evil.

Cooperative Cultures saw the Earth as sacred, a gift to them, and to all people equally. They were an integral part of nature, not separate and at war with it. Even their intertribal warfare was mostly minor skirmishes to establish territory and exhibit personal bravery. It was never to exterminate and dominate (this changed somewhat when tribes were forced on each other's tribal lands by the encroaching settlers).

Their wealth was in security, not possessions and money. Their goal was to secure safety and happiness for all the tribe: young and old, male and female, healthy or ill, feeble or strong. Instead of the production of goods they valued producing tribal security, safety and ample time to relate to others and the Creator.

Most Cooperative Cultures live in matrilineal societies that value cooperation. Competitive Cultures are patrilineal which value domination. In a matrilineal culture, each child belongs to the clan of their mother, not their father. This automatically insures respect for the women, something that is always missing in patrilineal societies. For balance, it also gives the hereditary power to the physically weaker sex, insuring respectful treatment by the physically stronger males.

Chief Standing Bear wrote of the Lakota's respect for women and their importance in peacemaking:

> Women and children were objects of care among the Lakotas and as far as their environment permitted they lived sheltered lives. Life was softened by a great equality. All the tasks of women - cooking, caring for children, tanning and sewing - were considered dignified and worthwhile. No work was looked upon as menial, consequently there were no menial workers. Industry filled the life of every Lakota woman . . . In marriage, as in birth, mother's influenced prevailed . . . Though married, the woman retained her identity and continued to do so throughout her life. She never took the name of her husband, assumed no marriage title such as Mrs. and never entirely left her own band . . . Not until the women of the land come back to the forsaken road, emulate the Indian mother, and again raise sons for peace, will there be any substantial move toward "peace on earth and good will toward men."

Another example of this respect for women, was told to President James Madison by a white woman who had run away as an adolescence servant of a white family to live with the Oneidas:

> . . . the whites treated me harshly. I saw them take rest while they made me work without a break. I ran the risk of being beaten, or dying of hunger, if through laziness or fatigue I refused to do what I was told. Here, I have no master, I am the equal of all the women of the tribe. I do what I please without anyone saying anything about it. I work only for myself. I shall marry if I wish and be unmarried again when I wish. Is there a single woman as independent as I in your cities?

All members of the Cooperative Cultures, old and young, male and female, infirmed and healthy, were respected and cared for. Especially the old were held in high esteem given the wisdom of their years. The grandparents were often the main caregivers of the young. In time, the home of the adult children became the home of their elders. Care for your elderly relatives was considered the highest form of personal integrity - a task that was greeted with enthusiasm and pleasure rather than reluctance and distaste as it has so often become in the modern world. As the Lakota Luther Standing Bear wrote: "There is something evil in a system . . . when it makes the young hearts callous and unheedful of the needs and joys of the old."

The new Competitive Cultures' leaders obtained power at the top of the hierarchy through force, birth, wealth and later through elections. Usually, the "takers" (those that put their own interests in front of others) control power in Competitive Culture politics. They are often the ones most ambitiously seeking power and wealth. Even those that are democratically elected today are almost always those that have also accumulated personal wealth and power.

On the other hand, Older Culture leaders did not *choose* to lead but *were chosen* by the tribe. They were viewed as servants of the people, never as their masters. They were the "givers," from youth known for their generosity, compassion and placing the tribe's interests above their own. Often they were the ones with the fewest possessions, having given much to those in need. There was no inherited royalty, no kings, princes or princesses, passed down within families, something that the early colonists mistakenly assigned to them.

Chiefs were natural leaders with much influence, but little authority. They had no power to force tribal members to obey them. Only the power of their integrity and wisdom was used to persuade. Their customs taught never to make a warrior a chief or he will lead his tribe to war, something that the modern world has yet to learn.

Iroquois elder Leon Shenandoah explained the different views of choosing leaders. He wrote in *To Become a Human*:

To be a chief you can't want it. If a man wants to be chief that means he wants power. It's up to the clan mother to decide who will be chief. If she sees a man desiring the position, she passes him over because he wants it for himself and he might not work for the good of the clan. So she goes to the one who doesn't want to be chief. She knows if he's picked, he will use the good mind and work for the good of the people.

Through custom and ceremony, self-importance and self-concern was stripped away so the leaders could focus on the tribe and how to serve them. There were seldom individuals portrayed as heroes but rather tribes and clans. In contrast, in Competitive Cultures, the political ceremonies, like inaugurations and coronations, are designed to enhance the egos of the leaders. This leads to people who desire to accumulate power and then devote all their actions to holding on to it. Often the most self-centered, not other-centered, aspire to power in the Competitive Cultures. As one Native American Elder noted: "Men who desire power are generally not good men, and good men generally do not desire power." Or as reggae recording-artist Prezident Brown sings about today's leaders, "I see worshipping of vanity and but no love for humanity."

In addition to the chosen leaders, there was also often a council of elders consisting of older people known for their wisdom. They often offered advice and guidance to the leaders. As Luther Standing Bear writes:

> . . . through meditation and prayer, wisdom was gained for which the wise man was greatly venerated. The wise men were always part of every council, but, unlike the braves and chiefs, seldom spoke at length. Their powers were felt in prayer, and blessings they gave were always effective.

Having the chiefs guided by the wise elders proved to be a very effective system for good governance. Unfortunately, in modern governments, the leaders proceed without the advise of these wise ones.

In essence, the Competitive Cultures saw a universe created by a punitive God who dispensed rewards and punishments according to how you led your life and how you praised Him. He could be a jealous, angry God; traits that Native Americans would never attribute to the Great Spirit. The Competitive Cultures believe they are separate from God and have to earn His favor to one day be allowed into heaven. Native Americans believed they were living in heaven, gifted to them by a loving Creator who provided for all His children's needs.

As Black Hawk, a Sauk Indian, noted:

How smooth must be the languages of the whites, when they can make right look wrong, and wrong look right. We can only judge what is proper and right by our standard of right and wrong, which differs widely from the whites, if I have been correctly informed. The whites may do bad all their lives, and then, if they are sorry for it when they are about to die, all is well! But with us it is different. We must continue to be good. If we have corn and meat, and know of a family that has none, we divide with them. If we have more blankets than are sufficient, and others have not enough, we must give to them that want.

To understand how totally the early explorers reflected the Competitive Cultures' point of view of dominance, consider a proclamation read by Spanish Conquistador Pizarro to the uncomprehending natives, who stood before him with gifts and food when he landed in South America in 1514:

I implore you to recognize the Church as a lady and in the name of the Pope take the King as lord of this land and obey his mandates. If you do not, I assure you that with the help of God I will make war upon you in every place and every way that I can. And I will subject you to the yoke and obedience of the church and their highnesses. And I will take your persons and your women and your children and I will make them slaves. I will take your goods and I will do you all the evils and harms which I can. The deaths and injuries that you will receive from hereon will be your own fault and not that of his majesty nor of the gentlemen who accompany me.

For 7000 years, the Competitive Cultures has developed societies based on commerce, separation and war. It was, and is, a greed-driven system. It views its world through the lens of separation - separate from God, separate from the natural world, separate from other humans. It values conquest and enemy-thinking, believing they must conquer the land, the wilderness, the oceans, the desert, the elements, even space and one only seeks to conquer what one believes is their enemy.

On the other hand, for over 200,000 years the Cooperative Cultures had developed a worldview based on harmony, unity and peace. Cooperative Cultures saw themselves as "one" - one with their Creator, one with their environment, one with other humans. Or as the Sioux greeting says "Mitakuye Oyasin" - "We are all related." By this they meant all - humans, animals, plants, and everything in the universe. These were two very different stories creating two very different societies.

Just as it is today, the settlers response to encountering these Cooperative Cultures had to do with commerce, with money - which to them meant land. The new United States government kept taking over land in the east and pushing the tribes further west to what the government deemed useless wilderness. To the eager advancing Europeans, the Native Americans, who were not easily broken to become slaves, were at best an annoying hindrance to their "Manifest Destiny;" at worse, wild vermin that needed to be eradicated like dangerous snakes or wolves. As more and more settlers came, these Western lands became desirable so the government just broke the treaties, killed many of the tribal people and took what they wanted.

These moral contradictions were glaringly obvious to foreign observers who were carefully studying this new, and apparently more enlightened, form of governance. Alexander de Tocqueville, the French military man, historian and philosopher, wrote in his *Democracy in America* published in 1835:

The Indians have been ruined by a competition which they had no means of sustaining. They were isolated in their own country, and their race constituted only a little colony of troublesome strangers in the midst of a numerous and dominant people . . . Moreover, the Indians readily discover that the settlement that is proposed to them is merely temporary . . . The United States pledges itself to maintain them there [on new reservations], but the territory which they now occupy was formerly secured to them by the most solemn oaths . . . and, as the limits of the earth will at last fail them, their only refuge is the grave.

By the time the invasion of Native America was over, millions of indigenous people had been killed or died and only a small amount of their ancient tribal land was Indian reservations - land that the encroaching culture now considered "junk land."

These Native Americans encountered the same unmerciful and relentless force that their counterparts in other parts of the globe had succumbed to centuries before. Once the Competitive Culture commercial and political system began spreading thousands of years ago, there was no stopping it. It was inevitable that it would run its course worldwide (that course is now almost complete). As large scale agriculture and commerce was introduced allowing for a larger population to inhabit any region, the Competitive Cultures began to grow and spread. Instead of living off the available resources of the land, agriculture led to surpluses and the control of the means of production. This, mixed with commerce, led to another level of power that complemented the use of physical power for the control of the masses.

More and more people began to live away from the land, removed from nature and needing money to survive. Today, almost all First World people live in cities or suburbs. Almost everything that surrounds us in our cities - concrete, glass, metal, plastic, sheetrock, etc. - is dead. Everything in nature is *alive*. And as Native American elder Walking Buffalo noted, "When people live far from the scenes of the Great Spirit's making, it is easy for them to forget His laws."

When the explorers landed in America, other areas such as Europe, the Middle East and Asia had been living under this unconscious Competitive Cultures for millennia. Most of the indigenous tribes of these areas had been destroyed and their wisdom long lost. The native tribes of North and South America were living on the last continent to be overrun by the Competitive Cultures. Their cultures were the last to be impacted by this aggressive commercial system. That is why their wisdom is so important. It is the most current. Except for a few small remote pockets of untouched indigenous living in the jungles of South and Central America or on isolated islands of Indonesia or other remote areas, Native American tribal wisdom is the most recent and the least contaminated by the advancing Competitive Cultures.

It would be easy to reason that surely the more militarily powerful culture must be the superior of the two. However, if there was ever any doubt about which lifestyles brought greater human happiness, it may have been put to rest by one European observer of early America who noted, "It hath often been seen that a Christian gentleman, well born and bred, and gently nurtured, will, of his own free will, quit his station and luxurious world, to dwell among savages and live their lives, taking part in all their savagery. But never yet hath it been seen that a savage will, of his own free will, give up his savagery, and live the life of a civilized man."

Pre-contact Native America was the first "affluent society" on the continent. It is no wonder that no one wanted to leave it and many fought so hard to keep the life they had and so few embraced the "comfortable, civilized life" of the newcomers. Native Americans intuitively understood that living close to nature was inherently healthy - mentally, physically and spiritually. It produced high self-esteem, the foundation of true happiness. As Alexis de Tocqueville wrote:

> They [the Indians] hold their customs with a degree of tenacity unparalleled in history . . . Not that he is devoid of admiration of the power . . . of the whites but he despises the means by which we obtain it . . . though he acknowledges our ascendancy, he still believes in his own superiority. They consider labor not merely as an evil, but as a disgrace . . . He considers the cares of

industry a degrading occupation . . . there is no Indian so
wretched as not to retain . . . a lofty idea of his personal worth .
. . with no feelings of inferiority towards anyone.

However, these tribes were no match for the newcomers and their
aggressive ways and powerful weaponry. Soon, these Competitive Cultures
overpowered the Cooperative Cultures, who were not as technically
advanced and knew nothing of cultural dominance and genocidal warfare.
Their defeat was inevitable. When the Cooperative Cultures encountered
the advancing Competitive Cultures they had three choices: either fight
them (and in doing so become like them), be assimilated by them, or flee.
In the end, none of the options allowed the Cooperative Cultures to
remain intact. Once the Competitive Cultures took over their land and
crushed their culture, within a few generations, this new worldview
replaced their more holistic tribal worldview. This new worldview
"infected" everything it touched. By the time it was over, Babylon had
absorbed Zion into itself - but not totally.

Within a few hundred years of the "discovery" of America by
Columbus, over ninety percent of the indigenous population was wiped
out. Of the millions that lived here before the invasion, by 1900 only
350,000 remained. Their political and spiritual leaders were systematically
assassinated, their religious shrines and artifacts defiled, their villages
and homes destroyed and their entire societies ripped apart by the
advancing culture. In the West, Indians who had been arrested, usually
for drinking, were auctioned to the highest bidder where they had to
work hard labor for their sentence in mines and ranches. Native women
were taken as prostitutes in miners' camps. "Abducting children," noted
one California paper in 1854, "has become quite a common practice."
Indian slavery in California, a state that never enslaved blacks, did not end
until 1869 - four years *after* the Civil War ended Negro slavery.

Ten white soldiers died for every one Indian warrior. It was estimated
that each warriors death cost the new government one hundred thousand
dollars. The cost to both sides never needed to be this great. Canada had
no Indian wars. They purchased rights to use the tribal land by treaties
that were often, though not always, kept. They set aside permanent reser-

vations for their indigenous peoples and seldom removed them. They chose agents of integrity to work with the Indians through the transformation. They viewed their tribal people as equal subjects of Her Majesty the Queen of England - probably one of the few benefits to emerge from belatedly adopting the fledgling democracy.

What the advancing culture did to the land and environment can best be described by Luther Standing Bear:

> Forests were mowed down, the buffalo exterminated, the beaver driven to extinction and his wonderfully constructed dams dynamited . . . Great grassy plains that sweetened the air have been upturned; springs, streams, and lakes that lived no longer ago than my boyhood have dried, and a whole people harassed to degradation and death. The white man has come to be a symbol of extinction for all things natural to this continent. Between him and the animal there is no rapport and they have learned to flee from his approach, for they cannot live on the same ground.

It was an American holocaust that is one of the most terrifying events in human history. For centuries it has been sanitized from our history books. Many died from the advancing culture's brutality, including being shot like rabbits. Many more died from their diseases often spread through infected blankets intentionally given to the tribes by the settlers (the first use of germ warfare). The Native American had no immunity to diseases, which are usually spread within cities. Believing that all animals had the right to run free, they also had no domesticated animals. Scientist now know that all human disease began with animals and then mutated and jumped to humans. It was not just these infectious diseases that led to the tribes' weakening, but the new enforced eating and living habits as well.

As Chief Luther Standing Bear writes:

> The tipi was never infested with rodents . . . we were not beset with insect hordes . . . The Lakotas were lean and thin, due to their outdoor and vigorous lives . . . The Lakotas were blessed with

good health, but this was natural, observing as they did all the rules that appertain to health. As far as I can remember there was no such thing as contagious disease. But when our mode of life changed and we began to eat "spotted buffalo" and learned to eat bread, sugar, candy and canned goods, we then realized the meaning of disease . . . Food, which had always been procured through the exercise of great energy and industry, was doled and rationed . . . Everything that was natural and therefore healthful, was displaced with things unsuitable, foreign, and unfitted.

Even millions of Natives dying by European diseases, was seen as God's blessing by the colonists. As Rev. John Elliott wrote in 1663, ". . . it pleased God to visit . . . with a pestilential fever whereby great numbers of Indians suddenly were taken away and the country left depopulated." If it was God's blessing, it was to spare them the nightmare that was to follow their conquest.

By making liquor a staple of their trade with the Indians, the English, who had invaded China by weakening them with mandatory opium trade, used alcohol to similarly weaken Native Americans. The evil was twofold. English plantation owners used enslaved Africans to grow sugar and make rum, referred to as the "Indian Exterminator," which was then used by other Englishmen to trade with the Native Americans to destroy them physically, emotionally and spiritually.

The United States presidents were no more compassionate or enlightened. As Thomas Jefferson wrote in 1807 to his Secretary of War, ". . . if ever we are constrained to lift the hatchet against any tribe, we will never lay it down till that tribe is exterminated, or is driven beyond the Mississippi. . . we shall destroy them all." He was following in the footsteps of George Washington who sent orders to General John Sullivan in 1779 to make Native American settlements objects of "total destruction and devastation and . . . to capture as many prisoners of every age and sex . . . that the country may not be merely overrun, but destroyed." Over a century later even President Theodore Roosevelt, a winner of the Noble Peace Prize, revealed his racism when he said the phrase "the only good Indians are dead Indians" applied to 9 out of 10 and he wasn't that sure of the tenth.

Adding insult to injury, Roosevelt's countenance, along with that of three other presidents, all of whom aided the annihilation of the Native Americans, was carved into the massive stone cliffs of Mount Rushmore in the Black Hills of South Dakota - one of the most sacred sites of the Lakota Sioux Nation. At least slave-holding Jefferson had some remorse. He later wrote, "I tremble for my country when I reflect that God is just."

This systematic and aggressive assault on Native Americans by the new settlers and their government, which de Tocqueville called the "most prodigious growth and rapid destruction" in human history, did not end in the 1800s when their land was seized. It is still ongoing today. Racial prejudice continues against them at all levels of society. True justice for Native Americans is often random and arbitrary where it exists at all. Government and business interest continue to desecrate and pollute their lands by pushing mineral, coal and uranium leases and casino operations through uncomprehending or corrupt tribal councils. Leaders, like Leonard Peltier of the American Indian Movement (AIM) are framed and languish in prisons for decades. Some are killed while trying to demonstrate against the abuses. The government agencies, such as the Bureau of Indian Affairs, meant to protect them and their assets, are some of the most corrupt in the country. Recently they were sued by tribes for mishandling billions of Indian funds over decades. Even Native American religions were illegal until Congress finally acted in 1978.

Of those that survived the onslaught, many have succumbed to alcohol and materialism. Diabetes and obesity are of epidemic proportions among the tribes. By choosing not to fight, your cultural death was assured even if your physical death was not. As they became wards of the state under the ruthless and corrupt Bureau of Indian Affairs, their new dependent lifestyle undermined the dignity and pride of all but the strongest. As Luther Standing Bear stated, "Incentive is gone. Old and young are meek to the point of docility, obeying every command of the agent. They settle no question for themselves; their overseer decides everything. The system has crushed them; they are nonentities."

Today, the spirit and wisdom of their ancestors still lives in many. In spite of the overwhelming assault, Native Americans have survived against all odds and predictions. They are *still* here. Indeed, their numbers have been growing and flourishing in the last 100 years. Lakota Elder Mat King noted that in the Original Instructions given to his people by Tunkashila, the Great Spirit, was, "The First Instruction is to survive as a people. Nothing is more important than that!" In most tribes, a few wisdomkeepers *have* survived and now their wisdom is being made available to all at this crucial time of planetary crisis.

THE INSANITY OF THE COMPETITVE CULTURES

Now let us fast forward to today and look at the true legacy of a planet dominated by the Competitive Cultures' worldview. It is not surprising with the ascent of the Competitive Cultures and the decline of the Cooperative Cultures has also come the degradation of the natural environment. Today, every life-support system is declining. Every 24 hours over 200,000 acres of rainforest, the "lungs of the planet," are destroyed, 13 million tons of toxic chemicals are released into the environment, 45,000 people die of starvation (most of them children) and approximately 100 plant and animal species become extinct. Over 2 billion people, 40% of the world's population, do not have clean water to drink.

It took 200,000 years to produce our first one billion population; 130 years our second billion, 30 years our third, and only 12 years our sixth. Clearly this Competitive Culture system is not sustainable and we are very close to its collapsing point, and in many countries, especially in Africa and parts of Asia and South America, that collapsing point has been reached. Today less than one percent of the planet lives tribally, and even they are threatened and diminishing.

Along with this loss of our First People and their tribal lands, has come the growth of corporations, the logical extension of an economy created under a Competitive Cultures' point of view. The plundering by the early United States government of tribal lands to sell them for a profit has now morphed into the plundering of resources and labor globally by modern-day multinational corporations who now control the United States government. It has been a seamless progression of greed.

Until the mid-1800s, corporations had little sway over public policy.

However, President Lincoln predicted their ascent when he stated, "As a result of war, corporations have now been enthroned and an era of corruption in high places will follow . . . until all wealth is aggregated in a few hands, and the Republic is destroyed." A hundred years later another president, Dwight Eisenhower, issued the same warning in his Farewell Address to the Nation. He said, "In the councils of government, we must guard against the acquisition of unwarranted influence, whether sought or unsought, by the military-industrial complex. The potential for the disastrous rise of misplaced power exists and will persist."

That potential has now become a reality. The first modern corporation was the Hudson Bay Company chartered by King Charles II in 1670. At it's peak the company owned land larger than Western Europe, all stolen from indigenous people. It is still the world's largest dealer in furs. This was just the beginning. Today the leaders of large corporations make almost all public policy. It is these corporations, through their financial control of politicians at all levels, that truly have the power in the United States and many other countries. These corporations also control the World Bank, the International Monetary Fund and the World Trade Organization, all organizations that claim to help developing countries but in truth do just the opposite. Just as the Church once was the dominant institution, the corporation is now the dominant institution of our times.

However, before we declare this system a failure, let's take a look at the best this system has created for us as individuals. Let's look at life in modern America, which we still insist is the greatest society on the planet (though many now disagree). It is held up as the masterpiece, the grand culmination of capitalism and the Competitive Cultures' value system.

In reality, however, it has become for many a turbocharged life of frenzied activity and unbridled consumption. Life in the United States, and many other countries, has degenerated into an almost manic reality. It's a lifestyle that promised us more free time but has created the two-earner family that works longer each year. With more time needed to provide for our needs (or perceived needs), and with more people in our lives, we have less and less time for meaningful relationships, where true human happiness is found.

Americans are now subject to fear of job loss through massive layoffs by companies that have moved their operations overseas. Overseas manufacturing accounts for eighty percent of everything sold in stores owned by Wal-Mart, who, like other conglomerates, pay employees a near poverty-level wage. The minimum wage, unchanged for the last eight years, remains a scandalous $5.15 an hour. The gap between the rich and everyone else in the United States keeps getting larger. For every additional dollar earned by the bottom 90 percent of the population between 1990 and 2002, those in the top 0.01 percent earned $18,000.00. The middle class is mortgaged to the hilt and maxed out on high credit card debt. Everyone is just one serious health catastrophe away from bankruptcy. Many are just one layoff away from not being able to pay their bills.

This American phenomenon is not new. In the early 1800s, Alexander de Tocqueville noted that America's pursuit of prosperity was a "restless burning passion that increases with satisfaction." We have become addicted to striving for more, addicted to junk food, addicted to television and electronic stimulation, addicted to pleasuring, addicted to drugs, stimulants and alcohol, addicted to addiction. Tens of millions of Americans take anti-depressants. Almost half take at least one prescription drug. Fifteen million people are abusing these drugs. Fifty percent of us will have cancer in our lifetime and will have Alzheimer after 85.

We are a country where 2 out of 3 adults and 1 out of 2 children are overweight; where most of us work in unstable workplaces and we suffer from restless sleep patterns and chronic anxiety and stress. A Harvard Medical School survey in 2005 reported 46% of adult Americans say that they have experienced some form of mental illness, 26% within the last year. Twenty-nine percent have experienced anxiety and twenty percent depression. Many are living on the edge and have lost their presence of mind. Many feel they live pointless, empty lives and anesthetize themselves with shopping, television, eating and ingesting legal and illegal drugs. Yet we still insist that this is the greatest society ever. We may be the richest but that does not inherently make us the happiest nor the healthiest. In fact, any society glorifying things and pleasuring, will never advance happiness in its citizens.

There probably has never been a more lonely-making society in history than the United States. By adulthood, most people have moved away from the early roots, if they even had any. Many of our families are spread over 3000 miles, making contact with them infrequent and expensive. Our jobs often demand that we move repeatedly. Our political system has now divided us into "blue staters" and "red staters" and exasperated our political and social differences beyond reasonable dialogue. Our religions are desperately trying to convince us of which of our friends and relatives will join us in heaven and which may have been denied eternal grace, perhaps on a technicality. Most of our neighbors are new to us. Everyone is distracted by 250 television channels, massive shopping malls, and the all-pervasive Internet - all going non-stop, 24 hours-a-day, 7 days-a-week, 365 days-a-year. Perhaps we should consider the words of a Cherokee Elder who said, "As the world moves faster, we need to move slower."

World-respected psychologist Abraham Maslow, noted that the greatest motivator of most of humanity is to belong - to belong to the tribe, the church, the family, the peer group, the country club. Correspondingly, then our greatest fear must be to *not* belong, or in other words: being lonely. Modern society, while giving us unparalleled levels of comfort, stimulation, pleasure and distractions, has also created our worst fears. It is making us lonely. Loneliness was never an issue in pre-contact Native American tribes. Their lives were built around their relationships to the Creator, the Earth and each other. That's why they were inherently happy.

They designed societies that incorporated two essential mainstays of human happiness - tribe and tribal land - both of which are missing in modern life. Few of us in the First World have any sense of tribe or place that is relevant in our daily lives. It is more of a romanticized view that our ancestral home is Ireland or Africa or England; that we're Catholic or Jewish or Democrats or Yankee fans. Tribe and land is not an everyday experience. Since the loss of this is not part of our awareness, we have not even considered what it would mean to feel that we were part of a tribe that considered *everyone's* well-being essential and had roots in a place that was *always* home. If we do consider it, we can understand why indigenous people clung so tenaciously to their way of life and why the alternatives offered by the advancing Anglos seemed so abhorrent to them. And we would understand why our world has lost its balance - what the Hopi call a state of "Koyaanisqatsi."

Now that the situation that we, as a species, find ourselves in is somewhat clarified (at least if you agree with my reasoning), let us put it in an even broader perspective, hopefully one that will give us some peace of mind with the present state of affairs. In the past, many Cooperative Cultures valued unity, cooperation, security, love and friendship. This certainly sounds like "the Garden." Somewhere along the line, we made a "detour into fear" where we started to view ourselves as "separate" from all. We began to see ourselves as skin-encapsulated egos - sinful, competitive, hostile, combative. We came to value possessions, power and pleasuring, the outward manifestations of the belief in separation. We have done this as a species and we have done this as individuals. It *is* the human condition.

This was probably when we fell from grace and left the Garden. The Bible says that we left Eden when we "ate from the tree of good and evil." In other words, we left the Garden (unity) when we started to judge (separation). *I am good. My enemies are evil. I am right. You are wrong. My religions is correct. Yours goes astray.* And on and on, deeper and deeper into the illusion of separation until you have Planet Earth today, teetering on the brink of chaos created by this fractured and faulty worldview.

Looking back now, it seems inevitable that the Competitive Cultures and their point of view would eventually reach the worldwide dominance that it has today. Its philosophical base is to seek but never find - to never be satisfied. Since it seeks only on the material plane, never the spiritual, more is never enough. Or as Bob Marley sings, "When you get what you want, do you want more?" The Competitive Cultures will take all they can get, through "the ballot, the bullet, or the Bible," as our Havasupai friend Supai Waters, likes to say.

However, just as inevitable as it is that this vibration would eventually infect most of the Earth and its people, it is also inevitable that it will one day self-destruct and that day may be very close. The Competitive Cultures have developed their technology to the point that the entire planet is at risk, a phenomenon that only occurred around 50 years ago when we had built enough nuclear weapons to destroy all life. Now these technological threats are many: nuclear, chemical and biological weapons, overpopulation, pollution, global warming and terrorism.

Before August 6, 1945, the greatest weapon on Earth could kill a few hundred people. After that day, the atom bomb dropped on Hiroshima demonstrated that the largest weapon could now kill 100,000 people - a thousand fold increase. Until that day, advances in weaponry were traveling at an upward trajectory parallel with advances in consciousness - advances in noble ideas of justice, democracy and basic human rights. All of this has been slowly developing as we advanced our technology without wisdom, spiritual clarity or love. Or as an Indian Elder once said, "The white man is smart but he is not wise. He seeks knowledge but not wisdom."

Within 10 years of the dropping of what Hopi prophecies call "the gourd of ashes," the Soviet Union and the United States had developed nuclear arsenal that could wipe out the planet in an afternoon. Most of these weapons still exist. Some may be, or may soon be, in the hands of terrorists who are very willing to use them. The threat could not be more acute, for as Albert Einstein once said when asked what weapons would be used in World War III, "I do not know with what weapons World War III will be fought, but World War IV will be fought with sticks and stones."

However, this Competitive Culture system does have a self-correcting mechanism built into it. All conscious advances in civilization - the creation of democracy, the abolition of slavery and apartheid, the civil rights movements, the women's rights movement, the environmental and appropriate technology movements, etc. - have never been birthed from *within* this system by its leaders. In fact, the system and its leaders have always fought these advances and are often the cause of the problems. All conscious progress has been initiated by small groups of people from *outside* the main power centers.

The system responds, often very slowly, to intense and sustained efforts by these groups and individuals. Therefore, we can assume whatever efforts to heal the planet and draw us back from the nuclear-biological-environmental-population brink, will be envisioned and initiated, not by our political leaders, but by a few individuals and small groups of committed people. If a few can create mass destruction, a few can create mass healing. World-famous anthropologist Margaret Mead once noted, "Never doubt that a small group of thoughtful, committed citizens can change the world; indeed it's the only thing that ever has."

If the forces of destruction grew a thousand-fold in a short period of time after 1945, the forces of love and clarity need also to grow at this rate in order to infuse wisdom into the managing of these technological forces. In some ways it has. Historically, we must remember that before 1776 every human that ever lived on the planet, except a few kings, warlords and chiefs, lived under the rule of a tyrant who had complete control over their lives. Now over half the world lives in a democracy, imperfect as they are.

Human slavery is no longer legal in any nation where once it was a major piece of the economies of "civilized" countries (though illegal slavery and legal sweatshop slave labor is mushrooming). Women now have rights in many societies where they were once denied. Though watching the daily horrors on the nightly news may lead you to believe otherwise, the University of Maryland's 2005 "Peace and Conflict" biennial global survey, as reported in the *New York Times*, ". . . shows that the number and intensity of wars and armed conflicts have fallen once again, continuing a steady 15-year decline that has halved the amount of organized violence around the world . . . war between countries is much less likely than ever and civil war is less likely than any time since 1960." The paper went on to note that "so many other people are now living in peace that you don't have to be a dreamer like John Lennon" to foresee the end of war.

People are following their own inner guidance on their spiritual path, in a manner similar to the Native Americans. Sustainable appropriate technology, such as organic gardening, solar and wind energy, waste and water recycling, aquaculture, hybrid cars, and plant-based fuels have been developed, though not yet widely in use. Herbs once again help us to heal our bodies. Meditation, yoga and true wisdom help us heal our minds and spirits. From natural childbirth when we are born, to hospice care when we are dying, new and ancient holistic ways are now available. We have the answers, the solutions. We just need to recognize the problems - and we just need a little more time.

RETURNING TO THE GARDEN

There is much work to do and yet much to celebrate. It is crucial, however, to not let this information oppress your spirits. As the Hopi Elders, people who personally watched their once elegant, peaceful and sacred culture impacted by the advancing unconsciousness, tell us:

> Don't let the burden of worries trouble you into sickness. Let your hearts be filled with happiness, enjoy your lives to the fullest, for this is the best medicine for sickness. Live long, for there are great and exciting adventures awaiting you. So time passes on and the prophecies handed down by our ancient people unfold. Many great events lie before us, and we are witnessing today the fact that our ancients' words were right . . . The wisdom accumulated by anyone who is willing to stand up and be counted is respected.

In a way it seems so simple. When people saw themselves as one - one with their loving Creator, one with their environment and one with each other - they created societies that reflected this love and unity. As the Taos Pueblos said, "We are in one nest."

When people saw themselves as separate from all that - separate from their Creator and needing to win His approval, as needing to conquer and dominate nature and others - they created societies reflecting this disharmony and isolation. One story told that man belonged to the Earth. The other told that the Earth belonged to man.

However, if it was a fractured and faulty worldview that created many of our problems, then it will be a corrected and holistic worldview that will solve them. Though we may not be able to change the world as much or as quickly as we wish, we do have *total* control over our own decisions and the stories we, as individuals, tell ourselves. Each of us is only responsible to heal ourselves from this faulty, painful and unsustainable illusion of separation. As we do this, our own lives become healed, for as the Hopi teach in their sacred instructions, "Think of attitude as being equal to application."

This is not a call to passivity but rather to dynamic activity, in humble or public ways, guided by our clarity and love. We do not necessarily have to quit our jobs or move to the countryside. Though we may not be able to return to the natural lifestyle of the ancient Native Americans, we can heal our minds and hearts and infuse this unity in our modern lives thereby transforming them into channels through which we can bless the world.

As we heal ourselves from our story of separation, our way - our Beauty Path - will be made straight and clear to us. The Beauty Path is the path of love and leads us *Home*. All other paths lead us astray. Iroquois Tadodaho Leon Shenandoah gives us more of the Instructions when he writes:

> Sooner or later we will all remember to do the duties we were instructed to do. Sooner is better than later. Later brings the suffering that will cause us to remember the Creator. The decision as to when it will be is always up to each person. In the end everybody will be doing the same thing, and that is remembering. I'm going to always be following the Instructions now. You can wait to give thanks, if you want to. Not me! I know the pain the waiting causes. Nobody knows what specific suffering someone will have to go through that will bring them back to remembering.

Chapter 5
Bringing the Original Teachings to Jamaica

"I try to tell people that as you are walking about, and you think you are using the Good Mind, the Creator is talking to you, coming into your mind. You think it's your own mind, but words are being put in and you're not aware." —**Past Iroquois leader Leon Shenandoah**

"Life is one big road with lots of signs. So when you're riding through the ruts, don't complicate your mind. Flee from hate, mischief and jealousy. Don't bury your thoughts. Put your vision to reality. Wake up and live!" —**Bob Marley**

After our visit to the Hopi and Havasupai reservations, we continued our journey through Jamaica - a journey that had begun as a normal family vacation with our two daughters, Julie and Alicia, several years earlier in 2000. At that time, I had written two books, In the Spirit of Marriage and In the Spirit of Business, that explored exercising greater unconditional love in both our work and love lives. During our vacation in Jamaica, we were so taken with the vibration coming from the island, especially through the Rastafarians and the music of the late international reggae superstar Bob Marley and other conscious artists, that I decided to write my next book on the Jamaican version of unconditional love - One Love - as they call it. Over two years and many trips to Jamaica, I authored two books, Rasta Heart:A Journey Into One Love and The

Gathering of the Healers:The Healing of the Nation.

As a way to give back to the people of Jamaica, and as a way to reflect their own message back to them, we decided to sponsor One Love concerts and events. These events were held throughout the island, especially at inner-city schools, and featured many well-known conscious Jamaican recording artists and other "healers" (teachers of love). Needless to say, the youths were thrilled to have their "heroes" come and speak and sing to them.

(The concept of a "conscious," as opposed to a "slack" artist, is well understood in Jamaica, home to over forty well-known conscious recording artist, mostly Rastafarian reggae singers. A conscious artist sings about love, justice, freedom and forgiveness. A "slack" artist sings about materialism, vanity, sexuality and/or violence.)

These concerts were non-commercial, free, and involved no corporate sponsorship or government funding. All the artists and speakers donated their time and talents for free, as a gift of love to their people. Julia and I covered the costs out of our savings. Everyone joined us, not in self-interest, but to heal their "tribe."

For up to two weeks at a time, Julia, Alicia, Abijah (a conscious artist who performed at all of our concerts) and I would travel the island in our small rented car, doing two or three school concerts each day, sometimes separated by hours of driving on Jamaica's treacherous back roads. Some concerts were at large schools of over a thousand youths; others were small schools of a few hundred. Some were in the remote mountain areas, small coastal towns and villages, where white faces and reggae artists are seldom seen. Many were in the ghettos areas of Kingston, under constant patrol by the police and the army. It was in this area that Bob Marley spent all but the last few years of his life. Occasionally, we would use a local band but mostly we just used a sound system with recorded tracks for Abijah's songs. Few of the schools had an auditorium or a cafeteria so most of the concerts were held in their center courtyard or ball field, often in direct sun and ninety-degree heat.

At every school, the students went crazy. Having a well-known and loved recording artist like Abijah perform at the school was the highlight of the year - perhaps of the decade. Though Abijah would speak and perform for most of the concert, Julia, Alicia and I would speak a few minutes each about love and forgiveness. Alicia, being their peer, had the greatest effect. For a white, middle-class American teenager to tell them how their island and it's people had changed her forever made a big impact.

It was moving to see the love between the students and their dedicated, but severely underpaid, teachers. At every concert, Abijah would ask, "Do you love your teachers?" and this was almost always followed by a very loud, very enthusiastic, "Yes!" Then, we would ask the school bullies to come forward. We intuitively understood that converting the most disruptive on the school yard can often be the most effective way to bring peace. At first they were reluctant to admit being a bully but after everyone kept pointing at them, they would finally come up on stage. We reminded them that Jamaica's best-known bully was Bob Marley, who had a street gang until he began to use his talents toward good. We would then get them to publicly promise to no longer be a bully, but instead a protector and a peacemaker on the school yard and stop all fights. When they agreed, to the shouts of approval from their classmates, we would reward them with a beautiful "Unity" tee-shirt or cap - turning violent leaders into peacemakers.

Perhaps the smallest but most moving concert was at a home for 25 abused or abandoned boys deep in the Blue Mountains. Having heard of abuse at orphanages in many countries, we were a little concerned at what we might find. The home was located on a once impressive but now severely decaying "great house." When we arrived, it was raining so hard on the tin roof of their meeting hall that we had to shout to be heard. After the boys shouted their love for their teachers, I asked the five male staff to come forward and they expressed their deep love for the students. All of them had been residents at the home when they were younger.

Each concert was unique, each fulfilling. At the end of the long day, we would stay at accommodations donated by Jamaica's hotel association, sometimes an all-inclusive major resort, the next night a small country guesthouse. It did not really matter to us. We couldn't wait for the next day, to once again be greeted by so many smiling, excited faces.

In addition to our many school concerts, for four years we also hosted a large free public concert every year in Kingston on February 6, Bob Marley's birthday. Bob, who died in 1981, is Jamaica's best-known citizen. His birthday is observed with a week-long celebration. At each large birthday concert, we would invite Jamaican healers to join us on stage. To determine who these peacemakers were, we asked many Jamaicans from all walks of life one simple question, "Who teaches love in Jamaica?" After awhile we kept hearing the same names and we went to these people and invited them to join us and our efforts. All did.

Over time, more and more Jamaican healers joined our efforts and spoke and performed at our events, or interviewed us on their radio and television programs. This group of healers included elder Rastas, media personalities, newspaper columnists, university professors, a Jamaican senator, business, religious and civic leaders, the Minister of Tourism, and the Governor General - all teachers of love representing the many "tribes" of Jamaica. Their voices, much more familiar and eloquent than ours, reached the listening ear of the people.

Our first public event, called "The Gathering of the Healers," was on Bob Marley's 57th birthday at his home in Kingston, which is now a museum. A month before the event, I traveled into the hills of the back-country and spent an afternoon with Bob's mother, Mama B, who graciously allowed us to use his home after hearing of our mission. Five well-known teachers of love, three popular reggae artists, Abijah, Denroy Morgan and Luciano, well-known author Dr. Dennis Forsythe and Antonnette Haughton, a conscious talk show host who was also running for prime minister, addressed their people at the press conference in Bob's backyard. The message was carried by one newspaper and one television station. The next year, Bob's 58th birthday, we held the event at The University of the West Indies in Kingston, in front of several hundred students. It was a full concert with seven internationally-known Jamaican reggae artists (Abijah, Luciano, Mackie Conscious, I'ngel Chanta, Swade, Ernie Smith, and Denroy Morgan). It was carried live by Richie B, the island's most popular radio deejay and covered by both daily newspapers.

For our third concert on Bob Marley's 59th birthday, the Jamaican government, who initially kept their distance from our efforts, agreed to provide a large public venue and stage management for our concert in downtown Kingston. Several speakers joined us including the open-hearted Minister of Tourism, Aloun Assamba, plus eleven recording artists including Abijah, Ernie Smith, Prezident Brown, Warrior King, Junior Smith, Cherry and Little Natural, Mackie Conscious, Keteis, Mystic Revelation of Rastafari, and Bushman. The concert, with a live audience of thousands, was covered by most of the print press and by live or delayed broadcasts by all four television stations and the two largest radio stations.

Many of these healers also spoke or performed at our special "One Love Leadership Event" in October 2004 that was attended by many of Jamaica's political, business, civic and religious leaders. Knowing that we must change the hearts and minds of the leaders if peace was to prevail, all of us together invited these Jamaican "chiefs" to join us in leading the people into peace and love. The evening, held in the largest hotel in Kingston, was a combination of musical performances and addresses by well-known people who taught love on the island.

The room was full, and all of Jamaica's TV stations broadcast or rebroadcast the event, bringing the message to the entire island. Monsignor Albert, fondly referred to as the "ghetto priest" for his work with the poor, offered the opening prayer. The titular head of state, Governor General Sir Howard Cooke, who is known for his efforts to bring peace and reconciliation on the island, gave the introduction speech. (Though independent, Jamaica is still a commonwealth of England. The Governor General is appointed by the Queen of England. His official duties are ceremonial but he and his office carries considerable influence in the country.)

"Brothers and sisters," the Governor General said, opening the event, "this is a unique moment. It may well be a moment of history. For many, many years I have tried to devote my time to make some significant effort to bring peace wherever I am. I have now come to the conclusion that there is only one God and that righteousness is with all people and whether you are a Christian, a Muslim, a Jew, we are all one people seeking truth and goodness and mercy. So now I am comfortable with anyone who worships God. I thank God that at this moment I cannot identify anybody that I do not love. There's peace in my heart. I love people and I want people to love me. I'm not happy if you do not love me. I am speaking from my heart and I'm happy to be here. If we have peace in our lives, the creative genius of God will express itself in all sorts of ways. If the Minister of Finance really had peace in his heart and love, he would devise a strategy for financial health. If the Prime Minister had total peace and there was no anger, he certainly would do greater than the man who had no love. We *here* could change Jamaica overnight. Let this be a moment of peace and feel that God is working here."

"If a society is to define itself by the acts of a few let it be the acts of the best of its citizens, not the worst," I said in my address. "Jamaica must stop defining itself by the few gunman, thieves, drug dons and corrupt politicians. It must stop defining itself by its IMF debt, per capita income and number of potholes. Jamaica must begin to define itself by its over two million hard-working people who toil every day against difficult conditions to live a righteous and an honest life. Jamaica needs a national healing of its self-esteem by understanding what an incredible people you are and what precious gifts you have offered the world."

"Everywhere your people are known for their love. People come to your shores every day and experience your love. Many feel they have come 'home.' Through your conscious reggae music, this love has gone out as a wave of healing to every corner of the planet. Jamaica, as a society, has birthed this global drumbeat of love. You are an unbowed and unbroken people, a passionate people, expressing greatness in spite of your constant struggles. Can Jamaica be the first society to heal itself with love? It can be the first to try and even that is a great honor. And as I look around this room at the leaders God has gathered here all together, Christians, Muslims, Jews and Rastafarians, political, business, civic and religious leaders, conscious talk show hosts and recording artists, I have no doubt that it is the Father's will for us to heal this island through One Love. There is an untapped potential and power here within your people that once released will lead this country to its destiny to teach One Love to the world. So we ask you again to join us in healing this great nation through your individual acts of love in whatever way you feel guided. Let this be part of your personal legacy. We all hope and pray this healing will manifest through lower crime rates, a more vibrant economy and better vibrations island-wide. We would all like to see that. But we also must remember that no matter what the observable evidence, every act of love is inherently of great value, not only to the recipient but to the giver as well."

"I want to start out saying that it is obvious that love is the only way that this is going to work," Alicia said, speaking clear and strong, a teenager addressing a room of adults. "I tried to think of other ways to solve many of the world's problems and I couldn't. There is no other way. There is nothing that comes even close to love and peace in bringing this country together. And I also wanted to say 'don't give up.' Just like Thomas Edison took 2000 times to develop the light bulb and if he had stopped at 1000, we might not have light today. Most great things happen over time. So don't give up and never stop believing."

"I'm thinking about this group of people in front of me," Julia said. "I know each of you has worked so hard. I know that. I can see that you are truly givers and your giving has been so effective because the moment I stepped on this island of Jamaica, I felt the love. I feel like I have to speak from my heart and I feel comfortable in crying now. You have built an society so that people can feel that way and the students at the schools we have gone to have not forgotten. Let me tell you they have *not* forgotten. They *know* love and you know love. That's why you can feel it when you take one step upon Jamaican soil. It's in your heart forever. I meditate in the mountain's of North Carolina by my peace pond and I send a prayer for nonviolence and peace. It is a reality in the heart of every child and everyone of us is a child. You have created a wonderful country - all of you - and I give thanks."

Together we invited them to join us in leading Jamaica into a national healing through love. Their response was enthusiastic. The results are yet to be known.

One of our most powerful events was on June 14, 2002, when we held the "Fires of Forgiveness" on the eastern tip of the island in the small town of Port Antonio. This was the day of the "Tall Ships Event." These Tall Ships are the large sailing vessels of the 16th and 17th century. Every few years, they gather in a different country for a large regatta. This year the organizers had chosen Jamaica and several ships were to be moored in Port Antonio's harbor on that day.

The year before, Julia and I were in the Maroon village of Moore Town when we heard the Tall Ships would be coming to Jamaica. The Maroons were escaped Africans who lived free in the hills of Jamaica in the 1600s and 1700s. Being unable to subdue them, the English granted them their freedom one hundred years before general emancipation. For centuries, they have lived in several villages throughout remote areas of the island. When we heard these ships were coming, our first thought was, *The slave ships are returning to the slave colony!* We decided to use this as an opportunity to have a healing ceremony - hence the Fires of Forgiveness was birthed.

Basically, the vision was to have a large fire near the harbor, with the tall ships in the background, and to offer a public healing of African slavery. I arrived a month early and brought thousands of colorful "Fires of Forgiveness" posters to put up around the island inviting people to join us that night in Port Antonio or to light their own fire or candle or a lamp at their home or community. During that month, I traveled throughout Jamaica, often alone, sometimes with my Jamaican friend, Scram, asking people in small shops throughout the island to put up these posters.

Since few people in the countryside of Jamaica own cars, there are thousands of these little local shops throughout the island where people can walk to in order to get a few staples, cold drinks, cigarettes, Red Stripe beer, rum, or candy. Each shop is like someone's living room with the usual faces hanging around or dropping in. It is as much a part of Jamaicans' social life as are pubs in Ireland or neighborhood bars in New York.

Usually I would go into a shop where there might be a few people hanging out and just my walking in often brought the place to a hushed standstill. They see few unfamiliar faces in these small shops and on an island that is ninety-six percent African descendant, almost no white faces. I would ask the shop owners if they would mind putting up a "Fires of Forgiveness" poster.

"What is dis poster about?" someone would ask, in their beautiful lilting Jamaican accent.

"We are going to have a big Fire of Forgiveness in Port Antonio and we want to invite you to come or light a fire here that night," I would answer.

"What is it we should forgive?" was the next question.

"We're asking people here to forgive the four hundred years of African slavery," I replied, knowing exactly the response I was likely to receive - a combination of laughter, catcalls, raised eyebrows, and penetrating looks. As you might imagine, a white man from a once slave-owning country asking African-descendents in a former slave colony to forgive slavery brought up a range of emotions from anger to dismay. This would begin a group reasoning on the value of forgiving - not only ancient wounds but present ones as well.

"Why should we do dat?" someone would usually say in a voice anywhere from true questioning to amazement to anger. "Ya white people from America and England should come 'ere and beg our forgiveness and pay reparations. Den we can talk about *us* forgiving *you*!"

This was always greeted by grunts of approval from the group, which was now fully engaged if for no other reason than they thought the person standing in front of them must surely have lost his mind.

"I know it sounds crazy," I would reply, letting them know I had no illusions about how truly absurd what I was asking them to do sounded. "But follow my reasoning. Have any of you here had anyone who wronged you come back and ask for your forgiveness and offer to make reparations?"

Only rarely would anyone answer positively. Usually there was dead silence.

"Have any of you ever gone to someone you wronged and told them you wanted to make reparation and ask for their forgiveness?" I continued. This was usually followed by the same silence. "This is the problem on our planet. It is keeping the world bound in a vicious cycle of attack and counterattack that must be broken. Look, there's several hundred years of life experience in this shop and few of us have ever asked someone to forgive us or had someone ask for our forgiveness. If we are going to wait to forgive those that hurt us personally, or even those that hurt or enslaved our ancestors, we are going to have a very long wait. And all during this wait, which may last our entire lifetime, we are going to have a bitter heart and that means less happiness, less peace of mind, less health. The only other option is to forgive others, even if they never ask you or make amends. Forgiveness doesn't mean you have to like them or be in their presence any longer. It just means you forgive them."

"But dat don't seem fair," someone would often say. "Dat person dat hurt me must come and ask before I will forgive. Den maybe I will forgive dem."

"I didn't create this system, God did," I would answer. "If you want to be as happy as you can be in this life, and who doesn't, you've got to forgive. So if you don't like the system or thinks its unfair, get mad at Him, not me. Look, this is a human thing not a color thing. People will exploit their power if they can - physical power, financial power, sexual power. And what Gandhi called the greatest exploitation of all, is that of men over women."

This comment was usually followed by an uncomfortable silence by the men in the shop and smiles by some of the women and their calls of "Ya, mon!"

"Even if what ya seh is so," someone would say, "forgiving like dat is very hard ta do."

"You're right," I'd answer. "It *is* hard to forgive. It is the second hardest thing in the world to do. The only thing harder is to *not* forgive because you just keep reliving the attack and robbing your peace of mind. As a friend once told me, resentment does more damage to the vessel in which it is stored than the object on which it is poured."

"Are ya saying dat we should never ask for reparations?"

"Forgiveness does not mean we do not demand fairness or seek reparations. It only means that we do so not out of anger but out of healing. We seek justice rather than revenge. We can still ask, even demand, fair compensation from a state of forgiveness and love, like Mandela, King and Gandhi did - by the way, all men of color."

The whole encounter took only a few minutes and at the end everyone agreed to put up the poster (though I have no way of knowing if they threw it in the trash as soon as I drove off). What I *do* know, is that the vibes usually felt very good when I left and I never - in all those weeks, in all those shops, in all those encounters - felt any anger directed at me *personally*. Every shop was a healing journey. Every discussion uplifting, watching people move through anger and revenge to forgiveness. At the end of each day, I would return to my hotel feeling exhausted but exhilarated.

The event was held at a place called Folly Ruins. The ruins are from the Folly Great House built in 1905 by the daughter of Charles Tiffany, founder of the famous New York jewelry store. Seawater was used to mix the concrete of its foundations and the house began to collapse only eleven years after the couple moved in. At one time it must have been a beautiful mansion with a commanding view of the Caribbean Sea. Now it looked like an abandoned, decaying large Roman temple, with a lawn that gently sloped down to the ocean.

During the night, many people shared their thoughts on forgiveness through our open mike. Shortly before ten, Abijah took the stage and brought the crowd to a very loving state with his music. At ten o'clock, we all gathered around and lit our ten-foot high Fire of Forgiveness, inviting all Jamaicans, and people everywhere, to forgive, as much as they are able.

Chapter 6
Return to the Center of the Universe

"Coming here, I passed the place where the Algonquin massacred us last spring . . . I turned my eyes for fear of exciting my anger . . . Then striking the Earth and listening, I heard the voice of my forefathers massacred by the Algoquins. When they saw that my heart was capable of seeking revenge, they called out to me in a loving voice, "My grandson, my grandson, be good; do not get angry. Think no longer of us for there is no means of withdrawing us from death. Think of the living - that is of importance; save those that still live from the sword and fire that pursue them; one living man is better than many dead ones." After hearing those voices I passed on, and I came to you, to deliver those whom you still hold."
—**Mohawk Chief Kiotsaeton**'s *appeal to the French and hostile tribes, who were holding Iroquois prisoners in 1645. His mission was successful.*

"Overcome the devil with a thing called love." —**Bob Marley**

As we continued our concerts in Jamaica, Hopiland kept calling to us. We had stayed in touch with Karen Abieta, the reggae deejay, and told her we were interested in organizing a series of One Love concerts on the reservation to thank the tribe for keeping their Covenant. In September 2003, fifteen months after we first visited Hopiland, Julia, Abijah and I went to the Hopi Reservation to host five *Respect is Due:The*

Healing of the Hopi Nation Concerts, three at their elementary schools, one at their high school and one public concert at the Hopi Veterans Memorial Hall. We were joined by L.A.-based reggae artist Zema, Uproot reggae band from Yuma, Arizona and Joseph Israel and the Lions of Israel, again all providing their time and talents for free. Everyone spoke and performed at the Hopi schools and, as it had been in Jamaica, the youths loved it.

We knew that the Hopi had a strong belief in the healing power of song and that Kokopilau, one of their spirit *kachinas* who were sent to give help and guidance to the tribe, was a flute player whose music created warmth and healing. At every school concert, we put up a large banner that we had made with an ancient Hopi symbol, a circle divided into four equal quarters by two crossed lines with smaller circles in each quadrant. Underneath this symbol, it read: "Together with all nations we protect both land and life and hold the world in balance - Techqua Ikachi."

Our message to the Hopi youths reminded them that their prophecies instructed them to continue purifying their tribe to assist in a global purification. Mostly we thanked them for successfully keeping their Covenant with the Creator to do this. Several tribes share Hopiland today - Hopi, Tewa, Navajo, Zuni, Havasupai, and bahanna - and the tribes had never been better. Long-standing feuds and resentments had been put aside or reduced. Issues that in ancient times might have been settled with violence no longer were. Though issues still emerge, people were working together better and respecting each other more.

We thanked them for staying on their ancient land and working through the human drama for centuries - work that they were doing for *all* peoples. We thanked the tribe for keeping their Covenant, whether they had realized it or not. They stayed as instructed. They have forgiven their oppressors, learned to live peacefully with their neighboring tribes, and have kept the ancient ceremonies and teachings alive - even their ancient language. They have honored their name *Hopi* - Peaceful People.

I closed my talks by saying, "We do not come with the same message that many other outsiders have brought to your tribes. We are not here to say that Hopi should be more like the modern world but rather that we in the modern world should be more like the Hopi. Many of you here wish you had shopping malls and more restaurants and movie theatres and theme parks. That's understandable. But we want you to know many of us in the modern world, shop and eat out and go to movies and theme parks because there is something missing in our lives that we are trying to fill with these activities - something missing that you have. You have a tribe and a homeland. We outside this reservation have neither. We are tribeless and because of that we are lonelier. Treasure your tribe and land. They are precious and rare."

The response at the Hopi High School was overwhelming. When Julia danced down the center aisle toward the stage early in the concert, the usually reserved Indian youths quickly followed her. When Abijah started to sing a Bob Marley song, "Three Little Birds," more students rushed the front and danced and sang for the rest of the show, singing in unison other Marley songs. In the middle of the concert, their open-hearted principal, Glenn Gilman, came up to me and said, "The maintenance manager says the students are pulling the seats out of the ground by standing on them but I said, 'Let 'em. We'll fix it later. I'm not going to let anything stop this!' I've never seen the students so happy - even after winning a big football game!"

At that moment it became clear to us that the message of One Love was still deep in the hearts of these people. Here were over 850 Native American high schools students in the remote Arizona desert who knew the words to every song of a Jamaican artist who had died before any of them were even born. Before the coming of the commercial culture, the Hopi's flame of love may once have been one of the brightest on the planet. This musical message of One Love coming from Jamaica was fanning this flame. The scene later that night at the public concert, attended by over 500 tribal members, was the same.

At one of the elementary schools a young Hopi student teacher, Dawn Quamahongnewa-Mapatis, came up to us afterwards. She had the classic Hopi beauty of so many of the tribe, with long, beautiful jet-black straight hair, a full expressive face and a personal charisma that was endearing. As she spoke, you could feel her passion, her joy, *and* her concern.

"I really like the message that you're putting out there to the kids," she said with tears in her eyes, "that this symbol, that together with all nations, we hold the balance of life and land and that this will sustain us as Hopi people. We're the ones that believe we're the caretakers of this land and that this is really important to us. I'm so emotional. This is our symbol and the kids are learning everything about the white man's ways and they're forgetting us. So we need them to remember and be able to sustain us, especially as Hopi people. They're the little ones. They're going to be the ones to help us to survive and to keep being Hopi. I'm so glad you have come here to remind the youths what it means to be Hopi. My father is the Snake Priest and he has been trying to tell them for years but often they do not always listen. When you and famous recording artists come and tell them it means a lot. To keep the Covenant is to *be* Hopi."

The real impact of our tour was not revealed to us until seven months later. In April, following these September concerts, I read online that the Hopi had voted against allowing casinos on their reservation. Over two hundred Native American tribes had said "yes" to casino gambling, even though many of their members were against it. The Hopi were one of the first to say "No!" What was even more amazing was that the planned income stream from the casinos, over twenty-five million annually, would have doubled the Hopi tribe's yearly budget, a budget that was about to be cut in half due to the loss of other revenue. They could easily have said "yes" because the casinos would have been a two-hour drive away from the villages on tribal land near Interstate 40. The casinos would not have affected the daily life of the tribe. And yet given all this, they had still said "no."

The article went on to say that the effort to defeat the gambling was lead by a young Hopi teacher, Dawn Quamahongnewa-Mapatis and her father, Radford Quamahongnewa.

We immediately called Dawn to congratulate her.

"Thanks," she said. "And I want to thank you because your visit here last September inspired me. It reminded me of what a few committed people can do. And many of the people who voted gambling down had been to your concerts and heard your message reminding us of the important place Hopi has in the world - of how wonderful it is to be Hopi. Over two hundred youths came out to vote against the gambling. That has never happened before."

"How did you get so many people to give up all that income?" I asked. "Surely there must have been very powerful forces that wanted the casinos and the millions in tribal revenues."

"Before the elections, my father and I went to talk to all the villages. The pro-gambling people and many of the people on the tribal council did not like that we did that. We went anyway. We reminded everyone of two things: Hopi teachings say you must never benefit from another's weakness. Also, we were always told that Hopi should *never* accumulate wealth, that a permanent flow of money is not the Hopi Way. It will weaken the tribe. You must earn as you go. People listened. You and the artists helped."

As she spoke, I remembered about the two Hopi villages - Palatkwapi, which was destroyed because of gambling and Tikuvi, which was abandoned when their women were lost in a bet. The dangers of gambling was in their history, legends and collective consciousness. We sensed that their defeating the gambling initiative was a major milestone in the purification of the Hopi nation, which, according to their prophecy, would begin a global purification.

As we finished our phone call, we hoped that we would continue to work with Dawn and her family. As it turned out, this would happen sooner than any of us thought.

RESERVATION GAMBLING

Indian reservation gambling is a complex political, social and economic issue. Much good can come from the immense revenues created - roads, utilities, drug and alcohol abuse programs, community centers, hospitals, education for the youths, better tribal medical care, etc. However, these gaming funds, and those generated by the sales of tax-free tobacco on the reservations, are created at the expense of supporting painful and life-destroying addictions. Wherever gambling is instituted, unemployment and welfare often decline but it is also inevitably followed by problems in the form of individual and organized crime, loan sharks, suicides, alcohol-related disturbances and accidents, family disruptions, an explosion of personal bankruptcies, jails filled with drug arrests, and other human misery. Inter-tribal animosity increases and members fight over control of mass sums of gambling revenues, often leading to physical violence and, on occasion, contract killings.

Reservation gambling has also encouraged political corruption within the tribes, the same government corruption that has caused so much pain to their members - both past and present. In 2005, a prominent Washington lobbyist was arrested and in his subsequent confessions he revealed that several Native American tribes involved in gambling had given him tens of millions of dollars to pay to politicians in order to bribe them to pass legislation to protect and increase the tribes gaming profits.

In tribes awash in easy profit, it also reduces personal incentive, especially in many of the young. For years, we have visited the ancestral home of the Eastern Band of Cherokees, in Cherokee, North Carolina. After Harrah's opened a casino there, we noticed that we no longer saw the Cherokee youths working at the motels or restaurants. Instead they were replaced with young people from Eastern Europe, Jamaica and other countries. When we inquired, we were told that every Cherokee gets sixty thousands dollars when they turn eighteen and none of them want to work anymore. The village itself has changed. The main attraction now is the gambling, *not* the Cherokee people and their culture. Also, the tribal culture is tremendously impacted by reservation gambling - drawing in a powerful commercial vibration and thousands of visitors that have little to no interest in the tribal culture. From then on, that tribe and their land is known for the gambling - not for their themselves.

Also, Native American sovereignty issues are at stake. The longstanding and recognized federal Indian law does not include tribes having a relationship with the states or abiding by state laws. Tribes are perceived as one sovereign nation negotiating with another, nation-to-nation, not state-to-state. However, once gambling is allowed on a reservation, the tribe is required to work within state laws. This often diminishes the hard-won sovereignty which is held sacred by many - a loss that can be permanent. As Oneida author and musician Joanne Shenandoah says, "Are we willing to sell our rights promised to us in 1794 just to have alcohol and slot machines in the casinos? . . . Sovereignty is the right to define the present and future of a people. Sovereignty means self-governance, and that governance is only as good as the people involved."

Even gambling's economic impact is questioned by many who might profit should they allow it on their traditional lands. As Onondaga Faithkeeper Oren Lyons said in 2005, "We don't believe that high stakes gambling is good for anybody - in terms of economy, it's like chewing on their own arm." (The Onondaga, like the Hopi, have refused to allow gambling on their reservation.)

The spiritual ramifications of Native American tribes being the willing conduit for the gambling industry are clearer. It is the final step of many indigenous people succumbing to, and incorporating within themselves, the very unconscious commercial system that for centuries they witnessed create such pain and degradation for their tribes. As one Native American gambling opponent wrote, "The proliferation of gaming is a spiritual cancer eating away at what is left of the soul of Native American communities."

As in the past, Indian gaming will remain an intensely controversial issue among Native Americans. It straddles the debate of their need to survive economically in today's world and their ancient spiritual covenant to help balance the world by moral action. Perhaps Sicangu Lakota artist and grassroots activist Rosalie Little Thunder outlines this struggle best when she says in Wilma Mankiller's *Every Day Is a Good Day*,

After nearly two centuries of existence in an oppressive society, many indigenous peoples' sense of survival is constrained within the framework of American values, which promote a lifestyle of physical comfort and convenience at the expense of other human beings and the natural world. It is this long-term oppression that sometimes blinds us to the greater challenge of being responsible for our survival of humanity and all of the relatives. Because we are silenced and devalued, it is much harder to maintain our knowledge system and culture and pass it on to future generations . . . The challenge of passing on this knowledge is further compounded by years of oppression, dependence, and shame. . . Expecting to be heard by the American masses is perhaps unrealistic. Our values are too threatening for the American sense of comfort and sense of self."

THE HOPI

For thousands of years, the Hopi have followed their spiritual guidance. In their sacred songs they are taught to ask, "Who are we? Where do we come from? Why are we here? Where are we going?" Their songs answer, "You were made by the Creator. You are to become *Hopi* - the Peaceful People - and share this peace with all humanity. You were to leave evil behind and you must search for the place where all migrating Hopi would meet again." They believe that place to be Hopiland, their home for almost one thousand years. Because of this, their entire religion is bound up in their land. As former tribal chairman Abbot Sekaquaptewa said, "Without our land, we are nothing."

Each Hopi village is like a separate world, with its own leaders, religious societies and ceremonies. These villages were not established at one time but rather over centuries as their migrating clans were all directed there by divine signs from their spiritual guides. Their legends tell of these centuries-long migrations - migrations which began when they emerged from their underground "Third World" through the "sipapuni," a sacred hole in the Earth located in the Grand Canyon.

After the Emergence into this, the Fourth World, different Hopi clans migrated in all four directions - from the Atlantic to the Pacific shores, from the tip of South America to the frozen ice lands of North America. Their migrations formed a huge cross. The North-South and East-West axis crossed in Hopiland, which they call "The Center of the Universe."

During their migrations through North and South America, they had lived in many lush, fertile areas, many with unimaginable abundance. Once in Hopiland, they could have simply walked a hundred miles in several directions and found water, trees, vegetation and fertile soil. One can only imagine what they thought when they were told their final destination, their final *home*, was to be the most desolate, inhospitable place they had ever seen. However, for almost a thousand years they had tenaciously clung to these isolated, barely fertile - yet breathtakingly beautiful - mesas, eking out their food and shelter in a very hostile environment while living a sacred life.

As they settled in Hopiland, each clan had different migration histories, different myths and different worldviews. Even the dialects vary from different villages, which before roads were built, were very isolated from each other though only a few miles apart. This clan system is a vital part of Hopi life. They cross-fertilize relationships between villages and families. The gathering clans contributed different ceremonies to the Hopi's sacred year-long Ceremonial Cycle, which became a repository - recorded in song, dance, drumming, and spoken word - of *all* human wisdom.

This complex and revered cycle is the key to keeping this wisdom alive and to the Hopi successfully attaining their goal of being the Covenant People - the Peaceful People. Core human values that bring out the best in us are expressed, to various degrees, in the cycle's many ceremonies and rituals. These values include prayer, cooperation, gratitude, respect for women, courage, patience, wisdom, certainty, responsible childrearing, compassion, joy, clarity, understanding, depth, generosity, abundance, and agape (unconditional love for all - One Love).

Through their clan's particular ceremonies, everyone who chooses to has a place in the cycle. And to be sure no one takes themselves too seriously or becomes judgmental, the Hopi "clowns" keep everyone laughing at themselves, reminding their people that it is an imperfect world with imperfect people and they need to be gentle with themselves and others.

Even today, "Hopi tradition" remains a collection of traditions from the various clans and villages. As Alph H. Secakuku writes in *Following the Sun and Moon:The Hopi Kachina Tradition*, "The complex cycle of interrelated responsibilities and concepts that is the Hopi religious system is all the more complicated because each of the twelve Hopi villages possess the autonomy to carry out Hopi religious practices independently. The timing of ceremonies, the underlying concepts may vary among Hopi villages. Nevertheless, throughout the land of the Hopi, the religious mission is the same: to promote and achieve a 'unity' of everything in the universe."

Their legends say when all people emerged from the corrupted underground Third World, each tribe could choose a different ear of corn to represent them. All tribes, the Navajos, the Comanches, the Utes, the Apaches, the bahannas (white race), etc., chose an ear, leaving the Hopi with the shortest, stubbiest ear - a plant that, like the Hopi themselves, is rooted deep into the Earth. It has a fifteen to twenty-foot root system searching for water, for survival.

Understanding that thoughts manifest in form and thereby create individuals' realities, the Hopi are taught from infancy to avoid revenge and bitter thoughts, which they view as "harming someone in your thoughts." Gossip and anger is seen as "wounding someone else's spirit." They understood that mistakes are being made everyday by everyone and that these "mistakes" are really just lessons for us. Generosity is held in the highest esteem. Their teachings instructed them that "if your house is gleaming with beauty and good food but not shared with kindness, it is empty, without spirit. The humble home that is shared is beautiful."

Theirs is a belief in non-resistance - don't fight, don't try to get revenge, even when someone hurts you. To seek revenge is to hurt yourself more than you hurt them. They were told not to accumulate possessions and to be generous with everything. They were told that they never walked alone - Great Beings always walked with them. Their religion taught that to live this way, with respect for the Earth and all life and in harmony with each other, was the true *Hopi Way* and walking this Path would help all people of the Earth, not just the tribe.

Underlying this peace was the Hopi respect for women, without which no real peace and happiness is possible in a society. Motherhood was highly respected and gave women a sense of worth. Hopi women own the gardens, fields, houses, and cisterns. Hopi understood that since the house, field and mothers are inseparable, all must rest with women. The Hopi traditional society revolves around their strong matrilineal clan system.

Though Hopi are known for their peaceful nature, Hopi life before the coming of the white culture was not idyllic. Violence and human corruption were not strangers to them. For generations, they too had wrestled with these issues. Their legends tell of entire Hopi villages that were destroyed or abandoned by the tribe because of human weakness. One ancient village was destroyed by a neighboring village due to envy and jealousy. Another split in two because of greed and the misuse of leadership power. Another village, established in South America during their migration, was destroyed by several neighboring villages at the request of its leader. His people had degenerated into a disrespect for women and sexual promiscuity was rampant, even in their sacred kivas. According to Oraibi legends, generations later, gambling lead to the destruction of another Hopi village, an issue that would reemerge in recent times. The ancient village of Tikuvi lost all their women while betting on a foot race with the neighboring village of Payupki.

In 1680, the Hopi joined with other Pueblo tribes in a revolt against the brutal "slave church" of the early Spanish missionaries, who more resembled slave masters than spiritual teachers. As ancient Hopi prophecies had predicted, these explorers and priests appeared out of nowhere and claimed these ancient villages as their own. They profaned the Hopi religious ceremonies, destroyed their sacred objects, took their women as they pleased, often murdering their husbands. The Hopi and the other Pueblo tribes of the area conspired together and revolted against the Spanish, killing nearly 500, tearing down the churches, sacking Santa Fe, and driving the survivors back to Mexico.

By 1690, the Spanish re-conquered the tribes - all but the Hopi. Ten years later in 1700, another village, Awatovi, was destroyed by neighboring villages when it welcomed back the Catholic missionaries and some of the villagers converted to Christianity. The village once again sank into depravity and violence and the chief of Awatovi asked the chiefs of the neighboring villages to destroy his people, including himself. "The Castilla (Spanish) sorcerers are among us again," the chief explained to the other chiefs, "causing people to turn against one another. They are causing the young to despise the old and to ridicule the ceremonies. Girls and women are being raped. Awatovi has broken into pieces. It has lived out its life." The village was burned, many killed and their fields and young women and children were divided among their avengers.

Though they never warred against neighboring tribes nor against the United States or its army, time and time again, human frailty or contention between individuals, villages and clans caused dissension and conflicts. Even in modern times, this has been true but these issues no longer lead to violence. Harmony on the reservation has perhaps never been greater.

As Hopi travel about their reservation today, every few miles they pass the ruins of an ancient destroyed village. In some ways, their collective remembrance for these past corruptions, and their belief that the prior "Third World" was also destroyed due to human immorality, motivates many Hopi to strive to live a undefiled life in this, the "Fourth World," which according to their teachings *will* become purified.

In recent times, their struggles to become the Peaceful People have involved conflicts with the bahannas and with their neighbors, the Navajos. However, the conflict within the tribe itself, between the Traditionalists (Hostiles) and the Progressives (Friendlies), is a constant issue. These Traditionalists, those that want to live the old ways and practice their ancient religion, are often seen as anti-progress, which they are materially but not *spiritually*. Many Friendlies or Progressives, those that want to adopt bahanna's way and often their religion, feel their ancient ways keep the children from a better future and is not in the best interests of the tribe. The Friendlies believe that if they are to survive, their children must adopt the white culture's ways. Believing it is part of prophecy, some Friendlies have even made sacred their religion's decline, saying that once the Ceremonial Cycle became corrupt and impure, it was better to discontinue it than continue in a profane form.

The Hostiles and Elderly Elders (the elder Traditionalist leaders) see it differently. As written in their newsletter, *Techqua Ikachi*:

> [Modern conveniences] . . . would be good if there weren't spiritual problems associated with them, and if one could get them freely without the danger of involvement in obligations that will later be regretted . . . allowing our life to be controlled by outside interests. A person's life easily becomes ruled by his pocketbook and by foreign rules - even jail . . . And they are not aware that by falling for this temptation they place themselves at the service of a worldly power greater than themselves, which is at least as

selfish, and which intends to gain at their expense . . . Overdue bills cause pressure, and dead-end jobs drive them to drink . . . The word 'unemployment' meant nothing to us before such government programs were introduced . . . Yes, there are many good things that we are trying to preserve for the future of our children. The best of these are what "progress" wants to destroy.

These Elderly Elders, many of whom remember when the tribe was living self-sufficient in the ancient tribal ways, have observed what has happened to some of the people when modern conveniences are introduced. Bodies, once strong from farming, cutting wood and carrying water, have become unhealthy and obese. Diabetes is at epidemic proportions as the tribe has adopted the convenience of packaged, devitalized foods. Instead of spending time with family and friends and in tribal ceremonies, some tribal members are glued to their televisions, and more recently, their computers. Instead of working their garden plots and providing for their daily needs, they are working in jobs, often very low-paid ones, in bahanna's world. This life has lead to some degree to alcoholism, indebtedness, confusion, suicide, sickness and a splintering of tribal, clan and family cohesiveness. This they view is the result and curse of introducing these "wonderful, modern conveniences" into their villages.

The Progressive-oriented Hopi Tribal Council has endorsed an attempt to introduce casino gambling and has sold mining rights to vast areas of the Black Mesa to the Peabody Coal Company, who is presently strip mining this sacred area. The relentless influence of the United States Government, The Bureau of Indian Affairs (BIA), the Friendlies, The Hopi Tribal Council, the churches and missionaries and certain corporations, has diminished the bright flame of spiritual striving somewhat but as we later learned, it is still *very* strong.

The environmental effects of recent Hopi Council-approved development on the reservation are extreme. The only man-made object visible from the Gemini 12 spacecraft in 1971 was a plume of smoke that covered over 10,000 square miles of the Earth's surface spewing from the coal-fired Four Corners Generating Plant near Farmington, New Mexico. The mines mix the pulverized coal with large amounts of water and pipe it over tribal land two hundred miles to power plants in Nevada to provide electricity to cities as far away as Los Angeles. Tapping into the underground water supply has driven wildlife from the mesa and caused many Hopi sacred springs, wells and creeks to go dry, further inhibiting the Traditionalists ability to live their Covenant of living close to the land.

Many of the Progressives feel that they too are following the Creator's instructions by adopting bahannas' ways to some degree and that they could not maintain a "good heart," as they were instructed to do, by constantly resisting modern ways. Also, they felt that since the prophecies outlined these painful events, even by their abandoning the ceremonial ways, they too were fulfilling prophesies. They understand that prophecy tells that this abandonment of the Ceremonial Cycle will precede the global purification. In some ways they welcome it so that life can begin anew and pure, fresh from the "giver of the breath of life." To them, even this abandoning of some of the tribal ways and ceremonies is *sacred*.

The Elderly Elder say once they are all gone, Hopis of good intention will seek right leaders. Three people were named to help the Hopi: The Paiute, the Navajos, and if neither of these can help, the bahannas. They write in their newsletters that "the leadership will pass to some person who is clinging to the Creator's great laws . . . someone who will stand not for himself, but for all people, land and life . . . At the end, all who are of one heart . . . will be safe and secure." They added that you can change your course, from materialism to that of the Creator's, at anytime - on whatever day you decide.

THE HOPI PROPHECIES, WARNINGS & INSTRUCTIONS

(Note: The following information was revealed only by the elders from Oraibi and Hotevilla. The elders from Shungopavi, the Mother Village, still await a divine signal before revealing *their* sacred information to the world. They believe this signal will not come until they have completed their Covenant to become Hopi - to become the "Peaceful People.")

According to Hopi prophecy, Maasaw (or Masau-u), a spirit messenger from the Creator and the Guardian of the Earth, appeared to the Hopi at their Emergence and welcomed them to share the planet with him "in poverty, but in peace." At that time he gave them the "Sacred Covenant" - detailed prophecies, warnings and instructions, all etched into four sacred tablets, which are now in the possession of the Hopi Elders. These tablets also contain "the laws by which the Hopi were to travel and live the good way of life, the peaceful way." In doing so, Maasaw told them he had placed in their hands, together with certain other ancient people in other lands, the fate of humanity.

This information was to be kept secret from all but the tribe until the world was in chaos and engulfed "by efforts to force one's will upon others" to the point that these efforts will have pushed mankind to the brink of self-destruction. They even have a word for this situation - "Koyaanisqatsi," or "crazy life." The Elderly Elders have recently explained this ancient term as follows:

> It is a power of temptation, a charm used to induce, almost without their knowing it, a change in life from the old ways to the new. It is a way of charming people into seeking power and wealth without regard to the means they use to get it. Of charming people into believing an army and weapons will make peace. Or charming people into immorality and unnatural sexual acts . . . Koyaanisqatsi can be charming people into believing that there is nothing wrong in abusing the Earth and universe . . . we will arrive at a point of confusion because of the fast life resulting from the change from good to bad in our moral principles . . . the lives of the people and the leaders will become corrupted by greed and power. Honesty and truthfulness will wane. This will affect our children, who will hassle us with nagging and annoyances which will finally cause us mental distress resulting in the failure of our health . . . You name it, for you are living in the midst of Koyannisqatsi.

For almost a thousand years, the tribe carefully chose young men to be their spiritual leaders and trained them in their sacred kivas to understand and memorize verbatim these complex secrets. These initiates had to memorize the information word-for-word as it was given to their ancestors by Maasaw. This provided an exact and unbroken "mouth-to-ear" chain of ancient sacred information. Once a year, the tribe would gather and the "warnings, prophecies and instructions" would be spoken aloud to the tribe by the new initiates and the Elders. Their story is the oldest and most comprehensive existing oral history of any Native Americans.

The instructions and prophecies told that the Hopi were to keep this information secret until Koyaanisqatsi ruled the Earth and then it was to be shared, first with other "tribal leaders" and then with all people. They would know when this time had come by two prophesized events. The first event was when "a gourd of ashes falls from the sky and glows brighter than the sun, make the oceans boil and the land burn - causing nothing to grow for many years." This occurred on August 6, 1945, when the atomic bomb was dropped on Hiroshima. When this happened, the Hopi Elders were to go four times to the United Nations ("eastern shore to the house of mica (glass) where leaders meet"), to warn them. There they were to present the prophecies, warnings and instructions.

Their first visit to the U.N. was in 1949. The second in 1962, but it wasn't until the third in 1986 that they were allowed to address the assembly during the UN International Day and Year of Peace. Again in 1994, the few remaining tribal elders went to the United Nations to present their prophecies. For the most part, they got a deaf ear. Only the French seemed mildly interested.

The second prophesied event, instructing them to release this sacred information to "all tribes," began occurring in 1975. Maasaw had instructed the Hopi that when only a few Elderly Elders could still recite the prophecies, warnings and instructions in their entirety, they were then to reveal them directly to all people, not just their leaders.

Over an eleven year period (1975 to 1986), five of these elders published an underground newsletter, *Techqua Ikachi*, that included all the secrets. In 1997, the last remaining keeper-of-the-secrets, 104-year old

Dan Evehema, contacted Thomas Mails, an American writer on Native American culture. Dan, who was born in Hopiland in 1893, transferred his tribal secrets to him from which Mails published in two books, *The Hopi Survival Kit* and *Hotevilla:The Hopi Shrine of the Covenant.*

In these ancient prophecies, Maasaw foretold that a race of white people ("bahannas") would come and would "multiply like ants." It was told that they would appear and then leave the Hopi in peace for generations until they reappeared. This happened when Spanish invader Pedro de Tovar arrived at their mesa-top towns in 1540 and, finding no gold, continued on. It was over one hundred and thirty years before whites appeared again - this time to stay.

Their coming might be a blessing to the tribe, their prophecies stated, if they met "the right bahannas" and their long-separated "White Brother" who had wandered towards the east after the Hopi's Emergence into the Fourth World. Hopi believe that *all* races emerged together and therefore *all* are Hopi. For Instance, they believe that the Mayans were Hopi who did not complete their instructed migrations.

Prophecy said if this was the "good bahanna," he would bring a missing piece of one of their sacred tablets and they would live peacefully together, correcting each other's laws and faults and establishing a faith that reflected the truth of life in a spirit of universal brotherhood. For centuries before the bahanna brother came, every year in Oraibi a sacred ceremony was held to mark his welcomed arrival.

If they were unfortunate and met the wrong white brother, they would be cursed with "two-hearted people" who would disturb the Hopi land and tribal ways ("they will erect their own kingdom upon our land"). The Hopi would be forced to develop their land and lives according to the dictates of the new rulers. They were not to resist but to wait for the "White Brother" to deliver them. Even nature would be affected ("the vines of their kingdom will spread throughout the land, diluting and dissolving everything that gets in its way"). The prophecies foretold that if the Hopi resisted their land seizure by force, the bahannas would attempt to annihilate all Native People, but a remnant of these people would survive to carry on in the future.

The bahannas would possess "high knowledge," but little wisdom and would create man in their own image rather than the Creator's. They would be cunning and sly and speak with a "sweet but forked tongue." The prophecies also told of "the people of the cross," who would be "kind and helpful with good hearts" but would be "instruments of bahanna's kingdom and will seduce you into forsaking the laws of our Great Creator."

The prophecies went on to say that the possible final destruction of the ancient tribal ways would come from within, from the Hopi leaders selected by bahanna to do their will ("a new leadership will be established on our land, our own people with short hair will take positions . . . disguised as the ear and tongue for our Nation"). This has come to pass as the Elderly Elders have been in a struggle with the United States Government-created Hopi Tribal Council concerning the adoption of modern technology and the bahanna religion and way of life.

The Elderly Elders do not claim to be the only people holding the Truth. As they say in *Hotevilla:Hopi Shrine of the Covenant*:

Very often we hear the tune, 'Do the Hopi really hold the key to survival in their mysticism?' We do not want to undermine any religious groups. Hopi does not claim the key, for all people on Earth are responsible for holding the key to survival. The Traditional Hopi merely teaches alternatives by basing his knowledge on the past histories of mankind from previous worlds. We were instructed to tell of the Great Purification just ahead of a time when humankind would once again be highly civilized . . . Survival is up to each of us to consider. Furthermore, we believe the instructions were given to all people long ago, according to where we were placed and how we were commissioned to fulfill our duties. Hopi brings this message to the world, hoping that there are pillars, however feeble they seem to be, still standing by the strength of His knowledge. Only His way will endure.

Now we must look at each other as brothers and sisters. There is no more time for divisions among people . . . War only brings more wars - never peace. Only by joining together in a Spiritual Peace with love in our hearts for one another, love in our hearts for the Great Spirit and Mother Earth, shall we be saved from the terrible Purification Day which is just ahead.

Instead of the usual doomsday prophecies, the Hopi prophecies, of which there are about 100, is a well-rounded message of assurance, at least for those who learn to respect the Earth and live close to the Creator. It even states that "just two or three righteous people will be able to fulfill the Creator's mission - even only one." In these ancient prophecies, Maasaw referred to other races, modern accomplishments, pollution, and two global wars, fought under the symbols of the swastika (Germany) and the rising sun (Japan) - all situations for which ancient tribes would have no frame of reference.

Maasaw, on behalf of the Creator, purposely gave this information, not to the political sophisticated "civilized" people of the world but rather to a small group of Native Americans who would, as Mails wrote, ". . . outlast all the other tribes in North America in preserving their Traditional ways and vows." What better repository for sacred information than a small, isolated indigenous tribe living a highly spiritual life close to the Earth? Sacred instructions would be much safer there than in Washington, Moscow, Jerusalem, Mecca, or Rome.

The number of prophecies is large and only a few relate to major events of Earth-changing realities. Many talk of great changes in societies and new inventions such as trains ("moving houses of iron"), telephones ("people talking over cobwebs"), airplanes ("roads in the sky"), travel to the moon, television ("people will talk through the air"), and trailers ("houses built in a day"). They even predicted certain fashion trends ("men's clothing will be taken over by women") and warned against some ("women's skirts will be raised above the knee, devaluing the sacred body of the female, indicating that many things will be devalued from the original"). They foresaw a change in human consciousness as "human beings will have many evil ambitions in their hearts that they will pursue throughout their lives." They viewed materialism as "the great seducer" and that those who worshipped it and made it their "god" would have a greatly impaired ability to recognize the truth.

Unlike other prophecies that seem to take the form of difficult-tointerpret, almost coded messages, the Hopi prophecies are straightforward and easy to understand. They are offered by the Creator so that we would have the tools, the "active ways," to avoid some of the more direful possible outcomes. The instructions allow us to live with hope and optimism. More importantly, these instructions are what we need to do now, even if there were no threats. As Mails writes: "We are not left to sit, to wonder, or to live in fear. We can get to work immediately on specific solutions. More importantly, we are trained to be constantly doing, as an automatic process of life, everything that is necessary to keep us alert and ready. Therefore, we are able to live in abiding hope."

Many of the prophecies, including two "great wars," have already come to pass lending credibility to the future prophecies; however, all the prophecies are full of "ifs" and "maybes" and always remind us future outcomes are direct results of present and future human actions. No certain dates are ever given and nothing is predetermined. Though some of the prophecies and warnings are alarming, the accompanying instructions allow us to lessen their impact, delay them or avoid them altogether. We do this by following the "Road Plan and the Pattern of Life." As the book points out, "Maasaw implants a special kind of assurance within those who respond to his call to serve." The prophecies also tell us that the final outcome rests in the hands of the Creator Himself.

The prophecies foretell of a time "when a mystic fog will dilute the minds and hearts of all people" [television? consumerism?]. Wisdom and true knowledge will be weakened and the "Laws of our Creator will dissolve in the minds of people. People will become very materialistic, not sharing in the old ways and many will no longer follow the Original Instructions . . . The white man will tempt the Hopi with many things. Children will be out of control and no longer obey the leaders, immorality and the competitive war of greed will flourish." The prophecies tell that as the way of life of the bahannas invades and gradually takes over the Hopi life, everyone - bahanna and Hopi alike - will have two choices: to follow the way of the Creator (the "Pattern of Life") or the way of the "two-hearted forces" (materialism). How people decide will make a difference not only in their own personal life but in the final global "closing of the Fourth Cycle."

On the more hopeful side, the prophecies also mentioned that "the men with ambitious minds will decrease, while the people of good hearts, who live in harmony with the Earth, will increase until the Earth is rid of evil . . . There will be a new dawn of time when the world will bloom into peacefulness."

So what are the secret Hopi instructions to help us usher in this "new dawn?" Maasaw has asked us all to join him and the Elderly Elders on the "Spiritual Ark" and live the "Pattern of Life."

His instructions are as follows (from Mails' *The Hopi Survival Kit*):

1. **Make your own covenant with the Creator.**
2. **Live simply, as Maasaw himself lives.**
3. **Practice self-denial.**
4. **Practice self-sufficiency.**
5. **Change your priorities. Make careful choices.**
6. **Recognize that it is the Creator's wish to rescue us, and that, together with the Hopi, we can rescue the world.**
7. **Think of attitude as being equal to application. Be in good humor. Do not be angry or have sad thoughts. What we think, we create.**
8. **Make your attitude regarding life and the environment a reverent one.**

At first, it is easy to dismiss them as too simplistic, too low-tech. However, when you consider them in reflection, they are powerful, effective and complete. It is clear that if many people would follow these instructions, we could transform the planet and heal our societies. The Creator and Maasaw are asking us to totally change the way we view our lives and our environment.

The Elderly Elders tell us in *The Hopi Survival Kit*:

Fighting only brings destruction, sorrow, and increasing problems to the multitude of common people - no matter who wins the war . . . We have also been taught that those who are not given opportunities will sooner or later revolt and seek to gain attention [terrorists?], so that they will get their share and be like any people who are able to get it without revolting . . . common people will become concerned and frustrated because they can no longer cope with their hectic world. They will be particularly against bloodthirsty politicians and the deceitfulness of world leaders. The unrest will become worldwide as people foresee that any possibility of living in peace has become hopeless. They will realize that their leaders have failed in accomplishing peace. Then the world over ordinary people will band together to fight for world peace.

The Elderly Elders do not believe we should just turn our backs on our political leaders and pursue this dream. As Mails writes:

The Traditionalists have paid a great price for keeping the Covenant with the Creator. They have been scorned, persecuted, beaten, imprisoned, and ridiculed. However, they understand that you "never throw away this gift of Divine wisdom." They believe that as our perceptions and attitudes change so does our outer world, without a single visible event taking place. Slowly, without most people even noticing, problems that existed before begin to disappear. Many people resist the concept that the Hopi instructions of love, peaceful thoughts, blending with the Earth and striving to follow the Creator's path can really solve so many worldwide complex problems - problems that have been ingrained for centuries.
The ancient Hopi correctly understood that thought is creative power, that it is a seed that would bear fruit over time. Our attitudes, feelings and rhythms will reach out to those who are causing problems and get them to change their minds and practices. I know this sounds foolish, and if it were just the Hopi and I, as mere human beings, suggesting it, it would be. But remember that it is the Creator who makes this promise. He is putting divine power to work through those who follow his instructions.

We have become convinced that only modern concepts and more advanced technology can replace the natural order on Earth, failing to realize they *are* the problem. We believe we just need cleaner fuels, cold fusion, a faster Internet, more solar and wind energy, stronger environmental laws, bio-fuels, etc. Some of these are indeed needed, but they are not the solution, but rather the outward manifestation of people desiring to solve the problem by their inner changes of wanting to live in harmony with the Earth and each other. The Traditionalists say that their goal is to change the attitude of people the world over. From these attitudinal changes new forms of behavior will emerge and problems will be solved.

Our present predicament may be "the darkness before the dawn." Hopi believe what we are now going through is part of a Divine plan - one in which the final outcome is known and beatific. Hopi instructions for this Fourth World are clear. As outlined in Frank Water's *The Book of the Hopi*:

Man is created perfect in the image of the Creator. Then after "closing the door," "falling from grace" into the uninhibited expression of his own human will, he begins his slow climb back upward . . . The Fourth World, the present one, is the full expression of man's ruthless materialism and imperialistic will; and man reflects the overriding gross appetites of the flesh. With this turn, man rises upward, bringing into predominant function each of the higher centers. The door at the crown of the head opens, and he merges into the wholeness of all Creation, whence he sprang. It is a Road of Life he has traveled by his own free will, exhausting every capacity for good and evil, that he may know himself as a finite part of infinity . . . the highest function of the mind was to understand how the One Great Spirit worked within man. The spirit or kachina people taught this was so that the people would not become evil again and this Fourth World be destroyed like the first three.

In our own personal lives, as we more closely follow these instructions, a new rhythm will develop. We begin to heal our relationships and from this place of greater healing, we experience greater energy and a sense of fulfillment that we have indeed begun to walk in the "Pattern of Life" - the Beauty Path - the path we have been seeking all our lives. Traditional elder Dan Katchongva says in his *A Message For All People:*

> Those gifted with the knowledge of the sacred instructions will then live very consciously, for they will remember and have faith in these instructions, and it will be on their shoulders that the fate of the world will rest.

As the last of the Elderly Elder Traditionalists approach their Earthly transition, they truly feel fulfilled that they had completed the mission Maasaw and the Creator had given them - to turn the task of saving ourselves and the Earth over to us, a global One Love tribe. They tell us that if we follow the instructions in our own lives, things will work out. It was foretold that the Earth will not purify itself and settle its problems in the closing of the Fourth Cycle until the Hopi tribe purifies itself. As Dan Katchongva writes:

> Therefore it is only the Hopi that still have this world rotating properly, and it is the Hopi who must be purified if this world is to be saved. No other person anyplace will accomplish this. . . As we say, the Hopi are the first people created. They must cure the ills of their own bloodline so everything will become peaceful, by the will of the Creator. He will cure the world . . . If the world is saved, you will all be saved, and whoever has stood fast will complete this plan with us, so that we will all be happy in the Peaceful Way.

Chapter 7
Return to the Heart of Mother Earth

"It's our commitment to follow the ways for the Creator that put you here. If you don't have a belief that you follow, you are just out there roaming. That is where a lot of people are . . . We believe that once, all of humanity came from the same source. And because we all came in as one, we're supposed to get back together as one sometime. There is always hope that this will happen. It depends on how we communicate with one another. Right now, the races of the world are still trying to find out who has the power."
—**Radford Quamahongnewa, Hopi Elder**

"I don't stand for the black man's side, I don' t stand for the white man's side. I stand for God's side." —**Bob Marley**

After our concerts in Hopiland, we returned to Jamaica several times and continued our One Love tour there. We were also in contact with our Havasupai friend, Supai Waters. He had been selling reggae CDs to raise money for a One Love concert in the Canyon. Between his efforts and our contribution, we scheduled the concert, *Reclaim the Grand Canyon*, for June 25, 2004, the following summer.

Supai Waters strongly believed that this concert was needed. He and other tribal members knew that their land was continually threatened by government and business interests. For millennia, they have been the

Canyon's only inhabitants. Their reservation stretches for thousands of acres along the Canyon and they impede the government's ability to "harvest" the resources - now thought to be the most abundant in the continental United States. Because of this, in the past the government has referred to the tribe as the "Havasupai problem." The tribe is in danger of having their land pillaged and polluted. Only a tribal council strongly committed to protecting the land could prevent this.

"We need to have this concert," Supai Waters said on one of our phone calls to him. "Some of the teenage boys here are bringing back some bad things they got into outside the Canyon. They are dressing in black and listening to the violent hip-hop music that degrades women. They are being argumentative and giving everyone a bad vibe. We have never had this problem before. We need to get them into conscious reggae to get them back on track."

Our goal for the concert was to "big-up" the tribe and remind them that they *do* indeed have a Sacred Covenant with the Creator to guard the Heart of Mother Earth. We knew that if we could change how the tribe perceived themselves, they would take their power back. An enhanced self-image would not only uplift the vibes in the village but the tribe would recommit to their Covenant.

We also decided to ask several others to join us in bringing this message to the tribe. Uproot, a conscious reggae band from Yuma led by George and Roberto Flores, would be our tribal drummers. Radford and Dawn came in from Hopiland with their families. We knew they could be effective in encouraging the Havasupai to protect their land and culture from commercial interests just as they had done by keeping gambling out of their reservation. Supai Waters also invited Raquel Burnett, an articulate and dedicated Native American woman from the Leonard Peltier Defense Committee.

A week before the concert, Supai Waters, Julia and I drove to northern California to the Sierra Nevada World Music Festival, a large three-day reggae concert near Yosemite Valley. The festivals organizers had invited the three of us to speak each day and to have a booth with our books. At that time, a week before our planned concert in the Canyon, the tribal council was still debating whether to give us permission to use the schoolyard or not. Roland Manakaja, a very conscious Havasupai tribal leader, was left to convince them. As we drove to the festival, Roland called us on my cell with the good news that the council had approved the concert. He explained to them the need to keep the youths on the right track with conscious music and bring events like this to the tribe.

The Sierra Nevada festival was great - ten thousand reggae fans living and camping together for three days in the beautiful California foothills. We parked our small camper van in the vending area and set up our booth directly in front. Each day we would address the crowd from one of the two stages and we would spend the rest of the time at our booth talking with the myriad of people that passed through. Many had heard of us or had read our books. It was an enjoyable, relaxed way to meet our readers.

The three of us had a great time together for a week on the road. Though Supai Waters can be the classic stoic Indian with strangers, with us he is playful and fun, always quick to laugh and joke. He also has an uncanny sense of people, probably from years of navigating the minefield of American prejudice. On the last day of the festival, an eccentric self-proclaimed Rasta "prophet" from San Francisco came by our booth talking a mile a minute, unsuccessfully attempting to engage Supai Waters in his monologue.

"Does he speak?" the man finally said in frustration, gesturing toward Supai Waters.

"He's not a prophet," Supai Waters said after he had left. "He's a non-prophet."

Leonard Peltier, perhaps more than any other living Native American, has become a symbol of the ongoing oppression of America's Original People. A great-grandfather, artist, writer, indigenous rights activist and nominee for the Nobel Peace Prize, Leonard is a citizen of the Anishinabe and Dakota/Lakota Nations. Leonard is part of a new generation of Indian men and women who began in the mid-1950s to protest the violations of Native American rights by the state and federal government with a renewed resolve and militancy. Along with the civil rights, women's rights, black power and anti-war movements, it strengthened in the 1960s and 1970s.

Their activism helped convince the government to pass the Indian Self-Determination and Education Assistance Act in 1975, which permitted the tribes to run their own federal programs for the first time. It was also during this period of renewed pride that the Native American Rights Fund (NARF) was formed by Indian attorneys that began fighting legal battles over treaty violations. Their success included the Passamaquoddies and Penobscots of Maine being granted 300,000 acres and $27.5 million.

A participant in the American Indian Movement (AIM), Peltier went to assist the Oglala Lakota people on the Pine Ridge Reservation in the mid-1970s. During that time, the Indians on the reservation were under constant threat of being attacked, raped or even killed. Their reservoirs were being poisoned and women were being sterilized - all because they desired to keep their traditional ways. The traditionalists called on AIM for help. Tensions grew and it soon escalated into violence. On June 26, 1975, a tragic shoot-out occurred ending with several deaths, including two FBI agents. Accused of their murders, Peltier fled to Canada believing he would never receive a fair trial in the United States.

On February 6, 1976, Peltier was apprehended. The FBI knowingly presented the Canadian court with fraudulent affidavits, and Peltier was returned to the United States for trial. Key witnesses were banned from testifying about FBI misconduct. Testimony about the conditions and atmosphere on the Pine Ridge Reservation at the time of the shoot-out was severely restricted. Important evidence, such as conflicting ballistics reports, was ruled inadmissible. The prosecutor, who convinced the jury that Leonard had killed the agents at "point blank range," years later admitted, on the record at one of Leonard's many appeals, "We did not have any direct evidence that one individual as opposed to another pulled the trigger." At the time, though, the jury was unaware of these facts.

As acknowledged by the Courts, he did not receive a fair trial. As recently as November 2003, the United States Court of Appeals for the Tenth Circuit stated: "Much of the Government behavior at the Pine

Ridge Indian Reservation and in the Prosecution of Mr. Peltier is to be condemned. The Government withheld evidence. It coerced witnesses. These facts are undisputed."

Leonard was convicted and sentenced to two consecutive life terms. All his appeals, many conducted by his legal council, former United States Attorney General Ramsey Clark, have been denied in spite of the overwhelming proof of his innocence and that the government manufactured and withheld evidence. Though no shred of evidence has ever linked him to the killings, he was found guilty of "aiding and abetting" simply for having been on the reservation that day. Abroad, he is seen by many as a political prisoner in his own country. Recently, the European parliament, as well as the governments of Italy and Belgium, have passed resolutions calling for clemency and an investigation into his case. He is currently imprisoned at the United States Penitentiary in Lewisburg, Pennsylvania.

Leonard remains spiritually free though physically imprisoned. In his book, *Prison Writings:My Life Is My Sun Dance*, he writes:

> Let us forgive the worst
> in each of us
> and all of us
> so that the best
> in each of us
> and all of us
> may be free.

(Leonard needs our ongoing support in his attempts to have justice prevail and himself freed. For more information please visit his website at www.leonardpeltier.org.)

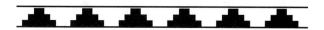

The day before our *Reclaim the Grand Canyon Concert*, everyone involved in the project gathered in the village, spending most of the day in the sweat lodge and swimming in the pools below Havasu Falls. Dawn came with her husband, Duane, and her young son, Rad; Radford brought his wife, Lorna. Around midday George and Roberto and the Uproot band flew in. It took six helicopter flights to bring in their equipment - all precariously hung in slings thirty feet below the helicopter - as they nervously looked on. The next evening, as the sun dipped below the canyon walls and the oppressive heat gave way to the pleasant evening, our event began on the playground area next to the school. Several hundred tribal members joined us.

"It is time that the Native American people will be honored again," Roland said opening the event. "As prophecy states through the thousands of years, these days would come when the winds would blow, the Earth would shake. There would be wars. There would be famines. There would be all kinds of chaos. Our culture, they say, may shatter like glass. But I believe that we can unify our people - the indigenous people - the people that has been oppressed by the government and we still are. But I have a lot of respect for the government. They've assisted the Native People in many ways. I thank them for that."

"There are many good people that are coming together in protection of the elements," he continued. "We hear good music. That's why we're here. We hear the beauty of the eagle as it flies across the sky. We have many sacred sites. The National Park Service is using the Native American Protection and Repatriation Act as a tool to benefit their research of our ancestors' remains at archaeolgical sites. The Havasupai people do not disturb these sites. It is taboo for us to even disturb a pottery shard, an arrowhead. Nine tribes have been involved in the Grand Canyon Environmental Studies for over a decade. These Indian tribes have documented their traditional cultural properties - their sacred sites. Our tribe has documented its sacred sites and then the government comes along and says, 'These sites are not eligible to be protected under the National Register.' The Native People want the Grand Canyon protected forever by the National Register from rim to rim. When we were fighting the uranium industry, they sat in Washington with their lobbyists and drew up agreements and tried to get our leaders to sign those documents. They told our people, 'If you will not fight us on religious grounds again, we will honor and protect four sites for you forever.' It wasn't those four sites that we wanted protected. We wanted the *whole* Earth to be protected."

"This Earth is a breathing Mother. We were in the womb of our Mother today - those of us that were in the sweat lodge. We suffered a little bit for you. As we sprayed water on the hot rocks, we suffered. The breath of our ancestors came into our being. The breath of our ancestors still lives today. That's why Leonard Peltier is in the spirit of Crazy Horse. I admire that man. When I read about what they've done to him, tears come down my face. When I hear about the Trail of Tears, about Wounded Knee, the massacres, it hurts us. And yet our ancestors looked at the canyon walls and said this is a powerful, powerful place. They did not have to desecrate it, dig it up and create a nuclear bomb to prove that it is powerful. They knew it. Their body, their being - they could feel it. Sometimes here when we have sickness or death come into our homes, we can feel it."

"The youths, they are the ones that will be taking over what we are doing here," Roland continued, his voice becoming more impassioned. "I told the council, 'This is the opportunity to talk to our children - to teach them, to talk to them about respect of our land.' They are proposing to build a ski resort on the San Francisco Peaks near Flagstaff. They want to spray city wastewater from the sewer plants on our sacred peaks - human waste on our sacred mountain. This will taint this water here, this pure water that we drink. It will no longer be pure. We will die from sicknesses. It breaks my heart to see the way they are abusing the elements. We have been told to protect these things. Thirteen tribes are opposing this."

"All the hard work that we've done to get rid of the aircraft, I've fought them all the times in the meetings, arguing for our people. Our leaders were afraid to speak up. One of these days, they may send someone to neutralize me, to get rid of me. But remember, I stood up. Sometimes I felt like I was standing alone but I stood up and believed what was right, our birthright. The Creator gave us these instructions. This is my foundation. Sometimes I tell the council, 'I feel like resigning when I get frustrated because things are not happening.' And they said, 'Roland, if you leave us, who's going to take your place? There's nobody here that can do that.' I heard that from our leaders. I had pity on them and I said, 'O.K. I will stay.' People, I beseech you, especially my own people here. Let's all come together at least once a month like this. Be strong, my people and I ask the Great Spirit to bless us all."

Raquel made a moving address to the tribe and read a letter from Leonard Peltier, which read in part: "Greetings, friends and supporters, let me thank you for inviting the Leonard Peltier Defense Committee to your gathering. I'm doing O.K. I feel healthy in body and spirit but determination for freedom is still very alive and active. It has been a long hard fight. We cannot believe how this justice department has so much disregard for the Constitution that they are sworn to uphold. Every appeal that I have, is filled with Constitutional violations by the Justice Department. Of course, to us Native people, none of this is a surprise. The treaties we made with them, were all violated before the ink was dry. We know from firsthand experience, they lie, cheat and manufacture evidence against anyone who has displeased them in one way or another, especially if you chose not to be one of their puppets . . . In short, I have not surrendered."

"I know this gathering today is to bring unity among all nations and I know you are all in it for the long haul and you will accomplish your goals no matter how long it takes . . . In what was known as the 'reign of terror,' we lost a great many people of the Oglala-Lakota Nation. We were also taught by our elders that though the enemy was vicious and cruel, there were a lot of good people in their race of people and that we should accept and welcome them as they come and stand by our side. So when we come together as nations, we must never forget to invite people of different races. I was taught by my elders that in order to be able to unite people, we must be able to pray together, then break bread together. I have always agreed with this."

After Raquel read Leonard's letter, Radford spoke to the tribe. "I am a Hopi. I am a snake priest. I am a warrior chief. I am a spokesman for the *kikmongwi*, which is the highest priest in the village of Shungopavi and I also speak for the leadership of the village of Shungopavi. Shungopavi is the Mother Village of all Hopi villages. Shungopavi is the only village that, to this day, is carrying on most of the traditional religious activities and events. This is why I am here, to tell you that you have your traditional events, too, and you are to keep them all the time. I have been in my position for thirty-four years. I am almost the last of my clan who are responsible for these activities. Tonight, I want to talk about how hard it is to preserve and help the people to maintain their ways."

He then outlined the problems the Hopi have had maintaining their traditional ways. He started with the first arrival of the Spanish in the mid-1600s, the taking of Hopi children away to schools in the early 1900s, and the building of the roads and school buildings on sacred snake-medicine ground in modern times, and finally he spoke of the recent gambling issues.

"We are still living our way of life," he continued. "We are still initiating our young men and women. There are new challenges with the new technology, the televisions and computers. People who left the reservation long ago are now returning with ideas they got in the cities. These are the people we are now having trouble with. They are coming back and trying to change everything. They have not been with us trying to fight for what our beliefs are, our religious activities are. They want to change everything to the way it is in the cities. There are still elders there that still want to keep the culture and the way of Hopi life continuing and perpetuating. And I am one of the people that are trying to help the leaders to make this happen. There are others that help me in trying to get this message out to the Hopi people. Not just in Shungopavi but other villages. It is hard work. Some young people are now trying to find out what their clan responsibilities are and what they can help do to revive their villages."

"This is my first time here. In the past, we have been friends, we have been brothers. Hopi has developed a dance that we call the 'Havasupai Dance.' We try to use your language in our songs. It was hard but the languages are similar. Last week, there was a dance at First Mesa with Supai dancers. When we came into this world, we made a covenant with the Creator that we would help Him take care of this world. When I came in the helicopter, it was my first time in one, and when I came over the edge, my heart was still up in the air and the plane was down below. Your home is so unique, so rich. When I saw your home, when I went to your waterfalls, my heart was so enthused. This is *your* place. Don't let anyone take it away from you. I want to encourage you to maintain it as natural as you can. Don't let this area be destroyed or be modified in any way or it will not be the same." "You have everything here that you need to survive with. In Hopi, it is so much different. We are a semi-arid area. We have to work real hard to get our crops to grow. Here you have your river, the most beautiful river. I think it will be up to the young generation to unite together to keep this place natural as you can. You are the ones that will carry on the future of this tribe, of your people. Don't get into situations where your personal lives are in danger. You have a good mind. Don't destroy your physical bodies. Don't destroy your minds. Stay away from things that will hurt your mind and your body. You are the ones that will be here to continue the ways of your people. Parents, guide your young people the right way. Tell them the history, the stories, the Supai way. Teach them how to be a Supai. You have a unique place here - so beautiful. Stay together and make this place *your* place and don't let *anyone* take it away from your. I will pray for you so that maybe with my help, things will be better. Thank you very much."

"My message to you is to be proud," Dawn said after the enthusi-astic applause for her father had quieted. "Don't forget who you are. Don't forget where you come from. I know sometimes you want to get out and go somewhere else. You have such a beautiful, beautiful land. When I first saw your waterfalls, I wanted to cry. It was really blue! Be strong. Be happy. Always, always remember who you are, Who made you, why you are here. The sign says 'Reclaim the Grand Canyon.' You don't have to reclaim the Grand Canyon because it was always yours. We - the Indigenous People - are still here."

"Since time began," I said, addressing the tribe, "the Havasupai tribe has lived in honor and, for the most part, peace. You have kept your Covenant with the Creator as the Guardians of the Grand Canyon. For the last century, the dominant culture controlled much of your ancient land and attempted to mold the hearts and minds of your youths by removing them and sending them to schools. Many of the tribe began to adopt the dominant culture's view of themselves - an interpretation that does *not* take into account the Creator's view and is therefore incomplete and inaccurate. It is now time to reclaim your power by re-instilling within yourself individually, and your tribe collectively, the Creator's image of who you *truly* are. You are the chosen people - chosen by the Creator as caretakers and guardians of the 'Heart of Mother Earth'."

"Yours is a Sacred Covenant and one for which you have been perfectly prepared. To keep your Covenant all tribal members do not need all of the skills demanded in modern society. To keep this Covenant, you do not need to know how to drive a car, work a computer or understand complex contracts. You need only to love your home and each other and claim your legal and spiritual rights. Only trust those leaders, both elected and un-elected, who truly understand and cherish this Covenant. Anyone who doesn't, does not see the tribe spiritually - only physically and financially - and therefore must be treated as a younger brother or sister, from whom guidance is seldom taken. They must always be viewed as a people with a limited perspective and dealt with as such."

"Your home is not only the most beautiful place in the country but it is the most remote," I continued. "It is the only town in the continental United States that you cannot drive to by car. This is not by coincidence. It is the Creator's plan. You have been protected from much of the onslaught of technology and commercialism. This too is the Creator's plan. Many of you were meant to stay on this land. Some of you were meant to leave for a period of time. You are all still *His* guardians. You are perfectly prepared to keep your Sacred Covenant - as a tribe, as individuals. In all your dealings regarding your tribal rights and land, look *only* to those leaders that put the tribe and its Sacred Covenant first."

With a combination of mostly original and a few Marley songs, Uproot opened everyone hearts and minds. Between songs, their lead singer, George, shared his message with the tribe.

"Havasupai, you are the chosen people, as you've heard all night," he said. "You need to remain strong and come out into the light and take the veil out from your eyes and realize you've got to be yourselves. Keep the story going, with yourselves and the children. A beautiful place like this can only hold beautiful people like you. I'm telling you - right from my heart. For me to perform my music for you in this place, with the walls all around us, is a spark to the fire that's got to be lit. We've got to keep this fire burning of righteousness, of claiming yourself. Claim your place of home. Just like Bob Marley says, 'There's One Love in the house!' "

For five hours, all of us took the Havasupai on a journey into One Love, thanking them for keeping their Sacred Covenant with the Creator to guard the "Heart of Mother Earth." Our message rang clear and strong on that summer night and, especially with the help of Uproot's music, went deep into the heart and soul of the tribe. The conditions for them to continue and complete their task as Guardians were in place - their remoteness, their legal rights, their love of their beautiful land, their desire to stay there, their love of reggae music and their newly emerging conscious leaders. Many will never again see themselves through the eyes of the dominant culture but rather through the eyes of the Creator. The healing had begun. Before we flew out, we left copies of our message on handouts at the cafe, post office and the store.

A few months after the concert, Supai Waters called to tell us the youths in the village, who had started to dress in black and listen to violent hip-hop, had stopped. As Supai Waters said, "They embraced their 'Indianness' after the concert and now they listen to conscious reggae."

The following December, the tribe elected a pro-environmental tribal council. Rex Tilousi, one of the few remaining traditional elders, is now the tribal council leader. A year later in January 2006, Damon called to tell us the vibes were even better.

"It's no longer the twentieth-century vibes in the Canyon," he said. "It's the twenty-first century vibes. The long-haired people have prevailed. The shortened-dignity people have lost the war. They didn't carry the culture. But I'm not making them my enemy. It just makes me stronger."

For now, The Heart of Mother Earth is safe.

THE EFFECT OF TELEVISION
ON INDIGENOUS PEOPLE

I was curious to see how the Havasupai had been affected by the introduction of utilities, especially TV, into such a remote tribe. I knew that it was the presence of the TV satellite dishes that represented one of the greatest threats to the traditional tribal life. More than that, I had come to believe that it also represented one of the greatest threat to *all* life. Along with weapons of mass destruction and global pollution, which are easily recognizable as threats, television's influence on the planet is much more imperceptible and subtle, hence more dangerous.

There is no greater mechanism for destroying human diversity and long-established mores and values, than TV. As Jerry Mander states in his book, *The Absence of the Sacred:The Failure of Technology & the Survival of the Indian Nations:*

> By its ability to implant identical images into the minds of millions of people, TV can homogenize perspectives, knowledge, tastes, and desires, to make them resemble the tastes and interests of the people who transmit the imagery. In our world, the transmitters of the images are corporations whose ideal of life is technologically-oriented, commodity-oriented, materialistic, and hostile to nature. And satellite communications is the mechanism by which television is delivered into parts of the planet that have, until recently, been spared this assault.

That is not to say that television has not helped to advance the planet at all. The televised horror of African-American youths being attacked by police dogs assured the final success of the civil rights movement. When the fledgling Russian democracy was threatened by a military coup, the television and Internet revealed the military's lies about their progress. The televised resistance in Tiananmen Square encouraged China to listen to the outcry of their youths. Recently, the mass demonstration in Ukraine assured that the corrupted elections would not stand. Television opens our hearts to the victims of natural disasters, encouraging aid to flow to the needed areas. Television can be used to bring people together and to reveal governments' lies and deceptions.

In the past, and to a much smaller degree today, most tribal cultures were based on communal ownership, respect for the Earth, respect for elders, sharing, generosity, sexual abstinence, co-operation and non-materialism. All these values are debased by modern television, which presents values in direct opposition to those held by tribal cultures.

Before the introduction of TV into their tribal life, these values were passed on from generation to generation through the storytelling, songs, dances and rituals. These were not just entertainment but moral instructions telling the youths how to live. Once satellite television, videos and DVDs enter a village, this storytelling almost always ends. The storytellers cannot compete with over 200 television channels running 24 hours a day. Often, the elders too become seduced.

After a few years of television, the ancient stories disappear from the tribal collective consciousness, and with them their way of life and perception of their universe - replaced by the trivialized, materialistic view of the television and advertising producers. In many ways, television, especially satellite TV, is a form of electronic colonization whereby the indigenous culture is replaced by the advancing "civilized" culture. Once introduced into a culture, it is like a Trojan horse that takes over from within.

Television watching also changes the tribal time-honored relationships between men and women. Respect for women is difficult to maintain if people spend hours watching TV where women are often portrayed as sexual objects or victims of violence. Television also effects the health of the viewer as it promotes unhealthy eating choices while encouraging passivity of sitting nearly motionless. In affluent societies, where people can afford several televisions, people no longer eat together or even watch together but are often isolated in their own rooms - silent, alone, in front of a flickering tube.

As soon as television is introduced in a indigenous society, its negative effect can most quickly be seen on the children. Once obedient and respectful, they often become argumentative and unruly, mimicking the behavior they witness on TV. Once honor-bound to uphold the moral code of the tribe, they now begin to believe that all forms of behavior are acceptable. Once co-operative and sharing, they often become hyperactive, greedy and violent. Once slim and fit from constant play, they now become obese and unhealthy. These changes are much more observable in isolated cultures where TV has recently been introduced. The effect of television happens so quickly, with so much power, it is difficult to understand its impact until it is too late. All this happens with no warning or even intelligent discussion of possible negative effects. There is no going back as a society - only as individuals.

Recently, the Canadian government decided it was time their indigenous people living in their remote northern areas, to be more in contact with the rest of the world. Generators, televisions and satellite dishes were given to the tribes. Until that time, the Inuits spent their long nights telling ancient stories and playing with the children. Within a year, all that was abandoned as the tribe, including the elders, spent the long nights glued to the TV. It was not long before the children, once peaceful and respectful, became restless and disrespectful. It was not long before their centuries-old Sacred Hoop was broken.

Hours spent talking with family, friends and neighbors, walking in nature, doing chores, reading, playing music, doing arts and crafts, and just "being" - all intrinsically life-uplifting activities - are now replaced with hours absorbing the values of those that control the commercial media. In its wake, it destroys the family and community life of the tribe as well as the relationships among many individuals. Television stifles creativity while encouraging uniformity. It alters the way tribal people view their environment, animals and plants, and their attitudes about property and landownership. It encourages the young to leave the tribe in search of all the things and experiences the TV has told them they must have.

Television's fast-pace makes it more and more difficult for people to be in nature, where the pace is much slower and changes more subtle. It even speeds us up to where it is difficult to be calm, read, relax, meditate or contemplate. We have created the first society that moves at machine time. We are only just learning the effect of this massive experiment. One Japanese cartoon TV series moved at such lightening speed that eight hundred children went to the hospitals with seizures during its first episode. It had to be re-edited for future shows.

The negative effects are not just those created by television's introduction to tribal societies. It has the same negative effect on *all* societies. Television, by its nature, is not a "give-and-take" relationship. It is a one-way street to what appears to be a dead-end as it reveals the awesome power of the few speaking into the minds of the many. The only thing that will limit this effect, will be individual decisions to partially or totally unplug from the tube and replace that activity with more life-giving alternatives. Or as some recent bumper stickers put it, "Unplug the Drug!"

Almost all television programming is now controlled, including the news reporting, by major corporations. In essence, large corporations are now establishing the value system of the *entire* planet. It is estimated that 75% of everything on TV, both programming and commercials, is created by fewer than 100 large corporations.

Corporations are created with one common goal - their function is to maximize the profits for the shareholders in whatever ways are legal (though that criteria too is being stretched). This is the legally stated intention of *every* corporation (except non-profit corporations). That is their sole reason for existing. By law, they are *amoral*. In fact, they are required by law to put profits in front of everything else. Corporate leaders can be sued if they do not. The capitalistic system was set up this way. Corporations (except non-profits), by their stated nature, have no altruism.

Most large corporations lack commitment to their employees, the environment, the communities and countries in which they exist, often leaving them more impoverished when cheaper labor can be found elsewhere or by incorporating overseas to avoid taxes. Capitalism has created these huge soulless and heartless beasts and they now have taken over our government, educational system, health care, media, and all the industries in which they operate. They take no moral responsibility for any of their actions and little legal responsibility believing they should be "as bad as the law allows." They are Frankensteins out of control.

Large corporations with their unbridled power are wreaking havoc on the planet, subverting democracies, polluting all they encounter and supporting a system of exploitation and poverty. Few corporate or business leaders will admit to this. An exception is Ray Anderson, the CEO of Interface, the world's largest manufacturer of commercial carpets. In a recent presentation to civic and business leaders at North Carolina State University he stated:

> Do I know you well enough to call you 'fellow plunderers?' There
> is not an industrial company on Earth, not an institution of any

kind, not mine, not yours, that is sustainable. I stand convicted
by me, by myself alone, as a plunderer of Earth. The first indus-
trial revolution is flawed. It is not working. It is unsustainable. It
is a mistake and we must move on to another and better indus-
trial revolution and get it right this time.

Or as Ojibway environmentalist Debra LaFountaine noted, "We are
allowing the destruction of the very systems that we need to stay alive -
water, air, trees, animals - as if they were of no consequence to us."

Most large corporations have lost their moral compass and by their
control of government, they threaten democracies everywhere. They are
convinced that more technology will solve the world's threatening problems, failing to realize that technology *is* the threat. This capitalistic
system, which seeks out the lowest wages worldwide and then pays
desperate people only enough for 2 or 3 meals a day for 10 to 16 hours
of sweatshop labor, is destroying people and communities everywhere.
It is fostering a legal form of slavery, one that is more profitable for even
slaves had to be provided with not just their food but shelter and health
care as well. Can it truly be said that these masses of people are living
better than they would have under the Cooperative Cultures' tribal
system?

Every year the average TV viewer watches 21,000 commercials, each
one trying to convince us to buy or do something that is in the advertising
corporation's best interest, whether that coincides with ours or not. In
addition to this, we sit for hours every day absorbing the value system they
have created. Because of this, corporations are beginning to control more
and more aspects of human consciousness. They are training us and
interpreting for us how we see ourselves and our world, what is important and what is not, how human relationships, from those among
individuals to nations, should be handled, and what it means to be
human in the 21st century.

The corporations are becoming the "global tribal elders," passing on
their "wisdom" to the planetary tribe by capturing the tribe's attention,
just as elder storytellers once did in teepees, mud huts, grass lodges and
igloos all over the globe. The problem with this, is that these new "elders"

have no wisdom and do not have the best interests of their tribe in mind. I think the fact that we are proud to have become a "consumerist society" says it all.

However, we do not need to perceive ourselves as victims of this massive worldwide system. The exit door - healing our minds and spirits from this faulty separation thinking - is in front of us and easily swings open. Just give it the slightest nudge and it will pull you through. It has always been open but our eyes have been shut. Babylon has never really blocked our path to Zion - only in our imagination, never in *Reality*.

To heal the planet and our societies, we must remove this faulty worldview from our consciousness for it is *this* worldview that is doing much of the damage. As we do this within ourselves, we assist others in no longer seeing themselves as victims and in remembering who they *really* are - spiritual peacemakers sent here to bless the world through their love. No outside entity, no matter how powerful it may seem, can impede us in carrying out this Divinely-given assignment.

As Iroquois leader Leon Shenandoah teaches, "Everybody must bury all the hatred for what the Europeans and big corporations and politicians have been doing . . . We will not be ruled by our own hatred. Nothing will make us be filled with fear. The politicians have no power over us. The corporations don't have power either; not even the government."

Chapter 8
Walking in the Footsteps of The Peacemaker

"While we actively become aware of our thoughts, especially those that have a kind and loving intent, we naturally allow ourselves to become spiritually in tune with the Creator's wishes. This allows us to use our talents to fulfill our purpose on Earth. This is my motivation to follow the Good Mind. When it is time to leave this earth, I would like to feel that I fulfilled the purpose that the Creator sent me here to accomplish."
—Onondaga Clan Mother, Freida Jean Jacques,
in describing the "Good Mind"

"Life and Jah are one in the same. Jah is the gift of existence. I am in some way eternal, I will never be duplicated. The singularity of every man and woman is Jah's gift. What we struggle to make of it is our sole gift to Jah. The process of what that struggle becomes, in time, the Truth." **—Bob Marley**

A fter our concert in Supai Village in June 2004, we began to plan for Bob Marley's 60th birthday event in Jamaica on February 6, 2005. We knew that this would be a huge celebration on the island and after organizing concerts there for the previous three birthdays, we felt guided to do something for this milestone day. We also began to feel this might be our last event in Jamaica - that our message had gone out

loud and clear and our work there might be coming to an end and a
new assignment dawning.

For almost four years, our odyssey through the island had unfolded
one step at a time - like a twisting road where you can only see a short
distance ahead. We seldom knew what our next step would be until after
we had completed the previous one. We knew we had been effective in
getting our message out in many ways. Not only had the public exposure
of our concerts reached nearly every Jamaican with our invitation to join
us in teaching love but it had been delivered in a way that almost anyone
could accept. If you were from the broad base of the working poor, we
were with elder Rastas, reggae artists from grassroots origins and going
mainly into the inner-city schools. If you were uptown, the Governor
General, the Minister of Tourism, business and civic leaders, a senator and
a college dean were speaking at our events. If you were Christian, we
were working with gospel artists and several Christian newspaper columnists. If you were Rastafarian, reggae artists and Rastafarian talk show
hosts and dub poets were performing with us. There was someone to
whom you could relate, whose words might speak to you.

Bringing forward a message of love, you will always encounter resistance. As we became better known, a few spoke out against us, mostly
privately but occasionally publicly in newspaper columns or on radio
or TV talk show. Some were angry, still too hurt and wounded to forgive.
Others were making money or amassing power by keeping things churned
up. Still others were threatened, feeling we were doing what they *should*
have been doing and were not. Others felt that we should stay in our
own country which they felt needed more healing than theirs. I reminded
them that by that logic, their conscious recording artists should never
leave the island to bring a message of love and forgiveness to other countries.

In early January, five weeks before Bob's 60th birthday, I flew to
Kingston to plan the concert. Given that almost 40 conscious recording
artists live in Kingston, I always have an easy time filling the available
performance slots. Though none of the artists are paid, usually I have
more artists wanting to perform than I have spaces. During the month,
I had a series of meetings with the Jamaican government and the Marley

family to see if we could work together. The Marley family, who every year had a birthday concert and a cake-cutting at the Bob Marley Museum, liked the idea. Stephanie Marley, Bob's daughter and a beautiful person - inside and out - agreed to bring the annual birthday cake-cutting to the concert. This worked well for them since Rita Marley, Bob's wife, was also planning a huge concert that day in Ethiopia that would include performances by many of Bob's children.

The government was willing to stage the event for us and only asked that several slots be given to two musicians and two dance troupes they had invited. They were eager to see a resurgence of conscious roots reggae music, hoping that it might affect the youths. Recently there had been much speculation in their press that the escalating crime rate might be tied to the growing popularity of their dancehall music - much of which glorifies violence, sexuality and disrespect for women.

The month leading up to the concert, to be called "Bob Marley:The Legend Lives On," myself and our group of Jamaican healers appeared almost daily in the press and on TV and in radio interviews, encouraging love and forgiveness. One of the group, Barry Chevannes, an author, recording artists and a dean at the University of the West Indies, organized a "Violence-Free Day" campaign including a week-long bicycle club tour across the island bringing forward the message and ending at the concert. I asked Elaine Wint, a healer, event organizer and talk show host, to assemble of group of conscious women, from all religions and walks of life, to invite the women of Jamaica to lead the way in healing their country through love. In the weeks leading up to the concert, their efforts were also constantly in the news.

However, when I wasn't in meetings or with friends, much of my time was spent in a hotel room in downtown Kingston. To pass the time, I had brought many books on Native American cultures, including several on the Iroquois Nation. As I began to read the Iroquois history as to how they formed their Confederacy, what it said amazed me - not only because of their own epic but how closely it overlaid our work in Jamaica.

THE FIRST DEMOCRACY

Our efforts, as outsiders bringing a message of peace, matched closely an ancient tribal healing that occurred over 600 years ago (some believe thousands of years ago) in the forests of northeastern North America and Canada. This ancient healing has advanced human freedom world-wide.

Let us begin with a true but little known historical fact. True democracy did not begin with a few transplanted English in thirteen American colonies as is generally believed. When the first colonists arrived, there was already a centuries-old Native American democracy in place called the "Iroquois Confederacy," "The League of the Iroquois," or "The Haudenosaunee Confederacy" (in their language, their name is "Haudenosaunee" or "People of the Long House"). It consisted of five Iroquois-speaking tribes - the Seneca, the Oneida, the Onondaga, the Mohawk, and the Cayuga. The Tuscarora joined the confederacy later.

This democracy, which served as the pattern for the United States democracy, was complete with a constitution, a legislature and an executive body. It included freedom of speech and religion, women's rights, freedom from unauthorized entry of homes, clear procedures for replacing dead, incapacitated or corrupt chiefs and leadership by consensus. The Confederacy embodied such key elements as a convention system, which they called the "Grand Council," political caucuses, the separation of military and civilian leadership and the admission of new tribes as equal members to the union. It had been in place for generations *before* the original colonists landed.

For decades after the colonists arrived, the Iroquois counseled them in the "Art of Union," urging them to unite their separate states into one union, if for no other reason than for the colonists to speak with one voice in negotiating with the Iroquois. In fact, Thomas Jefferson and Benjamin Franklin, two of the key founders of the new democracy, studied the Iroquois Confederacy's political system. In his *The Politics of Thomas Jefferson*, historian Richard Matthews noted, American Indians "provided the empirical model for his [Jefferson's] vision." As Franklin stated to the Founding Fathers as they argued over key issues, "It would be a strange thing if Six Nations of ignorant savages [sic] should be capable of forming a scheme for such an union, and be able to execute it in such a manner, as that has subsisted [for] ages, and it appears indissoluble, and yet a like Union should be impracticable for ten or a dozen colonies."

On June 11, 1776, the Iroquois "forest diplomats" attended a Continental Congress in Philadelphia. Congress President John Hancock welcomed them as "brothers," recognizing the long and friendly dialogue between colonials and Iroquois on freedom, law, democracy, and government. Three weeks later, the Declaration of Independence was signed, and a new democracy was born.

Many of the principles developed in the Iroquois Confederacy were later adopted and integrated into the Constitution of the United States. Even modern leaders have acknowledged this. President John Kennedy wrote in 1960, "The League of the Iroquois inspired Benjamin Franklin to copy it in planning the federation of States." President Bill Clinton addressed the Iroquois Nation in 1994, stating, "Because of your ancestors, democracy existed here long before the Constitution was drafted and ratified."

It is not by accident that the concepts of freedom and democracy did not blossom with Europeans until they reached the home of the Iroquois. The physical borders and personal boundaries between the natives and the colonists were very porous, at times non-existent. Exchange of ideas and beliefs was constant. Exchange of indigenous subsistence methods was essential for the early colonists survival. The Native American notions of personal freedom and liberty were totally new to the Europeans, who had always believed themselves to be the "loyal subjects of the divinely-anointed royal monarchs." The Iroquois concept that no person or leader had any right to deprive anyone else their freedom, was revolutionary to them.

The settlers had lived under an accepted system whereby all the aristocracy, comprising a very small fraction of the population, had rights over the larger populace. There existed no European model of sovereign political entities, like colonies or states, with a strong central government. At the time, England was autocratic, France dictatorial and Russia serf-ridden under the Czar. These were societies of rich and poor, powerful and powerless, controlled exclusively and brutally by men - be they priests, governors, kings, nobility or male heads of individual families. Even the Greek and Roman "democracies" had always been oligarchies, never true democracies.

Only the Iroquois had developed a true egalitarian democracy. Therefore, it should be no surprise that the American colonists developed a similar institution soon after coming in contact and close proximity with them. Observing the freedom of their Native American neighbors could not help but create stirrings within the colonists for similar freedom from the monarchs of Europe. In fact, the new colonial society refrained from being too oppressive, knowing that the settlers were surrounded by examples of freedom. Soon these settlers began to adopt insubordinate attitudes that eventually led to the American Revolution. It was not by accident that the colonists at the Boston Tea Party were dressed as Mohawks.

There was a key foundation pillar of the Iroquois Confederacy that the Founding Fathers consciously chose *not* to adopt - the equality of women and their active guiding participation. This weakened the new democracy and was responsible for the United States entering into more wars then it might have had women had a voice earlier. As present Tadodaho Sidney Hill, Leon Shenandoah's nephew, recently said when asked by a reporter why our American democracy had gone so far astray, "As soon as they [the colonists] left the women out of the choosing. How can you not respect the thoughts of the woman who brings up the children? These are the ones who see your leaders. They see the mistakes. They see who learns from their mistakes. When you take that woman's thoughts out, there is no balance of power."

Almost a hundred and fifty years later, the Iroquois Confederacy was instrumental in finally getting women the vote in the United States political system. The women's suffragette movement was initiated and led by Elizabeth Cady Stanton, Lucretia Mott and Matilda Joslyn Gage, all from upstate New York, Iroquois territory, where it was noted that they drew inspiration from the equal status of Haudenosaunee women.

As women's rights activist, scholar and author Dr. Roesch Wagner, the foremost authority on Gage, noted that these three feminists "looked to the Iroquois for their vision of a transformed society . . . Where else would feminists of that time find practical examples of gender equity?" Before the Women's Rights Conference in Seneca Falls, New York in 1848, Moot spent a month with the Seneca.

As Gage noted in her *Woman, Church and State*, "the modern world is indebted" to the Iroquois "for its first conception of inherent rights, natural equality of condition, and the establishment of a civilized government upon that basis." As Gage, who was later adopted into the Mohawk Wolf Clan, spent time with Iroquois women, she remarked on the "experience of really being listened to by the men." She also noted that she could walk around the Onondaga tribal village and have no fear of rape, something she felt she could not do in any white town.

In fact, though the rape of captured Indian women by white men was commonplace, it was very rare for a white women to report being raped by Native Americans. Their tribal respect for women extended to *all* women. The Iroquois women had real respect, not a romanticized, token type of respect. Their children belonged to them and their clan and there was no threat of their children being taken by their fathers. They owned their homes, fields and tools. Women had real authority and no fear of male violence. It must have been strange for early-American women, with no political voice and weakened civil rights and always under the oppression of men's political, financial and physical strength, to learn that Native American women where elevated to a far higher stature. Likewise, Native Americans found the treatment of white women by white men strange. When the Cherokees first met in council to negotiate with the early colonists, their chiefs, astonished at the absence of women in the white delegation, asked, "Where are your women?"

When the Founding Fathers fashioned the new American Democracy, they weakened it considerably, not only by disenfranchising women, but also by allowing slavery - the antithesis of *all* democratic values. By allowing slavery (as did the Greek model), and later withholding civil rights to minorities, it was a white-only, male democracy for its first one hundred and fifty years - only white, male property owners were allowed to vote. Finally, all Americans were assured the vote after the Civil Rights era of the 1960s. By then, the democracy had been corrupted by another threat that the Iroquois had not had to deal with - special interests.

Over time, the Iroquois' democratic history and their help in forming the American democracy, was intentionally deleted from history. (In the Capitol Building, where the history of the democracy is depicted in murals, there is no mention of the Iroquois' contribution.) It will not be given the honor it deserves until history books, which form our children's view of their country, are rewritten to truthfully include the contribution of this country's First People. It is after all difficult to acknowledge and honor a race of people your founders referred to as "ignorant savages" and systematically annihilated.

Respect is long past due to the contribution towards human freedom and liberty made by this ancient Confederacy. As Charles C. Mann, author of *1491:New Revelations of the Americas Before Columbus*, stated in his July 4, 2005 article in *The New York Times*: ". . . everywhere liberty is cherished - from Sweden to Soweto, from the streets of Manila to the docks of Manhattan - people are descendents of the Iroquois League and its neighbors."

THE EPIC OF THE PEACEMAKER

When the members of the Iroquois Confederacy were asked how their union came to be, four of the five tribes told the same story, with only slight variations (the Onondagas have never publicly told their version and the Haudenosaunee Grand Council does not endorse *any* written version of the epic). For centuries before their confederacy was formed, the tribes had warred against each other with the most brutal cycle of blood revenge, torture, even cannibalism, ever recorded in Native American history. In fact, Native American tribes were not known for their aggressiveness, brutality or viciousness. Usually their "wars" were more minor skirmishes and ambushes over hunting grounds. They never fought to gain territory nor to conquer another people. It was more like a rough sport where young men could prove their bravery and where touching the enemy was considered more honorable than killing them.

Somehow these five tribes had left this peaceful cycle and for centuries their tribal conflict had degenerated into tribal and personal blood revenge. Almost every tribal member had lost a loved one in a war to a neighboring tribe. When that happened, honor dictated that they must revenge their loved one's death by killing the murderer or one of his family members. Even the children played at war. Peace was considered cowardly. The cycle of vengeance never stopped until the confederacy was finally formed and all lived together in peace.

Their legends told of a Huron brave (the Hurons were *not* one of the five tribes) named Deganawidah, "The Peacemaker" (he will be referred to as "The Peacemaker" throughout our tale as the Iroquois do not use his name unless they feel they need his assistance). The legend was that he was born of virgin birth. His mother's pregnancy caused her and her mother to be ostracized from the tribe. All three lived in the forests on the edge of the village. Though they were isolated and shunned by their tribe, The Peacemaker was raised by his mother and grandmother with gentleness and love and a sense of destiny. While pregnant, his mother (some legends say his grandmother) was visited by the Great Spirit. In a dream, He told her He was sending His messenger of peace and that the two women should take good care of him as he was sent to do the Great Spirit's work on Earth.

The Peacemaker grew to be honest, intelligent, generous and handsome. Living on the "edge of the village" enabled The Peacemaker to deeply develop spiritually, free of the usual tribal relationships. The animals loved him and were his only playmates. At a young age, The Peacemaker told his mother and grandmother that he had a vision of all tribes living in peace - a vision he said was given to him by the Great Spirit. He called this "Kaianevekowa," the "Great Law of Peace." He had come to lead the warrior tribes out of darkness. "It is my mission to stop the shedding of blood among human beings," he told them.

His message had three parts: Peace, Righteousness and Power. Peace (the Law) means the people can travel anywhere without fear of being killed as they no longer know war. Peace was Righteousness, justice practiced between men and between nations, in action. Peace also meant health in body and mind, for that is what comes when minds are sane and bodies healthy. Power means the "Power of the Good Mind," when all the people think the same way without arguments or "throwing ashes on one another." It also meant the authority of custom and law, backed by such force as is necessary to make justice prevail.

When The Peacemaker began to speak his message, his own tribe, the Hurons, rejected it, viewing him as strange and foolish with his talk of peace. Soon he decided to journey first to the Mohawks and then to the four other warring tribes. However, The Peacemaker understood the difficulty of an outsider trying to bring peace to the warring tribes plus he had a speech impediment, a stutter, that made his mission even more challenging, though at the same time offering him a sense of vulnerability that reduced resistance to his message. He knew he could bring the message but only the tribes themselves could create the peace. In his twenties, with his mission clear to him, The Peacemaker said goodbye to his mother and grandmother and left his forest home, telling them he would not return. In a white stone canoe, he rowed across Lake Ontario to seek out the tribes.

Landing on the other side, he encountered a group of hunters.

"Who are you?" they asked in astonishment to this handsome man in a stone canoe.

"I am called The Peacemaker in *this* world," he told them. "Go back to your settlement and tell your chief that the Good News of Peace and Power has come, and there will be no more strife in his village. If he asks whence peace is to come, say to him, 'It will come.' "

This they did, awakening the hope in the war-weary chief and his people that peace was possible. Since the tribes already had a prophecy that in a time of great trouble, the Creator would send a messenger to help the people, immediately their minds and hearts began to open to that possibility.

The first person he encountered who accepted the "Great Law of Peace" was a wise, beautiful and peaceful woman who lived in a neutral village and who traded provisions to warriors from all tribes. However, her fascination with the warriors' stories of fighting only encouraged them to continue. She, like many women, were drawn to the warriors physical bravery.

He told her, "I carry the Mind of the Master of Life and my message will bring an end to the wars between east and west. The word that I bring is that all peoples shall love one another and live together in peace. You must no longer feed the warriors."

"But that is what I do," the woman protested. "I am the woman that feeds the warriors. It is my livelihood."

"Now you must serve a higher cause," The Peacemaker replied. "The path of war must run through the House of Peace. Don't nourish war or the warriors. Then you will discover who you *really* are."

And the woman accepted his message saying, "That indeed is a good message. I take hold of it. I embrace it."

"Because you are the first to accept the Great Law," he said, "you shall be called, 'Jikohnsaseh, Peace Queen, Mother of Nations.' When the peace comes, you - the women of the tribes - will choose and remove the chiefs. Their titles will be both political *and* spiritual and will always belong to the women, called 'Clan Mothers.' Women know the hearts of men better than men. Women are the connection to the Earth. They create and have the responsibility for the future of the nation. Men will want to fight. Women will now say 'yes' or 'no' to war. Men, whose nature it is to be warriors, may not always see clearly the path of Peace; but a woman who knows that she must bury her loved ones, the children she has suckled, she would see and know if the fight would be worth its cost in life and death. Women know the true price of war and must encourage the chiefs to seek a peaceful resolution."

He told her the tribes were to be matri-lineal, with children belonging to the mother's clan. When a man married, he moved into his wife's longhouse with her family. If they separated, the children, home, tools and fields stayed with the mother. There is great wisdom in this. The woman raised the children. A need for a home and means to provide for the children was of utmost importance. Men could always fend for themselves but for a woman with little ones to tend for, time would be limited for replacing much-needed items. Also, the children would belong to the lineage of the woman so that every child would have a family to nurture them even if the father left or died in battle. All of these customs insured that the women of the tribes would always be treated with respect. As recent Iroquois leader Leon Shenandoah writes, "The Instructions say that men and women are equal, too. They've got to learn that one is not above the other. It takes both to create the children who are coming behind us."

Jikohnsaseh immediately set about teaching the Good Message to all that came her way, especially the young warriors. Often she would feed two feuding groups on separate sides of a partition, everyone sharing from the same bowls. Then she would remove the partition and the adversaries would make peace since their custom was that all that ate from the same bowl were forever brothers. Men sought her wise counsel in hours of doubt and danger. People came with hate in their hearts and went away with love for each other. Such was her ability and her love for the people. Eventually, her great "stateswomanship" would become instrumental in the tribes finally accepting the Great Law of Peace.

Knowing he must find the peacemakers from within the tribes, The Peacemaker then went in search of others to help him spread the Great Law to the tribes. Soon he came to a vacant round house owned by Hiawatha (Ayowenta is his Iroquois name), a former Onondaga adopted by the Mohawks. Hiawatha (not the same as the fictitious character in Longfellow's poem) was a chief and a powerful orator. His tribe had been at war for years. During this time, Hiawatha's wife and daughters died from an illness thought to be inflicted by the sorcery of a very violent Onondaga chief called Tadodaho. In his pain, Hiawatha himself had descended into hatred and cannibalism.

The Peacemaker climbed on top of Hiawatha's home and awaited his return. Soon Hiawatha returned dragging the body of a slain enemy warrior, which he planned to cook and eat. As Hiawatha prepared the fire, he looked in the kettle water and saw the reflection of The Peacemaker, who was looking through the smoke hole above. The image was full of love, wisdom and strength. Hiawatha, believing the reflection to be of his own face, instantly remembered that he was sent by the Great Spirit to be a man of love, not a man of hatred.

Realizing this and how far he had gone astray, Hiawatha went outside and sat on a rock and wept and prayed that someone would come along and show him how to relieve his pain at having hurt others so badly. The Peacemaker climbed down and went to console him. Not mentioning it was his face Hiawatha had seen in the water, The Peacemaker asked why

Hiawatha was crying.

"Instead of a man of peace and love," Hiawatha said, "I have become a man of violence and revenge. I have killed and hurt many people. It was not the path I was to take. Because of my deeds, I will never know peace again. I cannot forget the suffering I have caused."

"Be consoled," The Peacemaker said, without judging Hiawatha's deeds. "You can be at peace again. Where you have brought pain, you must now bring healing. Where you have done harm, you must now do even greater good. The Good Mind has come to you but you are miserable because the Good Mind does not live easily with the old memories. Heal your memories by working to make justice prevail. Hiawatha, I have brought the good tidings of Peace and Power from the Great Spirit to *all* people on Earth. The word that I bring is that all peoples shall love one another and live together in peace. Bloodshed must cease in the land. The Great Spirit never intended that blood should flow between human beings. You must join me to bring the Great Law of Peace to the tribes. I am an outsider and do not speak the language of the tribes. I have a speech defect but you are an eloquent speaker and a chief of one of the tribes. We must tell them to stop telling the old stories or there can never be an end to war. But because I am tribeless, we can council with *all* the tribes. Together we must go to the tribes and reason with them about the path of love, forgiveness, generosity and cooperation."

Hiawatha's grief over the loss of his wife and daughters was so great, that he did not believe he would be of value in bringing a message of love and forgiveness. The Peacemaker then taught Hiawatha the "Condolence Ceremony," still used to this day by the Iroquois. Hiawatha recorded this and other ceremonies on wampum belts, a form of mnemonic writing, using beautifully designed wide belts strung with different colored small shells.

Using the first wampum belt, The Peacemaker said:

"When a person suffers a great loss caused by death and is grieving, tears blind their eyes so they cannot see. With these words, I wipe away the tears from thy face using the white fawn skin of compassion so that you may see. I make it daylight for you. I beautify the sky. Now you shall do your thinking in peace when your eyes rest on the sky, which the Master of All Things intended to be a source of happiness to man."

Presenting the second string of wampum, he said:

"When a person suffers a great loss caused by death and is grieving, there is an obstruction in their ears so they cannot hear. With these words, I remove the obstruction so that you may once again have perfect hearing."

Presenting the third string of wampum, he said:

"When a person suffers a great loss caused by death and is grieving, their throat is stopped up and they cannot speak. With these words, I remove the obstruction so that you may once again speak and breathe freely."

As Hiawatha mourned for his family, The Peacemaker reminded him that obsessive grieving weakened the creative powers of life, especially when it turned to thoughts of revenge. Hiawatha now forgave himself and joined The Peacemaker in his vision. By doing this, he taught us a great lesson - we must forgive *ourselves* as we move to forgive others. This is the dawning of the Good Mind - our willingness to look fearlessly at what we have created in our lives, no matter how painful it may be. The completion of the Good Mind is our forgiving ourselves *and* others for going astray.

Before leaving to bring peace to the tribes, The Peacemaker instructed Hiawatha to fetch water to prepare a meal. "Dip with the current," he told Hiawatha. "One must never go against the forces of nature." By instructed him so, The Peacemaker was telling Hiawatha they could not be successful by approaching the chiefs and angrily telling them what they had done wrong in the past. They must only be encouraged to do right in the present and the future. Otherwise, they would only encounter the chief's denial and resentment and would be "going against the forces of nature."

Over several years (legends range from five to forty years to generations), The Peacemaker and Hiawatha set out to meet with the many chiefs, called "sachems," of the war-worn tribes. They went from settlement to settlement seeking the people that desired peace. They approached each village singing a peace song, also known as the "Six Song," still sung today by the Iroquois. Since nothing travels faster than a song, this hymn of thanksgiving opened the hearts of the tribal members and made them receptive to the message of love.

In each village, they explained the Great Law of Peace, reminding the people it was the will of the Great Spirit. They reasoned with them that attack, violence and revenge as a way of life that divided them not only from other tribes but from themselves and those they loved. Since many would criticize their efforts, they explained that to bring the Great Law you must have "seven layers of skin so the magic darts of your enemies will not penetrate."

At first, the tribes were suspicious of The Peacemaker. Some believed that he was an agent for his tribe, the Hurons. They demanded The Peacemaker prove his message was Divinely-inspired by jumping off a high waterfall. When he emerged unharmed, the tribes began to listen. As The Peacemaker and Hiawatha reasoned with the leaders, more and more leaders agreed to follow this path *if* their neighboring tribes would also.

The Peacemaker and Hiawatha would often have to make several visits to the hopeful but still skeptical chiefs. Finally, every chief of every tribe agreed to join the league - all except one. Every time they approached Tadodaho (which means "entangled"), the vicious leader of the Onondagas who had caused the death of Hiawatha's family, would let out a blood curdling scream of "Asonkeneeeh!?" ("Is it not yet?!"). Sometimes he would wail, "Hwe-do-ne-e-e-e?" ("When will it be?"). These were mocking cries, meant to destroy their faith in their mission. When they approached by canoe, his cries created waves pushing them back but they just paddled harder, recommitting to their faith in their mission.

Tadodaho was a violent man who was horrible to look at, with hair like snakes and seven kinks in his body. He viewed their peacemaking efforts with contempt; however, The Peacemaker did not seek punishment or revenge. As Iroquois Leon Shenandoah says in his book, *To Become a Human Being*:

> The Peacemaker looked for the evil ones. The Peacemaker knew that if they were reformed, they would make good leaders. His mission on Earth was to reform them for the good of the people. Once he found them, they weren't evil when he left them. They were gentle then.

All their efforts to persuade Tadodaho failed. His participation was key as the Onondaga nation lay directly between the Mohawk and the Oneida on the east and the Seneca and the Cayuga on the west. Three times Hiawatha and The Peacemaker called for a Grand Council and each time Tadodaho's viciousness and threats broke up the gathering and caused dissension.   Jikohnsaseh had a plan. She had the Cayuga people join the effort to persuade Tadodaho and they approached him singing a peace song that had been composed especially for this meeting. Though Tadodaho was initially threatened, it was this song that transformed him and he finally agreed to listen to their message of peace.

Once again, The Peacemaker and Hiawatha approached his village hearing the anguished cry of "Asonkeneeeh?!" For Hiawatha, having to confront the man who had personally caused his family's death, it was truly an exercise in forgiveness, but the Condolence Ceremony had brought peace to his heart. Jikohnsaseh had gathered all the chiefs who had agreed to join the Great Peace so that Tadodaho could now see he stood alone.

"Tadodaho," Hiawatha said, "You keep asking, 'Is it not yet? When will the Peace come?' Every human longs for this peace and love. All the other chiefs and tribes have accepted the Great Law of Peace. They now live in peace with one another. Only you are still fighting. Peace will come to you when *you* accept it in your heart."

Jikohnsaseh also told him that he would become the "Keeper of the Flame" - like the facilitator - of the Grand Council. When he heard this, the Tadodaho accepted the law and brought peace to the Onondagas and the entire Iroquois Confederacy. First his body and mind was healed. The Peacemaker sang the "Peace Song" himself and then Jikohnsaseh massaged the Tadodaho's crooked body straight and combed the snakes from the his hair, symbolizing the straightening of his mind into the Good Mind.

"Now you too have a Good Mind," The Peacemaker told him. "All affairs of the Five Nations shall be conducted at this lake in Onondaga land and you shall tend the Council Fire of the Five Nations - the Fire That Never Dies."

The Tadodaho represented everything that stood in the way of peace: complete and unconscious power and control, unwillingness to change or accept the possibility of peace, charisma used to destroy, and a wounded and unhealed person wishing to wound others. When he accepted the Good Mind, this obstacle was removed. An "enemy" had been transformed, not destroyed. A man who once terrified people, now served them instead. A bully had become a peacemaker. (To honor this transformation of evil into good, his title has been handed down from generation to generation. To this day, the leader of the Iroquois Confederacy, always an Onondaga, is called "the Tadodaho." The Grand Council is held at Onondaga, and the Council Fire of the Five Nations is still tended and burns today.)

The Peacemaker now called a meeting, a Grand Council, of all the chiefs who had accepted the Great Law of Peace. The Grand Council was held on the north shore of Onondaga Lake, near present-day Syracuse, New York. It was on the shore of this lake that the confederacy fires were first kindled. Fifty chiefs, or sachems, were chosen from the five tribes. The sachems represented the fifty female-led clans of the nations. The names of these 50 original sachems have been passed down for generations to future sachems, thereby keeping a living reminder of the founding of the League. Some tribes had more than others but all were equal and each tribe had one voice, one vote. Though the Tadodaho was the Keeper of the Flame, there was no central leader more powerful than the rest.

There was to be no majority or minority, but rather consensus. Unanimity of "one mind" was the fundamental law of the new union. All the chiefs of one tribe would confer or caucus on an issue until they had consensus, then they would confer with their "brother" tribe (the Mohawk with the Seneca, the Oneida with the Cayuga) until consensus was found. Once these four all agreed, it was presented to the Onondaga, and if they agreed, the issue was settled. All meetings of the Grand Council, which would end at sundown to avoid weariness, would begin with gift-giving between tribes and prayers of thanks from each tribe to the Creator, thanking Him for all things.

"Now we are One People," The Peacemaker said addressing the Grand Council. "In truth, Reason brings Righteousness and Reason is a Power that works among all minds alike. When Reason is established, all the minds of all mankind will be in a state of Health and Peace. It will be as if there were a single person. I charge you never to disagree seriously among yourselves. If you do, you might cause the loss of any rights of your grandchildren or reduce them to poverty and shame. Your skin must be seven layers thick to stand for what is right in your heart. Exercise great patience and goodwill toward each other in your deliberations. Never, never disgrace yourselves by becoming angry. Let the good Tidings of Peace and Power and Righteousness be your guide in all your Council Fires. Cultivate good feelings of friendship, love, and honor for each other always. With endless patience you shall carry out your duty and your firmness shall be tempered with tenderness for your people. Look and listen for the welfare of the whole people and have always in view not only the present, but also the coming generations, even those whose faces are yet beneath the surface of the ground, the unborn of the future Nation."

He further explained that violence cripples people, physically and emotionally. When people are brutalized, they become either fearful and withdrawn or angry and aggressive. Violence breeds more violence and should never be used except in self-defense or we become as vicious as the things we detest. All attempts at revenge and retribution only make matters worse. True peace comes only with social equality. A peace founded on forcibly maintained dominance eventually breeds more violence. Peace can only be maintained indefinitely if everyone has a share in decision-making. He taught them the Condolence Ceremony that helped them release their grief and the accompanying desire for revenge.

The Peacemaker's vision was so broad, it encompassed and restructured every aspect of tribal life, while still addressing the major issues between the warring tribes. It was complete, concrete, detailed and outlined in a Constitution of 117 democratic concepts or codicils that were as concerned with constraining the Great Council as it was with granting it power and authority. It was designed to keep power out of the hands of any single individual. This Constitution was recorded on wampum belts. Each wampum belt enabled the chiefs to remember part of the law and, by holding the wampum, reminded the listeners and speaker that what they spoke was truth (in 1880, the Constitution was finally written for fear that future generations might not be able to decode the belts).

In another piece of political and social wisdom, The Peacemaker developed the clan system that knitted the nations together by encouraging strong friendship between members of different clans and tribes. Within each of the five tribes, were several overlapping clans (Turtle Clan, Bear Clan, Wolf Clan, etc.). If a Mohawk of the Bear Clan visited the Oneidas, he was treated as a cherished relative by the Bear Clan of that tribe. These clan relationships were as binding as family ties. Intertribal clans assured national goodwill, drawing together distant people.

Knowing the importance of symbolism, The Peacemaker also gave the tribes the "Tree of the Great Peace" as a symbol of their union. It was a white pine, the largest and most noble tree in their forests. The pine's four roots spread out in the four directions, spreading the Law of Peace everywhere. Others would see these strong roots and follow them to their source. Its full limbs sheltered and protected all those who chose to take refuge under the Confederacy. The tall, straight tree lifted the thoughts of the Iroquois to the meaning of peace - the Good News that Tarachiawagon - the Great Spirit - had sent to them through The Peacemaker. On top of the tree was the "Eagle That Sees Far," which signified watchfulness, to discover if any evil or divisiveness was approaching the Confederacy. If there was, the eagle would scream and give alarm to all the Nations of the Confederacy. It was a simple but effective symbol, familiar and friendly to people who knew the forest as their home.

Along with members from all the tribes, The Peacemaker dug up another large white pine and instructed all to throw their weapons into the hole, in essence to "bury the hatchet." The weapons fell into an underground river where they flowed to the nether regions, far away from human concerns. Another familiar symbol that the peacemaker gave the League was that of the Longhouse, called "Kanonsionni." The supporting roof rafters were the Law; its supporting vertical poles were the tribes. The fires of the tribes would burn separately, but all under one roof where all tribes would live in peace. A final symbol was a bundle of five arrows, hard to break where one arrow was easy to break. In this, he reminded them of the strength in their unity. (The United States later adopted two of these symbols. An eagle holds a bundle of arrows on the back of every one dollar bill.)

Innate spirituality and gratitude to the Creator was at the core of the League. As The Peacemaker, a messenger from the Creator, instructed the sachems, "It shall be the duty of all the Five Nations Confederate Lords, from time to time as occasion demands, to act as mentors and spiritual guides of their people and remind them of their Creator's will and words. They shall say: 'Harken, that the peace may continue into future days! Always listen to the words of the Great Creator, for He has spoken. United people, let no evil find lodging in your mind. For the Creator has spoken and the cause of Peace shall not become old. The cause of Peace shall not die if you remember the Great Creator.' "

Knowing that he carried only a piece of the vision, he empowered the Council to complete his work by using not just practical methods but dreams and visions as well. Once the Confederacy was begun, The Peacemaker left promising to return "if men should ever become indifferent to the league and if the Great Peace should fail." The tribes just needed to call his name. Because of this, the Iroquois today still refer to him as "The Peacemaker" instead of using his name, Deganawidah - which they would use only to call him back.

The Iroquois Confederacy, which at its peak spread over 12 states and parts of Canada, is a permanent government, not a loose association of neighboring tribes. The Confederacy is still alive and vital today. Each nation retains its own council and its decision-making of local affairs, but representatives from all tribes, meeting at the Grand Council in a "Longhouse," make decisions that concern the Confederacy. To curb warfare, no warrior was allowed to be a chief, a sachem. The women, the "Clan Mothers," still choose and remove the chiefs. Anthropologists have observed that no society has ever raised the status of women higher than the Iroquois.

Remarkably, the confederation was not to be a limited one. The design was to abolish war altogether. The Peacemaker wished that the federation would extend until all the tribes should be included in it and peace should reign everywhere. All neighboring tribes would be invited through reason to join the peaceful League. If they refused and continued warring, the Grand Council could bring a declaration of war and conquer the rebellious nation. After that, they would be considered "as brothers and sisters."

Then began "Pax Iroquoia," a peace among their tribes that lasted for many generations until the coming of the colonists. The League demonstrated that peace did not mean softness - that Peace armed with Power and guided by Reason could sway the hearts of people everywhere. They were the guardians of the peace throughout the forests of the northeast. Within a few decades they had broken the hostile ring that surrounded them.

With the coming of the settlers, the power of the Iroquois Confederacy weakened and finally succumbed, as did all indigenous people confronted by the colonists' aggression, superior military force and diseases. The Peacemaker even anticipated this. He told the Grand Council that if ever a great danger could not be avoided, they were to travel forth and seek protection under a swamp elm. There, at least a remnant of the Confederacy would survive - as it has until this day. The Iroquois Confederacy is unique in that they still maintain one of the very few traditional governments in North America. Their leaders are still selected according to the oldest constitutional democratic system in the world and their members can still travel internationally under their own Iroquois passports.

The tribes' successful efforts, later used as a pattern for the American political system, have served as the basis of *all* democracies on the planet today. It created a archetype - an ideal - that has subtly but profoundly affected human consciousness since its inception. However, The Peacemaker's vision and the Iroquois Confederacy could not stem the tide of history as the separation-based system of the Competitive Cultures rolled across the last continent yet untouched by its greed and aggression.

Just as Jesus' teaching helped diminish violence for over two millennia, the democracies that grew from the Iroquois roots have helped diminish conflict and violence among nations. The story of The Peacemaker and Hiawatha is like an Iroquois Bible. Just as Jesus' life and teachings shows us how to end our personal "wars" with others, in much the same way, the life and teachings of The Peacemaker are a guide to healing warring nations. The Great Law of Peace provides us the necessary guidance to heal our tribes, our countries and societies, with this same love and forgiveness.

Both of these teachers of love, Jesus and The Peacemaker, came with one key message: the appropriate response to any attack - verbal, emotional or physical - is love, not counterattack. After Jesus had been betrayed and deserted by his followers, and as he was dying on the cross for having done nothing more than bring a message of love, his final plea to the Creator was not to ask for revenge or punishment, but rather he asked, "Forgive them, Father, for they know not what they do." Jesus knew that they, like us all, had temporarily forgotten who they were. Likewise, The Peacemaker knew that no matter how twisted a person may have become, no effort is too great to make them straight again.

It is even possible that Jesus and The Peacemaker were the same being, incarnating in different places at different times but bringing the same message. Several sources have spoken on this. Since their beginnings, the Mormon Church has claimed that Jesus appeared to Native Americans. In her book, *He Walked the Americas*, anthropologist L. Taylor Hansen, spent thirty years researching the legends of tribes from North and South America that spoke of a "saintly pale prophet, bearded, robed and wearing sandals, whose hands performed miracles of healing, and whose strange eyes, gray-green as the ocean, looked down the vistas of the future. His symbol [a palm with a T cross on it] is woven into blankets; carved upon the walls of canyons; burned into pottery; danced in dances [of many tribes in North and South America]."

According to Hansen, this prophet appeared to the Toltecs, the Mayans, the Pueblos, the Pawnee, the Apache, the Shawnee, the Mississippi Delta Mound Builders, the Paiutes, the Yaqui, the Chippewa, the Cherokees and to many other pre-contact tribes. In Mesoamerica, the legends say that he lead them out of the atrocities of keeping slaves and performing human sacrifices. He brought them the original seeds of many of the tribal staples, such as corn, beans, and squash, and taught them how to grow them. (It is interesting to note that scientist have never been able to trace corn, the Native American staple, to a wild ancestor as they have other domesticated grains. It just seems to have "appeared." Also, corn will not seed without human intervention.) He told them to give thanks and to pray for any animals they needed to kill for the sustenance and to respect them by killing only if needed and to waste nothing.

In all these legends, He chose twelve disciples in each tribe to carry on His teachings after he journeyed on to be about "My Father's business." The Lakotas called their Twelve Wise Men, "Waki." This Teacher told them, "I bring to you a message from the God who has no image. He dwells beyond the rainbow. He lives in the lava, moves in the ocean, breathes in the wind storm and made all things. He has given us the Great Law. That law is this: *Love one another.*" He reminded them that "My Father's land lies deep *within* you."

A Shawnee traditional chant, given to them by "The Prophet," reflects his teachings:

> Do not kill or injure your neighbor, for it is not he that you injure; you injure yourself. Be good to him, thus adding to his days of happiness even as you then add to our own.

> Do not wrong or hate your neighbor; for it is not he that you wrong; you wrong yourself. Rather love him, for the Great Spirit loves him, even as he loves you.

To this Prophet, names meant nothing. When visiting each tribe, he asked that the people name Him. Some called him (in their language)

"The Prophet;" others the "Lord of Wind and Water" for his ability to calm the storms and seas. To the Mound Builders of Oklahoma, he was known as "Chee-Zoos." Some elders say that the Sun Dance of the Plains Indians, where young men hang themselves from a large wooden pole by leather straps connected to sticks pierced through the skin of their chests, is in remembrance of Jesus on the cross.

Past Tadodaho Leon Shenandoah also believed that The Peacemaker was Jesus, when he writes, "You [white race] got instructions too, but you put Him on the cross. He never got to finish His instructions. So you don't know what the future is because you never heard all that He was going to tell you. He went there to give instructions and they killed Him. I don't know if Jesus was a Jew or what, but He came to us. We knew Him as The Peacemaker. When he left here He went across the waters to give instructions like He gave us. What He told us became our way of life. We listened and did as He asked."

Could it be that the reason pre-contact Native American societies were so effectively designed to maximize human health, freedom and happiness, was because they followed the Instructions from a Teacher more effectively than their foreign counterparts? It is no more difficult to believe Christ could have carried his ministry to other continents at other times, than it is to believe He rose after three days. Indeed, in John 10:16, he indicated this when he said, "I have other sheep that are not of this fold: them also I must bring, and they shall hear my voice; and there shall be one flock and one shepherd."

In many ways, though not all, Native American societies reflected the values taught by Christ. Had Christ designed human societies, they would not have been dedicated to the amassing of power, money, materials good and pleasuring or with people living in cities were few are truly self-sufficient and a commercial system is required. Rather societies would have been devoted to a simple life lived close to the land with few possessions, led by caring leaders who could persuade but never command, and with care, common security and respect for all - old and young, women and men, healthy and sick. That is the way He lived.

These values are reflected By Chief Luther Standing Bear in his description of the values of his tribe:

Strength is evidenced not only in action, but in restraint as well, and in restraint the Lakota was schooled. Not only was he a man of brawn, but a man of will. In the distribution of food, this quality was uppermost. When food was brought into the village, the sharing must be equal for old, young, sick, disabled, and for those who did not or could not hunt as well as those who hunted. There must be no hungry individuals; so long as one had food, all would have food. There was never the hungry on one hand and the overfed on the other. All shared food as long as there was any to share.

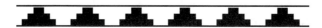

As I read about this Iroquois epic, I had a chance to share my realizations with our group in Jamaica. During my five weeks in Kingston preparing for Bob's 60th birthday, each week I hosted a Saturday update breakfast for our group of healers. At our last breakfast, the day before the concert, with almost everyone involved, including Julia and Alicia who had flown in a few days earlier, I told them the story of The Peacemaker and explained what I believed to be the similarities between our journey and his.

"All of us in this room do our work under the spirit of The Peacemaker - bringing a message of love to a nation where the tribes are at war with each other," I said to the twenty or so speakers and artists that were to join us on stage the next night. "Not that any of us are at his level but we work with the same goal as he did. Also, like The Peacemaker, Julia, Alicia and I come as *outsiders*, attempting to bring peace between the various religions, political parties and social classes. At first, like The Peacemaker, we were met with suspicion. Just as The Peacemaker had to prove himself by jumping off the waterfall, our willingness to go into the toughest schools in the ghettos eventually gained most Jamaican's trust."

"And like The Peacemaker, who stuttered, we too have a speech impediment. We do not speak patois, your grassroots language. And just as his stutter and his traveling with a woman, Jikohnsaseh, revealed a vulnerability that diminished attacks on him, so did our coming as a family, with Alicia's and Julia's soft feminine presence, disperse much negative energy. Like The Peacemaker, we are tribeless and outsiders; however, not being identified with any single group within the Jamaican culture made it easier for us to bring different groups together. We could council with *all* the tribes."

"Like The Peacemaker, we arrived in Jamaica at a time of great need, with your crime rate climbing and the economy declining and like him we often have no voice in our home village. During our time here, many others such as yourself joined us in our efforts, all under the spirit of The Peacemaker. Just as the Iroquois chiefs had heard of The Peacemakers message delivered by the hunters he met when he first arrived, so had many heard our message of love and forgiveness through news reports of our inner-city school concerts. Already hearts and minds were open to the possibility of peace on their island though a few rejected the message. They were earning their livelihoods by encouraging the warriors, by inciting anger and revenge, like Jikohnsaseh before she became the Peace Mother."

"Like Hiawatha, many people here have become cynical and disil-lusioned - embittered by Jamaica's and the world's ongoing problems. Many soon remembered who they were as they saw the faces of you - The Peacemakers - reflected in the kettle. We have counseled with many of your chiefs including the Prime Minister Patterson and Opposition Leader Edward Seaga, inviting them to join our efforts. Only time will tell if they have accepted our invitation."

"Like Jikohnsaseh and the Clan Mothers, we have invited a group of conscious women to speak tomorrow night and invite the women of Jamaica to lead in the healing of the country. As the Iroquois knew, it is always the women who more strongly desire peace."

"Like The Peacemaker, all of us also come on a musical vibration with songs of peace sung by your conscious artists. Many of these songs encouraged love for all humanity and forgiveness for past wrongs. As the "Six Song" was the Iroquois primary peace song, Bob Marley's "One Love" was ours. For a long time, you have understood the power of music to bring people together and spread a message."

"As The Peacemaker instructed Hiawatha when he dipped his jar into the stream, during our journey, we never went 'against the forces of nature' by making others wrong for their past actions but rather encouraged each person, especially the leaders, to remember that they were sent by their Creator to teach love to their people. We also did this on our school tour when we transformed the bullies into protectors."

"We are all working on developing our seven layers of skin. Everyday we encounter people under the spirit of Tadodaho, angry and pained that the peace has not come and that there is so much suffering in the world. Perhaps the hardest thing to do is to be able to look past their anger and know that in their pain they are asking, 'When will it be? When will the injustice, exploitation and violence stop?' To them we must answer as did The Peacemaker, 'It will stop for *you* when you accept the Great Law of Peace into your heart and life.' When their resistance continues, 'paddle harder.' You must continue to council with those under the spirit of the Tadodaho and comb the snakes out of their hair so that the Good Mind can take hold here."

"During our One Love tour, we have reached out to all - even the gunmen and corrupt politicians - reminding them that their lives, like those of the Tadodaho, are always redeemable. Our Fires of Forgiveness ceremony in Port Antonio was very much like the Iroquois Condolence Ceremony, encouraging everyone to forgive themselves and others - to bury their hatchets - and bring peace into their heart again. Like our ancient counterparts, we had recognized that forgiveness of ancient hatreds is the first, and essential, step towards peace. As The Peacemaker said, 'Stop telling the old stories or war will never end.' "

"We had no idea we were following in these footsteps when we all began this journey together. Tomorrow night is another Grand Council where all the tribes will be gathered to hear once again our message. Throughout history, different societies have been chosen to birth different advancements in human consciousness. The Iroquois birthed democracy. The English were the first to end legalized slavery. Gandhi's India was the first to overthrow oppression without armed resistance. South Africa, under the moral leadership of Archbishop Tutu and Nelson Mandela, was the first to demonstrate a course of truth and reconciliation after apartheid was dismantled. As each leap forward was made in these societies, enlightened people elsewhere looked to their example and implemented similar changes in their own societies."

"Looking back, none of these societies looked like they were well-chosen for the task at hand. The Iroquois tribes were at each other throats. The English were making the most money from slavery. India had no apparent strength to overthrow the strongest military power of its time. The tribes of South Africa were steeped in revenge and retribution. So for Jamaica, with it's high crime rate, to birth a movement of healing through individual acts of love and forgiveness, is not as illogical as it might first appear.

"Just as the Iroquois Confederacy has been the pattern for democracies worldwide, some society will one day provide a pattern of healing that can be imitated and emulated by societies worldwide. It is the next step in the conscious advancement of human societies. In fact, it may be the final step in a global healing. When we will reach this goal is not yet clear; what society it will be is not yet known. However, the Iroquois healing has shown us that societies embroiled in violence and revenge can be reasoned into love and peace *if* the hearts and minds of the leaders and the people are healed - if the Good Mind takes hold in them."

"We have often retreated to our mountain home in North Carolina, to our "edge of the village," to reinvigorate this vision. After tomorrow's concert we will return there. We do not know when, or even if, we will return to Jamaica but we will always hold all of you and your island deeply and fondly in our hearts. Like The Peacemaker, we cannot create the peace. Only you - the various chiefs of Jamaica - can do that. We can only bring the message."

The concert the next night was held in downtown Kingston. On the afternoon of the concert, Julia and I did a three-hour radio interview on our work and Bob's message of One Love on RJR, the island's largest radio station. Shortly before the concert, we returned to the hotel where we were joined by several of our friends who would be speaking. By the time our group left our hotel in the early evening to walk up the street to the venue, there was already thousands of people in the streets, streaming towards the stage.

The government had cordoned off the entire downtown area and erected a ten-foot high stage large enough to hold a 60-piece orchestra who played the Jamaican National Anthem. A huge backdrop showed a portrait of Bob with his kind eyes looking out over his people. Every TV station and most of the island's radio stations covered the event, making it one of the biggest concerts in Jamaican history. Photographers, radio broadcasters, and TV cameras were everywhere. One TV camera, mounted on a huge 25-foot boom, projected the concert to the home viewing audience and to large theater-size screens that were placed every block so the large crowd could easily see what was happening on the stage.

We're a long way from our first birthday celebration with six of us speaking to a handful of people in Bob Marley's backyard, I thought as we walked toward the huge stage. *How had it come to this? So easily? So gently? We just kept taking the next step. It all seemed so strange - almost surrealistic - yet at the same time, somehow so right, so familiar.*

Prime Minister Patterson was scheduled to make the introductory remarks to open the show but he cancelled at the last moment - a chief still reluctant to claim One Love. So with all of Jamaica looking on, our daughter, Alicia, then 17, and then Julia, introduced the concert and set the vibration. As I watched them speak so eloquently and confidently in front of tens of thousands of Jamaicans about how the island had taught them so much, I knew once again that only the Creator's will could have put the three of us on this stage, on this night.

"Greetings, our brothers & sisters, and welcome to Bob Marley's 60th birthday party," I said to the crowd after they spoke. "We stand before you as a American family who first visited this mystical land four years ago and returned home with our faith in humanity strengthened. We speak for those from abroad who have been profoundly touched by your people and your music. Like many here, our family is not immune to suffering. I was born into a Jewish family immediately after the Holocaust. I was raised by an black woman in the pre-civil rights South. I had to flee my government's attempt to send me to fight an immoral war in Vietnam. Even Alicia has not escaped the pain of a world out of balance. In the last two years she has buried 4 friends lost to suicide and alcohol and drug-related incidences. We are all here in pain together. And all of us here want, more than anything else, to love and be loved."

"To millions worldwide, Jamaica is a guiding beacon of love and inspiration. Like others who visit your island and met your people or listen to your music, we see you quite differently than you may see yourself. We see you as a country that has risen above great suffering both in your past and present to offer the world a beautiful message of One Love - a message that the world very much needs right now. And if God's currency is love, we see you as one of the wealthiest countries in the world."

"This is our 54th One Love concert our family has organized in Jamaica. Along with your conscious artists, we have taken an invitation to your schools island-wide. Our invitation is simply this: join us in healing your lives individually and your country as a nation, by claiming your God-given destiny to be a healer - a teacher of love - in your life. No matter what you have done in the past, no matter what has been done to you in the past, claim your heritage *now*. Get up each day and love and forgive as much as you can. As Bob Marley demonstrated, rise above the skepticism, the disillusionment, the hopelessness, the criticism, the negativity, and the anger and teach this One Love in your families, your churches, your schools, and your workplaces."

"God has not assigned any of us the task of ending *all* injustices and suffering in our countries. He has only asked that we do as much as we can in our own daily lives. No one alone can heal all of Jamaica but each one of us can heal our *personal* Jamaica, the small piece of Jamaica that the Creator has assigned to us. And we do this through our love, our kindness, and our compassion and mostly through our forgiveness."

"As Richie, the young man who washed motorists' windshields at the corner of Trafalgar and Hope Road, showed us, each assignment is vital. Before his tragic murder, he got up each day and gave every motorist he encountered a loving vibe. The outpouring of love and sympathy upon has death proves that every person's assigned path is important no matter how humble it may appear. Newspapers columnists wrote of his love. Television and radio commentators spoke of it. City commuters miss his gentle vibe. Richie, a humble windshield cleaner, in his sweet and simple way, may have done more to advance the consciousness of this island than many of its leaders."

"If you want a more peaceful Jamaica, become a more peaceful Jamaican. If you want a more loving Jamaica, become a more loving Jamaican. Claim yourself as a teacher of love. Keep your covenant with your Creator to love others as He has loved us. Let our anguished cry of 'When will the suffering end?' be transmuted to, 'What can I do to hasten it's end?' We as individuals need to heal our lives through One Love. Jamaica as a nation needs to heal herself through One Love and the world needs Jamaica to demonstrate the power of a people choosing unity over divisiveness, commitment over anger and love over fear. Jamaica heal yourself and let your motto become *Out of Many, One People. Out of One People, One Love*. Give thanks."

Later, Elaine Wint and the group of women healers addressed the women of Jamaica about their fascination with war, reminding them that they "must step up to correct those who are in need of correction and no longer dutifully wash the blood from their men's clothes." The concert featured over 30 well-known, conscious speakers and reggae and gospel artists, including Bunny Wailor, Culture, Luciano, Junior Reid, Abijah, Ernie Smith, Warrior King, Prezident Brown, Robert and Janine Bailey, The Fab Five, Stitchie, Fanton Mojah and Mackie Conscious.

Stephanie Marley and her children brought the huge birthday cake and invited The Governor General, The Education Minister and our family to cut it on stage. The event was flawless - with no technical or crowd problems. It was a huge success, bringing a six-hour musical message of One Love to a live audience of tens of thousands and to millions more watching or listening at home via TV, radio and the Internet. It ended near midnight with all the speakers and artists on stage singing "One Love," joined by the enthusiastic crowd. The next day, we flew home.

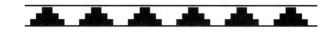

Several months after the concert, in July of 2005, Julia and I drove to the Onondaga Lake Peace Festival in Syracuse, New York, where we were invited to speak. Given our heightened interest in the Iroquois Confederacy, we knew that going to their homeland was meant to be. The festival was held at Long Branch Park just on the outskirts of the city. This was the *exact* spot where The Peacemaker held the first Grand Council once all the Iroquois chiefs agreed to live in peace. It was here - on this piece of land - that the Iroquois Confederacy was formed. As is anyplace on Earth where ancient hatreds have become present loves, this is sacred ground.

Though Onondaga Lake is one of the most sacred sites in the country, it is also one of the most polluted. As Tadodaho Sidney Hill said recently, "Our Nation looks at the ecological disaster of Onondaga Lake, the most polluted in North America, and we weep. A century of degradation caused by callous corporations and indifferent government officials has transformed the lake, the center of Onondaga way of life and culture, into a toxic pool hostile to fish, wildlife, and humans alike."

Abijah, who was appearing the week before at the Montreal Reggae Festival, where he had performed in front of 20,000 enthusiastic fans, joined us along with his road manager, Tony. We were all coming at the invitation of David, the festival's organizer, who we had met briefly the year before at a New York City peace festival. We had arranged to arrive five days before the festival to do a series of free One Love Concerts throughout the Syracuse area, especially in the inner-city areas. We were literally walking in the footsteps of The Peacemaker - and we were soon to learn we were also walking in the footsteps of Jikohnsaseh, Hiawatha and Tadodaho.

In the many emails we received from David to his staff, we could see that the vibrations were divisive and the infrastructure chaotic. In one email, David accused the Iroquois Clan Mothers of being "culture police" because they would not endorse the festival and encourage the tribes to attend.

"I'm beginning to think we shouldn't go," Julia said to me a few days before we were to make the 1200-mile roundtrip journey by car. "The

Clan Mothers hold the story of The Peacemaker. It is their responsibility to keep the story true. It is sacred to them. He has not shown them respect. I can understand why they are not endorsing this event, especially after I see how David deals with people. He may be honoring The Peacemaker but I don't feel like he's carrying His message."

"I'm getting the same feeling," I agreed, "but Abijah has made travel arrangements, our concerts have been arranged and I think it's too late to cancel, especially since were also speaking nearby at the Woodstock Museum two days after the festival. I think we're meant to go. I have a strong feeling there is something there for us too learn - something that needs to be in the book."

"I feel that, too," Julia said. "Let's just be very careful. David seems to have little good will in the area, especially with the tribes, and we will be closely identified with him."

A few days later, we drove twelve hours to Syracuse. As soon as Abijah, Tony, Julia and I met with David, the first thing he said, even before "hello," was, "There's been a lot of negativity in the last 48 hours. Today my festival coordinator quit. There's a lot of weird energy trying to crush the festival."

At dinner that night, he went on to explain all the problems he was having, including the staff's concerns of his ability to pay them if the festival was lightly attended. He was angry, and said he planned to stay angry a long time, at some corporate and civic leaders whose sponsorship had fallen through. He was also angry at the Onondaga Clan Mothers and other peace groups who were not supporting or encouraging people to go to the festival.

"David," I said, after he had laid out the grim scenario, "Abijah and Julia and I have done a lot of these events. We are here for one reason - to invite the audience to join us on what we believe is the path home. At the end of this week, we will have successfully done that but we want to be protected from the chaos that I can see will be churning behind the scenes. It will only drain us. So your problems are yours. Just let us know where to show and when."

During the week, we did five free concerts, at the inner-city schools, public parks and community centers. It was moving to see the commitment of the teachers to the children, reminding us that local healers are everywhere. Our concerts into the elementary schools were often met with the most enthusiasm. Often the message of love and forgiveness is best received by the young, who may not have yet experienced many heartbreaks.

Perhaps the most powerful event was at the downtown detention center, where around 700 people were being held awaiting trial - a time that may be one of the few teachable moments in their lives. Abijah and I spoke to a live audience of about 100, while it was simulcast to the other 600 people in the facility. I reminded them that they can claim themselves as teachers of love even behind prison walls. Abijah, who like many there was raised in an inner-city ghetto, was great at reasoning with them about committing crimes to be accepted by peers. He even got them laughing at themselves, often the first step towards forgiving yourself. We reminded them that once you turn towards love and forgiveness, your path becomes progressively smoother and clearer and your life becomes happier - even behind bars.

It was at the detention center that we met one of the most effective healers of our journey, Captain John Woloszyn, the program director. When we arrived, he was there to greet us with a welcoming smile, saying, "As soon as I saw your information come across my desk, I knew I wanted you guys to come and speak here."

When I told the audience of detainees that Captain Woloszyn had told us that after 18 years, he loved his work and that as far as he was concerned everyone here was innocent until proven otherwise and deserved respect and kindness, the entire group erupted in loud applause - detainees applauding a guard! Who would ever guess that the clearest example of The Peacemaker's message would have a gun on his hip and a badge on his chest.

At a small barbecue at a friend's home after rehearsal one night, I noticed Abijah on the front lawn looking sad.

"What's up, my brother?" I asked.

"I just talked to Sophie and my kids. My cousin, Eustis, the one who filmed some of our concerts, was killed tonight in Kingston. Gunmen made him lay on the floor in his own home and shot him in front of his wife and kids. Everyone is devastated."

We continued the tour, more committed than ever - our hearts torn open.   As much as possible, we kept a distance from the chaos churning around us. As expected, there were problems along the way. The crowds were small due to disorganization in getting the word out. Several were cancelled at the last minute. Events started late due to equipment problems. David showed little gratitude for our efforts, from the stage or privately.

Our final concerts were that weekend at the Onondaga Lake Peace Festival, designed to honor The Peacemaker, his message and the Iroquois Confederacy, and to re-sanctify this sacred spot. The park was beautiful - huge shade trees, open rolling greens and a river running through the back. The heat had finally broken and the days were perfect - mid-eighties and low humidity. Though small, the crowd was heartfelt and the speakers and musicians brought forward a clear message in the spirit of The Peacemaker.

By then, we had begun to perceive a rather remarkable pattern emerge. We began to realize that, as had happened in Jamaica, we were once again encountering all the various vibrations The Peacemaker encountered as we retraced his footsteps. However, something even more amazing began to occur. We watched ourselves come under the spirit of all these vibrations. At times we were centered and clear, like The Peacemaker. Sometimes we came under the vibration of Jikohnsaseh, amplifying the "warrior vibration" by agreeing with people that their anger is justified instead of trying to help them heal it.

Other times, like Hiawatha, we were reminded by seeing the loving faces and deeds of others. We even at times watched the Tadodaho within ourselves emerge, with thoughts of anger and judgment, as the behind the scenes organization became more chaotic, with broken commitments, unpaid bills, and everyone blaming everyone else. We began to understand that these vibrations are within everyone but *only* that of The Peacemaker represents who we *truly* are. It became clear that we must all pass through these first three levels - Tadodaho, Hiawatha and Jikohnsaseh - to truly be Peacemakers and for me it became clear that I still had much to learn on this path.

At the close of the festival Abijah, Julia and I, asked to meet with David to discuss our observations. We met at sunset. Marcine Quenzer, an inspired artists who has created an entire series of paintings of The Peacemaker's epic (including the portrait of Leon Shenandoah on the cover of this book), joined us. She had been one of the festival's speakers, beautifully telling the story of The Peacemaker.

It was a cool pleasant evening, under a huge white pine on the banks of a small river that ran through the park. The ancient gnarled tree looked like it could have been the same tree where the tribes buried their hatchets. Across the river was the headquarters of the rowing team for Syracuse University. As we talked, a team of women rowed back and forth behind us - powerful, vibrant women being lead by their leader shouting a single command through a megaphone - "Row Harder!!!"

Abijah discussed his feelings that the festival was not well attending because of the divisiveness created by David. He asked David why none of the other peace groups had come or help spread the word. David said they were always working against him.

"David," I said after Abijah finished and turned towards me, "you made many commitments that were never kept and you never addressed them. You just expected everyone to understand and roll with it. You keep saying that you hold the vision and you're not concerned with the money part of it. A visionary has to take total responsibility for their vision, including financial responsibility, and not leave everyone with unpaid bills and broken promises. You cannot expect others to make the same total commitment that you are making. I think you need to be grateful for everyone that helps you and not bitter and attacking when people cannot do more than they volunteered for. It splinters everyone and makes them afraid of your anger."

"I want to know what you plan to do about your relationship with the Clan Mothers," Julia said as the imaginary "talking stick" was passed to her. "Respect is due the Clan Mothers and I want to know what are your intentions. You must heal this relationship. You disrespect thousands of years of their culture when you disrespect them."

David said nothing and Julia closed her eyes and entered a yoga-like pose with her hands resting on her knees, silent but for the noise of the rowing team and the leader shouting "Row Harder." Most of what we said to him was met by his justifying his position but I had the sense that on a deeper level, it was being absorbed.

That night, Julia, Abijah, Tony and I had dinner together before we drove the next day to speak nearby at the Woodstock Museum and they headed to California to continue his concert tour. We were in great spirits - tired and reflective but feeling good about how effectively we had gotten out the message.

"You know, I think it was good to let David know our thinking," I said over dinner, "but I know that there was some anger and judgment in my communication. The Peacemaker taught that we are to heal divisive leaders through love. I don't think I really lived up to that ideal. By the end of the week, I was upset at David. David really needed me to be his friend but the hassles of the week just wore me down sometimes. I know my words would have been more easily heard if they come with more friendship."

"I know what you mean," Julia added. "But I felt like I was speaking for the Clan Mothers and I needed to be firm. You cannot disrespect the Clan Mothers. It is their responsibility to hold the true story of the tribe and if they do not want to endorse this festival, that must be graciously accepted. He is a leader and giving leaders honest feedback was part of The Peacemaker's wisdom. The Peacemaker told the Clan Mothers that if the leaders were going astray, they should warn them that they will lose their power if they do not correct themselves. He said they should give them three warnings. I know the Clan Mothers have already given David the first. I think I just gave him the second. I think everyone played their roles perfectly."

"Yes, man," Abijah said "This week happened just as it was meant to be. Everyone revealed themselves. None of us could hide."

From Syracuse, Julia and I traveled nearby to Woodstock, New York, where we had been invited to speak at a Bob Marley Film Evening put on by Nathan Koenig and Shelli Lipton, who run the Woodstock Museum. This area has always been known as a place of healing, especially after being the home of the 1969 "Woodstock Festival." The area is beautiful and the people we worked with were in a very supportive vibe and working well together in the true "spirit of Woodstock." The evening went well with a packed house of enthusiastic people. We showed video footage of our travels through Jamaica and Indian reservations and spoke about our experiences.

We also met a Mohawk woman, Rainbow Weaver, who gave the opening prayer at our talk. Rainbow Weaver has brought the Great Law of Peace to the troubled youths through a program she has developed called "Peace Keepers dreamcatcher."

"How did you develop you program?" Julia asked Rainbow Weaver as we sat on the lawn the day after our presentation.

"For twenty years I had the wonderful opportunity to apprentice with a Seneca Wolf Clan Elder, Yehwehnode Two Wolves. She taught me the wisdom and philosophy of the Haudenosaunee. I have traveled internationally to Russia, Australia, Italy, Canada and in the States, bringing the teachings of our Native People."

"How does your program work?" Julia asked.

"I use local materials for the youths to build a dreamcatcher," Rainbow Weaver answered. "Over four classes they build their dreamcatcher and I teach them the symbolism behind it. Native Americans believe that the night air is filled with dreams both good and bad. The dreamcatcher is hung over or near your bed, swinging freely in the air. It catches the dreams as they flow by. The good dreams know how to pass through the dreamcatcher, slipping through the outer holes and slide down the soft feathers. The bad dreams not knowing the way, get tangled in the dreamcatcher and perish with the first light of the new day. In my class, the youths learn about the web of life and their place in it. Through this, they learn to honor themselves by embracing a strong sense of self-esteem and self-respect. By the end of every program everyone, even the youths in the detention centers, are proudly standing up and saying who they are and want they want in life."

"Your program sounds really powerful," Julia said, as we said goodbye. "Maybe one day we can help you bring it to the Havasupai children. They are really starting to claim themselves."

"I would love that!" Rainbow Weaver said, hugging her. "I'm ready anytime."

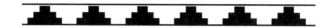

On the way back to North Carolina, we stopped in the Washington, DC area to visit my sister, Susan and her husband, Alan. While there, we visited the new National Museum of the American Indian, part of the Smithsonian Museum complex. The building is inspiring and very different from the more traditional public buildings in the Capital. The five-story, 250,000 square-foot building is on a 4.25-acre site, with almost three acres of gardens growing traditional crops for the cafe. Though still a large structure, a Native American feel is everywhere. Every step of the way, the Native American community was involved in the creation of the museum. Curators and designers of the museum met with nearly 150 indigenous communities from Central and South America, the Caribbean, Canada and the United States. Even the firepit-equipped kitchen of the museum's cafe serves Indian-inspired food.

The museum has an exterior cladding of Kasota dolomitic limestone that vary in size and surface treatment, giving the building the appearance of a stone mass that has been carved by wind and water. The museum's dramatic architecture was a collaboration of several talented Native Americans from several tribes, including Hopi, Blackfoot, Cherokee, Choctaw, Navajo, Oneida, and Caddo. Its huge overhang over the front entrance is aimed directly at the U.S. Capitol.

"I see the National Museum of the American Indian as a symbol or metaphor for something far more fundamental that transcends the fact that you are opening a museum," said Director W. Richard West, a Southern Cheyenne and Stanford-educated Washington corporate lawyer, at the museum's opening in September of 2004. "It is reflective of a turning point in American history where the United States is beginning to reckon with the history in various ways of the first citizens of the hemisphere . . . We are evoking the authentic voices of native peoples themselves in having a look at their own cultures."

The museum is not your typical anthropologists' approach to an ancient culture but rather a celebration of Native Americans - past and present. Though the history of their holocaust, genocide and land seizures are presented through their native voices, the tribes are not portrayed as victims. Rather, their entire millennia-long history is presented. You cannot help but leave there with a better understanding of the elegance, spirituality and power of these people. Ironically, the people who were here first had their museum built last.

Dr. Barry Chevannes addresses the Jamaican press at our press conference announcing Bob's 60th (Photo by Roy A. Sweetland-Kingston)

A Jamaican dance troupe performs at Bob's 60th in downtown Kingston (Photo by Roy Sweetland)

Alicia opens Bob Marley's 60th birthday in front of tens of thousands and over 2 million on radio and TV(Photo by Roy A. Sweetland-Kingston)

*Reggae legend Bunny Wailor performing at Bob's 60th
(Photo by Roy A. Sweetland-Kingston)*

Gospel recording artists Janine and Robert Bailey at Bob's 60th
(Photo by Roy A. Sweetland-Kingston)

Bicyclist club complete week-long, islandwide tour, asking for peace in Jamaica
(Photo by Roy A. Sweetland-Kingston)

Crowd at Bob's 60th (far right is Bob's daughter, Stephanie Marley, Governor General Sir Howard Cooke and Tourist Minister Aloun Assamba)

Respected Jamaican women address their people (LtoR:Charmaine Creighton, entomologist; Sharon Chambers and Pat Clarke, radio hosts; Juliette Dunbar, community organizer; Yvonne Coke, founder, Hands Across Jamaica; Elaine Wint, broadcaster/coach; Cherry Natural, dub poet

Cutting Bob's 60th birthday cake with his daughter, Stephanie, his grandchildren, Aloun Assamba and Barry Chevannes (Photo by Roy A. Sweetland-Kingston)

Recording artist Mackie Conscious inspires the audience with his lyrics (Photo by Roy A. Sweetland-Kingston)

Education Minister Maxine Henry, talk show host Elaine Wint, unknown,
Stephanie Marley, Tourist Minister Aloun Assamba enjoy the 60th

48. warrior king Conscious recording artist Warrior King (with mike)
entertains at Kingston crowd (Both photos by Roy A. Sweetland-Kingston)

Legendary conscious artist Ernie Smith entertains his people
(Photo by Roy A. Sweetland-Kingston)

International reggae recording artist Joseph Hill of Culture
(Photo by Roy A. Sweetland-Kingston)

Internationally-renown recording artist Prezident Brown
(Both photos by Roy A. Sweetland-Kingston)

Singing "One Love" at end of the concert (LtoR - Bunny Wailor, Abijah, Mackie
Conscious, Luciano, author, Alicia, Julia, Stephanie Marley, Bob's grandchildren)

It was incredible!
(Photo by Roy A. Sweetland-Kingston)

Abijah addresses inmates at detention center in Syracuse,
traditional home of the Iroquois Nation

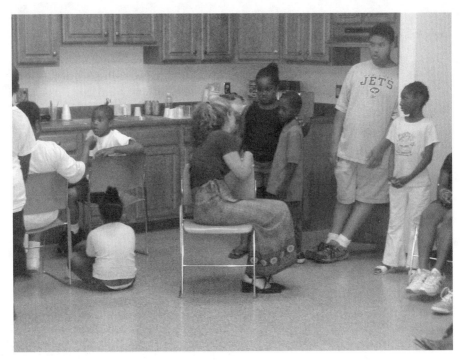

Julia playing with children at inner-city community center in Syracuse

Abijah with kids

Ashley Cox, a local singer, performs for the Syracuse youths

Abijah at Onondaga Lake Peace Festival

*Mohawk Rainbow Weaver explains her Peacemaker
Dreamcatcher Ceremony to Julia and a friend*

*Artist Marcine Quenzer tells the story of The Peacemaker the day of the
Onondaga Lake Festival (her portrait of Leon Shenandoah is on cover)*

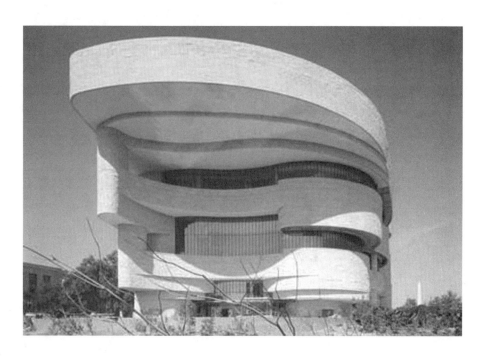

*The Smithsonian National Museum of the American Indian
in Washington, DC*

*Carol, Julia, John, Elaine and Abijah at Hualapai Hilltop
the day of our second Havasupai Concert*

Roland takes us to the sweat the day of the concert

John and Carol enjoy their first sweat

Damon addresses his people at our second Supai concert

The White Buffalo at Spirit Mountain Ranch near Flagstaff, Arizona

*Radford says a pray after our reasoning (LtoR:Duane [kneeling with Rad],
Julia, Lorna, Dawn, Carol, Elaine, Supai Waters, Radford, John)*

Radford takes us on a tour of his garden

Julia and Supai Waters in Sedona (Carol, John and Elaine in background)

*Leonard Peltier,
Native American leader,
Nobel Peace Prize
Nominee and author,
unjustly imprisoned for
over 30 years for his roll
at the 1975 Pine Ridge
incident*

Us

*Our "edge of the village" - the headwaters of the New River in our backyard
in the Blue Ridge Mountains of North Carolina*

Chapter 9
The Four Corners Calls Us Again

"Everybody is on a path. What you think about the most tells you which path you are on. The best path is the spiritual path. It's the only one that helps you become a Human Being . . . But everybody's path leads back to the Creator. To be able to see the Creator on the other side, you make sure you find your path in this life. If you don't, then the Creator has more lessons for you. That means you didn't learn what you were supposed to in this life, so you need more experiences . . . Nobody knows what specific suffering someone will have to go through that will bring them back to remembering . . . It's better to find and follow your path now. You know you're on your path because you become happy. It's like being contented or comfortable. That doesn't mean you just sit around. It's the opposite. You know what you're supposed to be doing and you're doing it. You're busy about your divine work . . . Nobody can tell you if you're on the path. You just know it inside. When you're ready, things come to you that pull you in a certain direction. That's you're path telling you that you're on it."
—Leon Shenandoah, To Become a Human Being

"Open your eyes, look within. Are you satisfied with the life you're living?" **—Bob Marley**

O n Labor Day weekend 2005, two months after our visit to the
Iroquois territory, we returned to do our second concert in Supai
Village with Abijah. Karen Abieta, the reggae deejay in Hopiland, had
arranged for him to headline at a two day reggae festival on her reservation, so we worked with Roland and Supai Waters to bring him to their
village for a free concert two days before his Hopi performance. Then
we would all travel to Hopiland for his concert and a reasoning with
Radford and Dawn.

Elaine Wint, our friend and co-worker from Jamaica, wanted to join
us on this journey, and Julia and I were excited about linking up our
Jamaican friends with our Havasupai and Hopi friends. Elaine invited her
friend and business partner, Carol Narcisse, to join us. Carol and Elaine
are both radio talk show hosts on the island and had just produced a large
wellness event in Kingston. They also invited their friend, John Fray, a
Jamaican-raised, Harvard-educated professor at the University of
Massachusetts Medical School. After a two-decade absence, John was in
the process of returning to his native island to train teachers to get the best
from their students.

On the Thursday before Labor Day, all of us flew into Phoenix. Friday
morning, we rented a van and Elaine, Carol, John, Abijah, Julia and I
headed across the desert to go to Supai Village and then on to Hopiland.
On the way to the Grand Canyon, we picked up Supai Waters at a friend's
house in Seligman.

We arrived at Hualapai Hilltop mid-afternoon and helicoptered into
the village. You could sense the vibes had changed. The new tribal council
had everyone more optimistic. Also, a bad flood during the winter had
damaged the campground, which the federal government was repairing.
As a result, there were more jobs - and money - in the village, which had
its advantages and disadvantages.

After settling in our rooms at the small lodge, we joined Roland,
Supai Waters and a few Havasupai friends for a sweat by the cold blue
waters of Cataract Creek. In the pre-contact Americas, the sweat lodge
was pervasive in cultures from the Eskimo in Alaska to the Mayas in
Mexico, as well as many other indigenous cultures around the world. It
was viewed as a threat and a heathen practice by the new culture and

the missionaries and they forcibly banned its use, though it went underground in many tribes and remains to this day as a living tradition.

To Native Americans, who believe that what is happening in the body is a reflection of what is happening in the mind and spirit, it is much more than a therapeutic instrument for keeping the body healthy. A visit to the sweat lodge is as much of a spiritual experience as a Christians visiting a church or a Jew going to synagogue. It is a sacred ritual for emotional and spiritual cleansing, as it reintegrates the physical and spiritual and reconnects one to the Earth. As Jaune Quick-to-See Smith, a member of the Flathead Salish tribe, says, "There is always a sweat lodge where you can resolve a lot of things, obtain information and advice, and talk over whatever is bothering you without fear that it will be shared with others."

The Havasupai's lodge was about a mile from the village, off the trail to the campground. It is an oval-shaped earthen structure around twelve feet wide and five feet tall. There is one small entrance hole covered by a blanket flap. Inside there is a fire pit to the left of the opening and room against the walls for twelve to fifteen people, maybe more. Outside is another fire pit where the rocks, called "little brothers," are ceremoniously prepared by the "sweat lodge people." They are then brought into the lodge and doused with water to create *very* hot temperatures inside.

After we walked down, I jumped into the creek while everyone else went into the lodge. Being heat-sensitive and extremely claustrophobic, I learned in my hippie days that sweats are almost impossible for me. I was joined in the creek by two Havasupai children, a boy about nine and a girl about five, and Shalini Nataraj, who was also resisting going in the sweat. Shalini, who works for Reebok's charitable giving division, had come to the concert as she has a personal interest in helping the Havasupai. In the water, we discussed the possibility of Reebok funding some of our future concerts.

"I'd love that, Shalini," I said. "We are always limited because we fund them from our savings, which aren't very large, but we couldn't use the sponsor's name and I don't think your company would go for that. A 'One Love Concert' brought to you by Reebok just doesn't feel right."

"I see your point," she said, "and I don't think we could fund it without name recognition. Too bad, because you could do a lot more concerts with corporate funding."

"We've thought about that," I answered, "but I think the Creator has provided just what we need, even if it's on a smaller scale. Once it becomes tied in to a commercial vibe, something is lost. That's why our concerts are free and the artists donate their time. We don't even sell our books there. Our efforts reflect what one family can do. It gives us total control without compromise and I think others need to see that."

After twenty minutes or so, everyone came out of the sweat and jumped in the water. For our Jamaican friends, Abijah, Carol, Elaine and John, it was their first sweat and they were exuberant, playing and splashing in the water like children. Encouraged by their joy, Shalini and I decided we would try it alone and went into the sweat, leaving the flap open. Much to my surprise, I was able to tolerate the heat and was enjoying it for fifteen minutes until the others rejoined us. As the lodge filled up and as Roland threw water on the rocks raising the temperature dramatically, I felt my fear rising. When it was packed with people and the flap was closed and the lodge became pitch black, I bolted - in the midst of Roland's opening prayer. I just couldn't handle it. (Shalini stayed and loved it.)

"Sorry," I said to Supai Waters and Roland, as they joined me after the sweat in the creek.

"It's O.K.," Supai Waters said, "I saw you go in and knew you couldn't stay. You went in head first. We go in backwards."

"That was very empowering," Julia said, as we all wandered back to the village. "I also felt like it was very familiar. Supai Waters took us there several times and I think that was the sacred waters mentioned in several books that we read where the tribe would swim and play for hours. As I was floating down the creek, both Supai children were watching me in amazement. The boy tried to float but he couldn't. I told him when I was his age I couldn't float either but now I'm more air than mass. As we were getting out of the creek, I showed them some watercress growing on the bank and told them it was good for healing. When I returned after the second sweat, the young boy had taken off his heavy jeans and he was floating in his boxers with a big smile on his face. The little girl proudly showed me some watercress she had pulled up, roots and all. I taught her how to snip just the tops and how she could replant the rest so that it would always be there. She liked that idea. It was good to feel that sense of family with all of us just playing in the water."

That night, under the beautiful Grand Canyon sky, Abijah performed and Roland, Supai Waters, Elaine, John, Julia and I spoke to the tribe, once again strengthening their commitment to be the "Guardians of the Heart of Mother Earth."

"Because of your extreme isolation, few tribes live closer to the pre-contact Native American reality than the Havasupai," I said to the gathering. "No other tribe is as removed from the frenzy of the modern world as you are. Your vibration of Native American wisdom, of Native American life, is very important to the planet at this time. Part of our mission is to bring this wisdom out to the world. So we are here to say 'thank you' for keeping your Covenant to guard this Canyon and for electing a pro-environmental tribal council to help."

"We come together to solve and resolve issues that we cannot do when we war with each other," Supai Waters said to his people, coming and going between English and his native tongue. "Our Indianness, our identity, who we are as a people - we've lost that. You are not supposed to be imperceptible of what's going on the outside. I hope you understand what we are trying to put together here. We are trying to teach you conscious strategies. Abijah's music says 'no' to drugs, 'no' to guns. We must get a better education, intellectual ideas, at universities and colleges. We need to get the young people to become the system. We are not supposed to be afraid of the changes. The changes are the opportunities our children are going to have to face. So we must teach and educate the youths and act wisely and respect the elders."

"There was a time," Roland said to the crowd, "that I was embarrassed because we did not have cars or toilets or electricity like the other tribes but now I am proud. Other tribes come here and say it is good that our children speak our native tongue very fluently. We must protect that. We must never lose that. That is the connection to the fire and to the elements here. That is the only way we can communicate with the elders here. We speak to our sacred sites this way to assist us in the healing to mend the wounds that we have. Be strong my relatives."

"Havasupai! Greetings!" Elaine exclaimed. "I bring you greetings from Jamaica. We understand that you are 800 strong. We are two million on a tiny island but we find that our size has never limited our capacity to reach across the world and today we find ourselves in the Grand Canyon. You have been given charge of a particularly wonderful heart of the planet. We want to encourage you to do that and to keep your own sacred rituals and your own sacred practices - your language, your culture, your stories - so that your culture will shine its own light as the only light of its kind on the planet, to show us a way - the way that all great masters have taught us. This way is that when we love and we respect each other, we create the harmony that we were designed for. So we bring you greetings from Jamaica and we say, 'Thank you! Thank you! Thank you!' "

Abijah invited the youths to join him on stage. He reminded the fifteen children surrounding him that they were the future of this ancient tribe - a future that was important to the entire planet. At the end of the concert, we all joined him on stage to sing "One Love."

After the concert, Julia, Supai Waters, Roland and I continued our reasoning back at the lodge.

"Now we must get stronger," Roland said after we settled in, "because the youths have jobs now here and the influences like alcohol and drugs is worse."

"I was just talking with one of the youths, David," Julia said, "at the hilltop. He's going off to Riverside School. It would be good if the tribe stayed in touch with him by phone and emails and letters so he doesn't lose touch."

"Yes. That would be good,' Roland said. "When I went off to school thirty years ago, I thought I was going for a horse ride and then I saw the buses. My mom and dad hinted that I was going to school but what was school? I didn't know what school was. Other students had to cut my food. We didn't know how to use a fork or knife or a toilet. We used to run outside and use the bathroom. They stuck the Supai kids in a school with all the misfit Indian kids."

"But now if we put our intention on this, we can heal it," Julia said.

"When we were in New York State, in the Iroquois area, we met Rainbow Weaver. She's this beautiful Mohawk woman who's been working with delinquent youths in a dreamcatcher workshop she has. These were tough kids, but by the end of her workshop every one of them was standing up declaring what they wanted for their lives. Maybe we could bring her here."

"That would be good for the youths. I can do many things as a leader, as a singer, as a shaman, as a practitioner. These are a gift the Creator gave me but I can never misuse this power. I could die if I did. It's a circle within a circle that I focus on," Roland said making a large air circle with his hands and arms and a smaller one inside that. "The outer circle is the past and the inner circle is the youths. But there's also the present there. When you make your decision, you always look at the past. Never disrespect the past and always try to benefit from the present, the people that are here now. Not for yourself but as a tribe, as a whole, and establish a foundation for those that will come, for 30, 40 years, so that they can fall back on it and say this is what our elders taught."

"The children you saw on stage tonight are not like us," Supai Waters said. "They have not gone off yet to Indian School where they learned to hate themselves. This is the first group in over one hundred years that will not. They may never hate themselves because those schools have changed. They are the future of Havasupai."

"The tribe needs to really understand that," I said. "Perhaps the tribe could make a commitment together - a tribal commitment - to try to correct this. Often the motivation to help for our children is stronger than one to heal ourselves. Then every time someone is drinking a sugar drink or a beer or eating bad foods, they will know they are letting the future down - letting the children down. That can be a powerful motivator. The world needs these kids. They are being raised far removed from the modern world. They will have much to teach their generation. You are the guardians of this precious generation."

"When I first shook your hand, yours and Julia's, I knew what I needed to know," Supai Waters said. "All that we are doing here is part of the Old Lady that is weaving the world and the little dog that constantly unwinds it so that she must weave it again. This now completes it. You're here to save a generation. To stop that unraveling. We are now revitalizing these kids in traditional ways. The old people sang songs to keep that going. I was brought in to bring those songs. I was taught those lessons through the songs from my grandparents. Some of those songs were about beings from other planets that had visited this Canyon and would one day come back. That is why I brought Bob Marley's songs here. I knew it could teach the youths. It was prophesized that Crazy Horse would return as a black man. He came back as Bob Marley."

The next morning, we helicoptered out and journeyed to Hopiland for Abijah's concert on Sunday. On the way, we stopped to visit the white buffalos at Spirit Mountain Ranch near Flagstaff. They now have seven white buffalos on the ranch. On a distant mountain behind the ranch, is a very distinctive light-colored image of a buffalo naturally outlined in the darker mountainside. Near the buffalo are two other figures similarly outlined: a wolf and the kokopelli - the humpbacked Hopi flute player whose figure is found on petroglyphs and pottery throughout the southwest dating back over 3,000 years.

Being with the buffalos was fascinating. As the owners of the ranch describe it in their literature: "These beautiful, divine energies touch all who come see them. People come to the ranch to pray and leave gifts for the sacred White Buffalo. Some weep, some marvel, and others are led to the ranch not knowing about the White Buffalo and their promise of peace and abundance. We believe the spirit of the White Buffalo calls out to the hearts of these people and directs them to the White Buffalo family."

We spent the night in Flagstaff and then left for Hopiland on Sunday morning. After checking in the lodge there, we headed over to Hotevilla, where Dawn and Radford had invited us to their traditional Butterfly Dance.

I was very interested in seeing this ceremony. The more I read, the more I realized that the Hopi were quite different from most other Native American tribes - a view shared by many indigenous people. In addition to being the most culturally and spiritually intact, their annual Ceremonial Cycle was considered by people both within and outside the tribe to be a repository of *all* human wisdom. It is a map of their Life Plan and helps balance the Earth. Within this cycle is the "Hopi Way." Each of these ceremonies are tied to each other creating a seamless and profound ceremonial portrayal of developing human life. In fact, their complete history - their Emergence, their migrations, and their life in Hopiland, past and present - can been seen as the Road of Life - from forgetfulness to Remembrance. It is neither symbolic nor an allegory. It is real.

As Frank Waters writes in his *Book of the Hopi*:

> The Emergence and the migrations are so beautiful in concept, so profoundly symbolic, one is tempted to accept them wholly as a great allegory of man's evolutionary journey on the Road of Life. Certainly the pure and perfect motherland the Hopi were seeking did not exist on this mortal earth.
>
> It is difficult to reconcile a people having such an enlightened concept of spiritual life with an actual primitive people wandering over a vast and undiscovered continent in prehistoric times. Yet such were the Hopi. Archaeological remains and ancient roads attest to this.

This Ceremonial Cycle is maintained and performed not just for the tribe but for all humanity. As the Soyal Chief prays during the Soyal ceremony, "May Mother Earth bless all your people and all life throughout the world, and may all seed come back for renewal."

This Cycle expresses their deep belief in a plan created by a divine power that supercedes limited human will. For thousands of years, their ancestors migrated across North and South America, abandoning their dwellings and villages, their fields and orchards, when they determined Divine guidance directed them to do so. Many could not leave due to health, pregnancy or young children. Others refused to leave. Those that stayed, such as the Mayans, continued to develop where they remained. (It is interesting to note that the Mayan culture abruptly declined in

900AD - the same time the Hopi clans reassembled in Hopiland.)

The ones that were the most devoted continued the millennia-long migration until they arrived at their final destination - Hopiland - possibly the most inhospitable place they had ever seen. Yet through all the centuries they had stayed on this barren plateau, living their humble lives and holding fast to their beliefs, their religions and their sacred Ceremonial Cycle. They understood that by depending only on the Creator to bring their life-giving rain would keep their faith strong, where those living near running water might abandon their faith more easily. The Hopi today are descendents from these highly devoted, spiritually guided and in-tune people. Their roots to the land and their beliefs, like the roots of their rugged corn, run very deep, far below what can be observed from outside.

Elaine, John, Carol, Supai Waters, Julia and I arrived at Hotevilla around noon, eager to observe part of this revered cycle. What we saw there truly amazed me and caused me to totally change my view of the present condition of the tribe. It also served to strengthen my belief that their Sacred Covenant to become Hopi - the Peaceful People - was near completion.

It is hard to describe the Butterfly Dance in words (and no pictures are allowed), but allow me to try. The dance is held in the plaza of the cliff-side village. The plaza is surrounded on all four sides by small stone and plaster two-story homes with flat roofs. The houses are all connected to each other like townhouses and except for the metal windows, they could be centuries old (and some are). For almost a thousand years, these villages have been their home. On the flat rooftops, and standing around the perimeter of the plaza below, were hundreds of Hopi and a handful of outsiders.

The Butterfly Dance is held in August after the harvest. It is a ceremony of thanksgiving for the abundance and especially for the corn. It is a petition for the much-needed rain and snow, for a long life and good health. We arrived around noon. The dance had already been going on since dawn. We took our place at the entrance to the plaza where the dance groups entered. Every thirty or forty minutes a new group of dancers would move into the plaza while the present group moved out to a feast table that was prepared for them behind the houses. Each group was made up of 30 to 50 young dancers, both male and female, of all ages from young children to elders. Many of the young maidens were wearing brilliant costumes with intricate headdresses, called *kopatsoki*, which had been made for them by their male dance partners, and which would become lifetime keepsakes. The boys wore loose-fitting velvet shirts and handsome quilts embroidered with rain and cloud symbols. They were not like any other Native American garments I had ever seen - detailed, elaborate and mystical.

For hours, one group after another danced in perfect synchronization, to complicated, yet soothing, rhythms (music authorities have noted that Native American music is the most complicated in the world with its half and quarter tones and complicated changing rhythms). Usually a group of men - uncles, fathers, brothers, in-laws - would be huddled to one side singing and drumming while the dancers were in the middle dancing in methodical, usually slow, fashion - a very peaceful, almost meditative vibration, every foot in unison. Their sounds, their rhythmic motions, their brilliant costumes, created a mesmerizing effect. You felt you had entered another time, another place, another planet. There were no celebrities, no stars on stage - a performance free of human ego. It was all equal, all tribal, all together as one.

From our vantage point near the entrance, we could sense their excitement and energy as each group prepared to go on. They took their performance very seriously and with excited anticipation. This was important to them. This Butterfly Dance was just one of many that occurred over the year during their Ceremonial Cycle. In fact, there was a similar dance being held the same day in another nearby village. This was not a rare or isolated event, nor was it a token ritual staged for tourists. This was their way of life - and had been for centuries.

As I watched the performances, I realized that the Hopi spirit and Ceremonial Cycle was much more intact than I had previously concluded. Here were Hopi of all ages dancing sacred dances as their ancestors had for generations on this tribal land. Each dance and song carried a message to themselves and the Creator. The complete esoteric meanings and spiritual functions of each piece of the cycle is known only to the Hopi - as

it should remain. Some were to bring the rain and the crops; others were
a moral teaching that confirmed that they were living the Hopi Way.
Each dance, each ceremony was part of a grand cosmic interlocking
pattern. They knew *who* they were and the power of what they were doing.
They knew that the outside world was not yet ready to understand this
and the incredible service and gift they were offering the world. And yet
they danced - confident in their reality and in their ancient Covenant.

We left the dance, all moved by what we had witnessed. On the way
back to the lodge, we stopped at the Prophecy Rock and prayed and
meditated. Each in our own private space, we retreated to our rooms to
digest what we had just seen before joining Abijah at his concert that
night.

In many ways, the concert that night was as powerful as the ceremonial dances. Many of the same people attended both. Before Abijah
came on, a very conscious Hopi reggae recording artist, Casper, performed,
with his backing group, The 602 Band. Casper was very powerful, singing
a message of love and justice to his tribe, who showed him love from
the minute he walked on the stage. I introduced Abijah, once again
thanking the Hopi for having kept their Ceremonial Cycle alive and
intact - for all of us.

Abijah's performance was perhaps the best I've ever seen (and I've seen
over seventy of his performances). It was almost as if the energy was
seamless, flowing from the ancient Butterfly Dance of love to the reggae
music of One Love. By the time it was over at almost three in the morning,
I felt as if that day I had truly witnessed the full power of Hopi life.

Reggae music in Hopiland started in 1985 when a group of reggae
lovers, Gerry Gordon, Tim Randolph, Karen Abieta, Burt Poley and
Hershel Talashoma, all tired of driving the 500-mile roundtrip to Phoenix
to hear reggae, invited a group called the Sons of Captivity to perform at
the Hotevilla School. According to Gerry, an Anglo who lived and taught
school in Hopiland for 25 years and now lives in Phoenix, the school that
night was packed, the vibes incredible, and the rest is history. Since then,

many of the top reggae artists have performed at Hopiland including Toots and the Maytals, Culture, the Wailors, Sugar Minot, the late Dennis Browne, Freddie McGregor, Third World, Black Uhuru, Mutabaruka, Black Rebels, Midnite, Mikey Dread and many more.

"The artists considered Hopiland the best crowd to play to," Gerry told me in a phone conversation recently. "Freddie McGregor told us that all the artists agreed it was the best vibes they ever felt. He said it was always city to city, one hotel to the next but when they got to Hopiland they were fed, taken to the traditional dances, given gifts of homemade *kachina* dolls and pottery. Artists and people like Dr. Dread of Ras Records were calling us, asking to play for a fraction of their usual fee. When Sunsplash USA was touring with lots of reggae artists, they'd come here for gas money instead of their usual twenty-five thousand dollar fee. It was not just about the music. It went a lot deeper than that. The artists felt it. The crowd felt it."

"Do you think the music has been helpful in Hopiland?" I asked him.

"Yes. You had Hopi, Navajos, Tewas, hippies, other Americans - white and black - all skanking [dancing] together enjoying the vibes. People would come from all over - New Mexico, Colorado, California. There were never any problems except occasionally when the police would set up roadblocks looking for alcohol or weed. Reggae music and Bob's music is all about trying to stay positive during, and after, oppression. The music helps you stay above it. Miles may have separated the Hopi from the Jamaicans, but their experiences are the same. It was like Bob sang, 'Same tree - different branch.' It was never about the money. It was about the music. It was a 'culture connection.' "

When I asked him why he moved off the reservation, he said laughing, "I traded peace and tranquility for pizza delivery."

Tim Randolph was equally as positive about the effect their efforts and reggae music had on the tribe, especially the youths.

"I first heard Bob Marley and reggae when I was at the Phoenix Indian School," said the 43-year old from Bacavi when I talked with him. "In 1983, we all went to Reggae Sunsplash in Jamaica. It was incredible."

"What was it that drew you to the music?" I asked.

"It was the music itself," he answered, "and the message. They were oppressed like us and farmers and cultivators like us. When Bob sang of the police roadblocks, we could relate. We had them in Hopiland. The artists sang about how oppressors keep us squabbling among ourselves so we don't look at the *real* problems."

"Do you think the music made a difference in the vibes there?" I asked.

"I think so," he enthusiastically answered. "It brought us all together, even with the Navajos, our traditional enemies. When Rasta Stevie, a reggae deejay in Colorado starting telling people about it on his show, a lot of hippies starting coming. Everyone got along great. A lot of us had been segregated and only lived and went to schools with other Native Americans. Now we were meeting whites, blacks, Mexicans, Jamaicans. It really broadened us. We got to know a lot of people and learned there are good and bad in every race."

"Was there much resistance in the tribe to the music?" I asked.

"A little from the older folks," he said. "The tribal government just ignored it but now they're using tribal funds to sponsor reggae concerts there. It was a good thing. There wasn't much to do and this gave the kids something to look forward to. The message was positive. It kept them out of trouble. It was all volunteer. None of us got paid. We never tried to change the Hopi ways, never preached Rastafari. It was just about the music - and the message."

INDIAN SCHOOLS

"What a difference between the vibes in Hopiland and in Supai," Elaine said as we drove back toward the lodge.

"That's because they have their own high school here now," Julia said. "They're not sending their youths away to Indian boarding schools anymore."

One of the main weapons the United States and local governments has used to destroy Native American cultures is to remove the children from the tribe and their elders and "Americanize" them in schools - in essence to "bleach them white." Once that happened, the child usually abandoned the ancient ways and no longer took an interest in the ceremonies.

Before their enforced enrollment in these schools, childhood for most Hopi and Havasupai, as well as for many other pre-contact Native American children, was rather idyllic. Theirs was an outdoor classroom and their teachers were everywhere - in the streams, the mountains, the plants, the animals, the clouds. This creates a much different worldview than is formed by formal Western education. As past Cherokee chief Wilma Mankiller writes in her book, *Every Day is a Good Day*, "I am convinced that there is an entirely different way of processing information among tradition-oriented indigenous people that is more whole and complete, and considers the contradictions and unevenness of life."

The tribal environment was very conducive to good childrearing. The pace of life was slow, gentle, and quiet. Adults spoke to each other quietly and courteously and seldom raised their voices, or were inconsiderate in their speech (there is no profanity in Native American dialects; they must borrow curse words from the English language). As the children roamed the village, *all* adults were concerned and loving parent figures; *all* other children were accepting friends and relatives. In their world, the *village* did raise the child.

E.A. Burbank, considered one of the greatest painters of the American Indians, spent time with the Hopi in 1898. In his book, *Burbank Among the Indians*, he noted the Hopi parents were devoted to their children, and he felt the North American Indian children were the happiest in the world. Though the children were never punished by their parents, they exhibited great obedience. He wrote:

Nowhere were children more charmingly treated than among the Pueblo Indians. It was rare to hear a Pueblo child cry or to hear him quarrel with his playmates. I think I never saw a Pueblo Indian strike or punish a child. And the children were polite, gentle and happy . . . How did the Indian parents accomplish this miracle? First by affection. Then, both men and women, young and old, always had time for the youngsters. The interests of the children were woven smoothly into the routine of the home. If the mother was making pottery, she gave the child a little piece of clay with which to work. She never said, 'No, no, you're doing it wrong. Make your pot this way.' She simply let the child learn by trial and error and by watching her skillful hands.

Before the invasion, every day children joined their parents, grandparents, other relatives and tribal members as they worked in the gardens, wove baskets, hunted, ground corn, cooked and built their dwellings - learning all the skills needed to maintain tribal life. At a young age, the children were taken to every tribal ritual, except the secret ones. It had been like this for thousands of years. Nothing broke this ancient sacred space. There was no bills to pay, no jobs to rush to, no traffic to wait in, no one trying to sell you anything.

With the coming of the white culture and the Indian boarding schools, all that changed. When the schools were first built around the turn of the century, most Hopi parents refused to send their children there, choosing instead to teach them the tribal ways through their daily instructions. The government sent in army troops to arrest the rebellious parents who refused to send their children away. They captured the frightened, hiding children and forcefully delivered them to the schools. Without even a trial, many of the Hopi fathers were imprisoned for refusing to enroll their children in the Indian schools. One of the Elders, Nasiwisima, tells of his imprisonment:

> As soon as we arrived in Keams Canyon, they threw us into the basement, six of us chained together. They starved us for five days. We got weak and started to see things. Finally they fed us, but then we got sick and each time one had to run to the outhouse, the other five had to come with him. We were lucky no one was hurt. Every day they came by with papers, saying, 'Sign them, then you can go home.' We refused to let them take our children away.

Often the fathers' trial-less imprisonments lasted for a year and a half, creating great hardship on the women, children and elderly who were left to fend for themselves in a harsh environment. During one period, the fathers were sent to penitentiary on Alcatraz Island, or put in chains and forced to work on the roads. If the father refused to sign, their children were held at the school all year, whereby the other children could leave in the summer. Except for a few brief visits, many Hopi children, taken from their families at age five or six, were raised in these schools until they were teenagers. The parents bore their tribulations with dignity. When the fathers finally returned from prison, they returned as they had left - tenacious about never agreeing to send their children to school and abandoning the Hopi Way.

Once enrolled in the schools, the children were submitted to even worse atrocities, with many, and in some years most, of them going blind or dying from diseases to which they had developed no immunity. Unhealthy conditions at the school also caused many deaths and much sickness. Many schools degenerated into child labor camps, with children being forced to work at hard labor for long hours - with total disregard for all prevailing child labor laws. As one official noted, the schools were often "workhouses" in which children were reduced to the status of "slaves." Hunger was a continual problem at many schools, both in the United States and Canada. Food rations meant for the children, were sold by corrupt administrators leading to serious malnutrition in many schools. As a 1907 government report on Indian schools noted, "Indian boys and girls [were] dying like flies . . . even war seldom shows as large a percentage of fatalities."

School officials immediately cut the children's long hair and dusted or dipped them in a delousing compound. To create an entirely new identity, and to sever them from their roots, the children were given "proper Christian names" and were no longer allowed to use their tribal names. They were whipped or their mouths were washed out with soap if they spoke their tribal language. Even if the children's parents came to visit, they were not allowed to speak in their native tongue, making much-needed communication between parent and child impossible. In time, the tribal language was forgotten by many students.

Many of the missionaries and teachers were brutal. After being forcefully, and often violently, captured in the villages, the children were beaten, humiliated and locked in storage rooms with little to eat for exhibiting any of their traditional behavior, even for speaking their native language or practicing centuries-old rituals. As one Hopi woman recalled, "Corporal punishment was given as a matter of course; whipping with a harness strap was administered in an upstairs room."

They were told they were "heathens" and their ancient religion of respect for One Creator and all His creation was evil and demonic. As one student recalled, "They told us that our parents, our grandparents, all our people, they were chanting to the devil." The result, she said, was that she learned to hate, not simply the people who oppressed her, but herself and her race as well. All traces of the injustices inflicted on Native tribes during the new country's expansion westward was deleted from their school curriculum and unquestioning patriotism to their new country was stressed.

The Indian students were introduced to the competitive system that was completely foreign to tribal values. As Sioux Chief Luther Standing Bear describes:

> In the course of learning, the strength of one small mind was never pitted against the strength of another in foolish examinations. There being no such thing as "grades," a child was never made conscious of any shortcomings. I never knew embarrassment or humiliation of this character until I went to Carlisle School and there was put under the system of competition . . . there was no sense of rivalry. We never disliked the boy who did better than the others. On the contrary, we praised him.

Eventually, 300 Indian schools would be established, most by missionaries and the government, all sharing the same philosophy. The view of the school administrators toward their Indian wards was made clear by Captain R.H. Pratt, who founded the Carlisle Indian School in 1879, when he stated his intention "to kill the Indian to save the man."

The motto of his school was "From Savagery to Civilization."

When they returned home, they could no longer easily converse with their elders, especially their grandparents, whose function it was to pass on their wisdom and values to the young. These schools broke the "sacred hoop" of many tribes. Even when they returned home for the holidays, they were often not permitted to attend any native ceremonies. When the students left the schools, they often fit in neither world. Soon alcoholism, idleness, suicide, obesity, broken families - all symptoms of self-hate, loneliness and the pain of racial prejudice - engulfed the tribes.

As Shoshone elders Mary and Carrie Dann recently said about tribal members returning from Indian boarding schools, "When they came back, they were completely different people. They were no longer Western Shoshone. They were not traditional indigenous people. They were hollow. I think we lost maybe a couple of generations of our people, and some of these lost people then became the so-called leaders of our nations. The boarding schools groomed these people for political leadership of their nations because the federal government knew they were no longer traditional people, no longer spiritual people."

In the 1920s, the government banned the religious ceremonies that was at the core of the tribe's soul and identity. They banned the Sun Dance of the Plaines Indians and "all similar dances and so-called religious ceremonies, shall be considered 'Indian offences' punishable by incarceration in the agency prison." The Hopi, and many other tribes, continued their sacred practices in secret.

The next morning, Julia and I went out on the mesa to greet the dawn before taking everyone to Radford's house.

"After seeing their dance yesterday," Julia said, "I understand why they have resisted Christianity taking root here. They were given their Instructions never to leave this land or their religion and they have kept that covenant. The Hopi are not judging other religions, they're just clear that their religion and beliefs were meant for them, just as Christians feel that way."

"Their beliefs of love and peace are in line with Christ's teachings," I said. "I'm really looking forward to hearing more from Radford. We have been guided to probably one of the best people to explain the Hopi and Native American worldview."

After a late breakfast, Supai Waters, Elaine, John, Carol, Julia and I went over to Lorna and Radford's house in Hotevilla where they lived with Dawn, her husband, Duane, and their son, Rad. Their house, a short distance from the village plaza, is off by itself with a large garden next to it. As with all Hopi gardens, it is dry dirt, almost like sand, but with healthy looking corn and bean and squash plants - each hand-watered.

(Like basketry and weaving, farming, often done together by clan members, is also part of their spiritual life. Farming is part of their Covenant with Maasaw that if they planted humbly and with a good and harmonious heart, their lives, though hard, would be good and full. Given that Hopi corn takes 120 days to mature and their growing season between frosts is only 130 days, their planting is exact and guided by their celestial-oriented Ceremonial Cycle.

Their simple but effective farming techniques are some of the most religiously significant activities performed by the Hopi. It connects them with the earth and with their ancestors. Traditional Hopi, who seldom seek "progress" and change but rather seek to bring repeated cycles from their past into the present, reject modern farming practices. Like Maasaw, they use digging sticks to plant their precious corn, believing that metal implements tear at the flesh of Mother Earth. Milland Lomakema, of Second Mesa, perhaps expressed this relationship of planting, corn and their ritual life best in John D. Loftin's *Religion and Hopi Life*,, when he stated, "In Hopi belief, if you want to teach a person the history or the song that is deeply connected to our history, you feed them corn. You're planting history in that person. Planting is really a life of Hopi.")

Inside their living room is spacious, welcoming and clean, with a two-story ceiling and bookshelves, comfortable chairs and sofas, and the usually personal pictures, crafts and mementos, most with a Hopi or Native American theme. A beautiful traditional headdress hung on one wall. A very large hand loom sat near a TV set - a foot in *both* worlds.

After brief introductions and updating them on what we had been doing since we saw them last, we all settled in their comfortable living room. I told them about our research revealing that perhaps Christ had once walked the Americas, as a white or red man, and asked Radford for his thoughts.

"As far as my knowledge about that, we have never been contacted," he replied. "And the reason I am saying that is that we have been told by our elders through our religious activities, that Maasaw was the one Divine Spirit that was here - not in person. So, that in spiritual ways we have accepted Maasaw's commission, our asking to be here in this world with him. We don't have knowledge of anyone seeing Christ, but the Peacemaker from the Iroquois Nation seems to me is reflecting the Christ."

"Did you see Maasaw in the flesh?" I asked.

"Maasaw could come in in any form," he continued. "It could be a bird. It could be some other animal. It could be a tree, a rock. Even in our moral teachings. It could be a person sometimes and it could come in as a ragged person. It could be a well-developed person. But there's a message in there that we have to look out for to see if that message is what we would want to see or what we would want to happen.

"When the Spanish came here and established churches," Radford continued, "they came in kind of a violent way as to establish domination upon us, upon the Hopi. They came from the pueblos in New Mexico, and then they came down here when they found out there were more pueblo people here that they did not know about. But we were native people and they had their own ways, their own government. The Spanish said, 'They cannot be like that. They have to be like the Spanish.' They just came in and just didn't mind the leaders of the villages. They made everyone work for them. They started to disrupt all their ceremonies. Like the ceremony you saw yesterday, they destroyed that. They came in that fashion and they wanted to do away with all our religious activities - everything. They built up churches. In those days, three churches were built here including one in Oraibi.

"When this was happening people from over near Taos, New Mexico, all the way to Hopi were warned that this was happening. People in Taos didn't want to have their ways destroyed either and so they sent runners all the way out to here to warn that we need to revolt, to do something about this. The runners came down and said this is the time we are going to have everybody revolt. So they had tightened knots on this leather tong and every day they would untie a knot and on the last knot, that was the day the revolt would happen.

"But when it came to Hopi, one of the villages, Awatovi, had already been consumed by the missions and they were reluctant to do this. But Oraibi and Shungopavi were still strong and revolting. In Awatovi, most of the people were already converted and baptized into the religion. And so the chief over there said, 'No. I'm not going to do it.' So when the day came, they didn't do what they were supposed to do so Oraibi and Shungopavi destroyed their missions - everything there was with the church."

"The village at Awatovi went on leading the Christian life but the villages that surrounding Awatovi village began to talk about it and make criticisms about the village. The chief there couldn't handle it and so he finally said, 'O.K. I'm giving up.' But the way he gives up the village is he says, 'All right. You come destroy my village,' asking the other villages to destroy Awatovi."

"To stop the spread of Christianity?" I asked.

"Yes," Radford answered. "He didn't want to be the one to do it so he said, 'You do that.' And so that's what happened. They went over there and destroyed the whole village. And that's how Christianity came over here. And that's one of our religious activities: Don't bring Christianity here. To this day, that is one of our religious activities."

"Is that a problem with those that have embraced Christianity in the tribe?" I asked.

"Yes," Radford said, nodding his head.

"What percent has embraced Christianity?" I asked.

"Not very much, maybe ten or twenty percent. Most of them that have converted, would leave the reservation."

"So eighty or ninety percent of Hopi still practice your traditional religion?" I asked. "That's very powerful."

"That is why the people that want to convert leave the reservation," Radford answered. "Because of that power that you just mentioned here on the reservation. In my village, Shungopavi, the village leaders and the village chief made provisions. If you want to convert, that's fine, but don't do it here and don't change my way of living here in this village. And they said, 'O.K. We will allow you to go in this direction, and when you leave Hopiland, you remain there and don't ever come back.' There is a place that we have for people that, as we always say, 'get tired of our way of living,' and want to live progressively. You can go there. If you want to change your religion, you can go there."

"With so many unconverted people, have missionaries continued to come here?" I asked.

"Yes," Radford nodded.

"So you're still seen as souls that need to be saved?" I asked.

"They are targeting our little ones, our children," Dawn said. "You will see a van in the summer driving through the villages honking the horn. It's from a church. They get the kids to go to the church. The parents don't know what's going on. They think the kids have something constructive to do. Even my nieces and nephews go over there because they get free stuff."

"Do you know what they are telling the kids?" I asked "Are they telling the kids they are going astray - in the wrong direction?"

"Yes. I'm pretty sure," Radford said.

"How much pressure are you getting to abandon your religion and beliefs?" I asked.

"I think the pressure is still there," Radford said. "We in Shungopavi just recently got our sovereign status from the Hopi courts that was established by the BIA. So now we are the only village on the Hopi reservation that is allowed to call ourselves a sovereign traditional nation."

"Is that because only your village took the matter to court and the other villages didn't join you?" Carol asked.

"Yes," Radford said.

"Plus, they're the only village that still has the traditional leaders," Dawn added. "Most villages don't have those positions any more and don't practice all the ceremonies."

"Our religion is still intact," Radford said. "Not one hundred percent but ninety-seven, ninety-eight percent of our religion is still intact. Some of the problems were from their own villages. Some of the practices were lost when the Oraibi split created this village here, Hotevilla, and the other village across the road, Bacavi. When they did that, they separated the practices, the importance of their religion, because the people that were supposed to perform certain ceremonies during religious activities, they moved away and the other group was left here without a completion of the religious activities. It began with accepting the government at Oraibi. That's what brought it in. That's what brought the separation. Some people at Oraibi wanted it. Others didn't want it. That's where the split came. And when they go, there goes the religion."

"I read that your elders were concerned that when they brought power into this village, Hotevilla," I said, "you were concerned that it would disturb the sacred object that your traditional elders buried here and that this would cause greater suffering during the period of purification. What's your view of that now? Has that affected what we are going to confront in the future?"

"I think so," Radford answered, "because the people from Oraibi really were into their religion and they are the ones that really didn't want to have these things happen. So when they came up here to Hotevilla, they were still that strong but because of the split, they do not have all their religion intact. Only those elders or the older people that knew the religion and had practiced it were gone and there was nobody to carry it on. That's why this village, Hotevilla, is without it. The same with Oraibi. That's why Oraibi doesn't have any spiritual function. One of our goals at Shungopavi, is that we are the village to maintain the unity of the Hopi religion. Shungopavi is the Mother Village of Hopi and from that village, other villages have been established. So we are saying that even though other villages will discontinue their practices, we will still have the unity there and if such time they want to come back and rebuild their Hopi religion and their own religion, we can do that."

"So in Shungopavi your full Ceremonial Cycle is still fully intact? Are you also holding some of the ceremonies for the Havasupai?" I asked. "Roland said you were preserving fifty songs for them."

"More than songs," he answered, after some silent thought, perhaps considering exactly how much to reveal.

"So you're holding this information for the Havasupai?" I asked.

"Almost all the nations. That's how we feel," he answered. "All over the world. Not only certain tribes, but for the whole world."

"So your whole life, all five of you have had in your awareness, that what you are doing here, you're doing for the whole planet? No matter how you were overlooked or degraded or ignored by the dominant culture, you knew the work you are doing here is for everyone?"

"Yes," they all answered, slowly, but proudly and firmly shaking their heads in affirmation.

"And all those people in the square yesterday were raised to know that the work that you do, you do for all and that one day, the world will understand?" I asked, amazed at the power of what was being revealed.

"That's the whole idea," Radford answered. "It's always been in the hearts of everyone that wanted to sponsor these ceremonies - especially the leaders of different societies. It's in their thoughts, in their minds all the time."

"How much of this is a public thought, a thought for publication," Carol asked, "and how much of this is an internal thought, a protected thought? In other words, does the publication of that view put it at risk?"

"It used to be the older people thought we should keep it to ourselves," Radford answered, "and not have it contaminated by different knowledge, different information from the outside because it may disrupt our way. But now *this* time, we're thinking that we need to go out to the people and say, 'Hey, we are still here and we are doing all this work for the universe.' And maybe with that we will have a little bit more respect from the United States government and other agencies. So we are now thinking that we should be out there saying that we are still here, still doing the ceremonies. All we need is respect."

"I feel that your information is really needed now by the outside world," I said. "Many of the problems were created because we did not listen to the advice of the Native Americans who told us we cannot abuse the planet like we have been. And as Native Americans have been telling us, in the end we just have each other, the leaders do not really care for the people."

"That's my feeling," Radford replied. "Things happen out there in the world because of who they are. In our ways, we are supposed to be in tune with nature. For some reason people get greedy and that's when they begin to diverge from the Creator's way. They believe they are a free person according to the United States. We don't believe that. There is no such thing as a free person. What I'm saying is that because of these kind of ideas and these kind of thoughts, they tend to only dwell on themselves and try to make an emperor of themselves, forgetting about the other people. In our way, we say, 'Don't dwell on yourself. You have other people to work with. You never work by yourself to achieve the glory or whatever it is that you desire. You always depend on other people and those are the people that you are working for.' That's how Hopi feels. So when we see someone doing something in that fashion, we feel that they're being out of line."

"In Hopi, we don't have anything called 'wealth.' But in the other society, there is wealth that they dwell on and there's also power that they dwell on. So we say these things are happening because they are not doing things in the Hopi Way or they're not focusing on the people, the helpers, the workers. They [the leaders] only give out things for themselves. We have a saying that when you're in that position or when you're focusing on those things, then you're starting to break away from the Hopi Way and there are some drastic things that will happen if you continue doing it."

"So you see this as part of those prophecies?" I repeated.

"You have heard some of our prophecies," Radford answered. "I was telling my wife that in Shungopavi, we have all of these prophecies but we are not talking about these prophecies. Hotevilla and Oraibi are the ones that are always talking about the prophecies and they always say, 'These are the prophecies so let it happen.' We don't see it that way. We know that the prophecies are made for *us*. We don't want to see those prophecies happen. That's why we don't talk about those prophecies. But up this way in Hotevilla, it's more open and to me, they are relenting ideas instead of trying to do something about it."

"What I'm hearing you say," Elaine said, "is that you prefer to give energy to the opposing possibility of creating what you *want*."

"Yes," Radford said. "Don't talk about it. Don't let it happen. When we go to our Hopi initiations for the young men, that's the positive energy there. At these initiations, there is knowledge being pounded into our heads. This is part of it. Don't do this. Don't do that. And so those that have gone through the initiation, know lots and lots of information about the whole world, the whole universe. But it's the way that you pick it up and the way that you use it, is something else."

"In our book, should we talk of the prophecies?" I asked. "Our book is not for the general audience. Our book is designed to reach out to the healers of the planet and assist the healers. Should I leave your prophecies out?"

"Just put it in there and bring it out the way I just mentioned it," Radford answered. "We don't want to energize that prophecy."

"In many ways your prophecies were comforting to me," I said. "Back in the sixties and seventies it became clear to a lot of us that our way of life was not sustainable. That's what the whole counterculture was about. We were looking for better ways - better ways to grow food, to make electricity, to heal our bodies and our minds, better ways to be born and to die, a better way to seek God. The prophecies agreed with all this and reminded us that only a few were needed for healing the Earth."

"I'd love to hear your words about freedom," Julia said, "because it's really the key to peace. I'd like to hear you say more on no one is free."

"In our society, we have the highest priest," Radford said, "and we look at him as the leader, the head of the Hopi society as well as the religion. Our way of life is intertwined with civil practices plus religious practices. We don't separate religion and society. It's all connected. Everything that happens, using of land, we have to ask the proper authority. We have lands that are given to different clans to maintain, to sustain, while they are here in this village supporting the village leaders. With permission, everything can be given. So to say that you want to be something on your own and just be by yourself and have no ties to anything, in Hopi you can't do that. There is always some kind of tie back to the village leadership or to the village religion."

"So when Oraibi split, some of them thought they would be free," Julia said. "They were going to hold that disconnection."

"That's what they were thinking," he continued. "They would split from Hopi and convert to Christianity so they would have more freedom there. They would have more access to the different things that the government offered to the people. That's what the whole fight was about. In our way, the Hopi Way, we still have to find out who we are and why are we here. That always brings it back to the young kids," he said pointing to his grandson, who had been playing happily around us. "You are Hopi and *this* is why you are here. And that again goes back to the time of Emergence into this world. We want to be here and we want to help maintain this world. That is what we told Maasaw and that is why we are here on this land. And that's why when you are at your own home, you do things for the family, you do things for the relatives, you do things for the village and you do things for the whole tribe."

"And that's the way eighty or ninety percent of the people here view the world?" I asked.

"I think so," Radford answered.

"You think in the next lifetime I can come back Hopi," I kidded.

"I hope so," he answered. "You are more Hopi than something else. That's what we say."

"So when I'm talking about freedom," he continued, "it's different from when I hear people, the native people, talking about freedom or sovereignty. When you listen to the tribes, they're still having their tribal councils operated or funded by the United States government. When they say they are a sovereign nation, it doesn't really say so. Because if you're going to be a sovereign nation, then you have to develop your own resources, your own ways of a society with your own ways of protection of your society. I don't think any of the tribes have that."

"Even Hopi?" I asked.

"Even Hopi," he answered. "Because we have the tribal council operated by the government. We have schools operated by the government. If we are to be totally sovereign, than we as the Hopi have to generate all of those resources to say that *we* are funding this program. If we were to really get united and then get into our own natural resources and then use those natural resources and funds to develop our Hopi Way, that's what the elders have always been trying to say. Is to develop things our *own* way. Whatever we are wanting to set as our goals and our goals is to keep our

Hopi religion going for all times - forever. And to keep the people in our Hopiland, we have to separate ourselves from the United States government. We have to start going into our resources. With that, we can then develop our own ways as to how we want to function, to make sure that the Hopi society is progressing, is healthy."

"Is the tribe moving toward cutting the cord with the United States government?" I asked.

"Not really," he answered. "We are not that progressive yet. We're not seeing that much of an improvement. The reason is, is that we still have this land conflict with the government. If we ever are ever at a time when the government says, 'O.K. This is your land, with no ties to the United States government.' At that point, the elders say, 'Now you can use the natural resources. You can sell it. You can use it. Whatever you want to do with it to keep your own society progressing.' "

"Given the power of the surrounding society," I said, "you may have found the most effective way to maintain by just staying here and quietly keeping your religion and Ceremonial Cycle going. This was probably the best you could, at least until now. And is this why your fought casino gambling? Because you knew this would push back efforts towards sovereignty?"

"Yes," he answered.

"How hard was it to defeat the initiative?" I asked. "Now that I see that eighty or ninety percent of your people view life your way, it seems that you only needed leadership to remind the people."

"We put out flyers." Dawn said. "One of them said 'Gambling is *kahopi*,' meaning 'not Hopi,' but if you don't go and vote, they'll build a casino in the name of Hopi. We had to convince them to vote, which is also *kahopi*. In our way, the consensus rules. But out there the majority rules. Fifty-one percent can impose their rules on forty-nine percent. In Hopi, my dad tells me that if an issue comes up, all the leaders have to talk it out. And it may take a day, a week, a month, or several years to come to a conclusion, but that conclusion is a consensus. Everybody has their say. In voting, nobody gets to say anything - only the people that put the rules out there. So we said that gambling and voting is not Hopi - it is *kahopi* - but if you don't vote they're going to make the casino the

'Hopi Casino.' In the past, if you didn't agree with something, if you didn't want to put your energy into it, you just didn't vote. That was what we were afraid of. So if only one hundred people voted and fifty one voted for the gambling, it would pass. That's the whole government system coming back in to play in Hopiland."

"What about the people that said they need this gambling money to educate their children, fix your roads and get good health care?" I asked. "They could just say that the casinos were going to be built two hours away on land you own on Interstate 40 and would not even affect your people here."

"At one meeting, a man said we could fix our kivas with the gambling money. I told them I don't think I would want to fix our kivas with any of that money," Dawn continued, "knowing that some soul, somewhere, is so addicted to gambling that she just has to go all the time to play bingo or slots. It's mostly older ladies. I had my students telling me, 'My grandma and my mom go Thursday night to gamble and we come back Friday and I'm all tired because we've been all over the place and we can't go in and we're sleeping in the car.' They *all* had stories. It blew me away. I didn't even tell them to tell their parents to vote against it. They were saying, 'Why do they want to build a casino. Why do they want to do that.' They told their parents *not* to vote for the casino."

"And that's why several of your ancient villages were destroyed by other villages," I said, "because gambling had gotten so bad that the women were not taking care of the home or children. And I've heard you're seeing gambling even now with new bingo halls starting up in Polacca, your Tewa village. What about the people that stood to make money from the casino? Did they hassle you?"

"It was the tribal council," Dawn replied. "They kept saying they were going to close the Peabody Coal Mine and the Hopi get a third or a quarter of their tribal revenue from that. They were trying to scare us saying in 2006 there will be no money. All these services that you enjoy are going to be gone. We're going to have to layoff 500 people from the tribe. We need this casino money. That's what they were pushing."

"How did you counter that?" I asked.

"I told them, and this is my dad's vision and goes back to the food and all of that, that we need to become sovereign. We need to start growing our own food again because that's what we did before anybody came here with any money. We knew how to grow cotton to make our own clothes. We knew what plants to eat. We knew what plants to use to take care of ourselves medicinally. We had our spirits that watched over us, that made rain for our crops. We need to go back to that. We were sovereign. We were self-sufficient prior to any non-Hopi that came here. We could take care of ourselves. We knew what animals to eat. The villages were built by hand. The whole village would go and wherever someone had their rocks that they were going to use, they'd pass it by hand. They did the same thing with the plastering of the walls. And so I told them, we need to develop that. And we can use technology to help you as long as you remember that it came from somewhere else. Someone up there (pointing upwards) helped us. I told them, 'We can do this. We don't need money. What's money?' The old people told us money will come and it will go. There was this article in a newspaper here and this woman said, 'We're so isolated here. When gas goes to five dollars, we can't even go to the casinos in Camp Verde.' "

"We have started eating so many unhealthy foods, processed foods full of sugar and fats," Dawn continued. "There are many healthy foods we have here that we can trade to organic stores. Like evening primrose that has one of the best fats that helps your brain and things in your system. It's just growing wild everywhere. We can market our corn and our healthy food."

"It was hard at first to talk to people about living this way," Duane said. "The first thing that came out of everyone's mouth was that it was hard to live like that now."

"In the late eighties," Dawn continued, "they tried to get a casino here but he [pointing towards her father] stopped them. It all started back then when these five ladies, who were the last of their tribe in California, had a bingo hall and they fought and got it to be a class A casino. They're the ones that started this whole casino movement within Native tribes. That was in 1976. And when we had Rad, I was worried what it would do to him. There's already people who would rather go to town than to watch our dances. I could just see all this stuff happening.

Duane's tribe has a casino in Parker and he saw the effects in his communities. Drugs, meth became a big thing there. They were selling in the casino parking lots. I just couldn't let that happen for my child."

"I started talking to a childhood friend of mine about what us young people could do about it. I used to think that I was the only young person that thought like this, that we had to keep the old ways going. I thought like that because I grew up in this house with these guys," she said, pointing toward her parents, "and I come to find out that my cousin, she's a clan relative, she went against Reliant Energy Company and stopped them from building a plant. So I followed in her footsteps, talking at the public meetings and brought up certain questions. The tribal council and their Gaming Task Team, their slogan was 'The Hopi People's Choice,' as if it was certain. I went to their first meeting and looked at what they had and then I went and did my own research. A lot of the information they gave was true but they didn't do the other side. You'll get 25 million in revenue but the state gets thirteen percent, the casino companies get so many percent, and in the end you only get three million. And they ignored all the social problems."

"And their answers to these problems," Duane said, "was that it's up to every person to decide what they are going to do anyway. If someone wants to go gamble, that's their choice. If someone wants to do drugs, that's their choice. It was really weird how they were promoting one vice and at the same time promoting other vices."

"Did you think you could win?" I asked.

"Oh, God," Dawn said. "It got to be when I would go to the meetings they would say, 'There's *that* girl again.' There was a man here, Lee Jenkins, he's the cultural preservation director, he was against it too. He had a story about some gambler who came here and said he would be able to lure us in this way of not being a Hopi. Lee said, 'I'm so glad you are doing this.' He was very helpful. He let us use his office and copying machines. I was praying all the time. There were a lot of people that I didn't know were thinking the same way as I was. They had a call-in radio show on KUYI the night before and only myself and another lady were the only one that called in that opposed it in the entire hour. So the ladies on the radio said, 'Well. It looks like there is pretty much a consensus among the Hopi people that they want the casino.' Come the next day, only three villages, Moencopi, Kykotsmovi and Keam's Canyon, voted in favor. All the other villages voted 'no' by almost ten or fifteen percent."

"Did those three villages vote for it because they are the villages that are most under the government's and tribal council's influence?" I asked.

"Yes," Dawn answered. "But even the people in Polacca that have the bingo halls there, didn't want it to pass either. But now some of the Navajo chapter houses are looking at bringing in casinos."

"But they are very organized here," Duane added. "The Gaming Task Team is still here. They didn't dissolve it. They'll try again. They told us, 'If we don't get it over the whole reservation then we are going to go to each village and propose it in each village to have their own casino.' "

"I think they'll try again when they think there are enough older people gone to go to the young people and tell them, 'We can get it through now that they're gone,' " Dawn said.

"Radford, did you ever think about leaving Hopiland?" I asked, feeling the casino discussion was concluded.

"When I was small, I was traditionally raised. It's always with me. The way they talk about different things outside, that everything is so free and easy to get and where's you work to get these things, that's what I was looking at. And then there were responsibilities that I'm going to have here because I'm never gonna to get in their position outside. I decided that I'd just have to do what I can at home."

"I was interested in engineering. But then my uncle told me, 'Our clan responsibilities, the Eagle Sun Forehead Clan, is that you are the educator. You are the healer. You are the counselor. You are the psychiatrist. You are the warrior. That's our clan responsibility.' They would be telling me this. At that age, I wasn't understanding very much of what was going on until I got into the Hopi religion and got initiated. Then I began to realize what they were telling me. As clan members to the village, we are the warriors *first*. We are like the Marines of the village. We go to the enemy before anyone else in the village goes. If we do poor, *then* the other villages come. That's the kind of responsibility that we have. And we are also the guardsmen of *all* the ceremonies of the village, the whole year round."

"The only place that our men folk don't have the responsibility is in the women's societies. They have their own. And that's where my sisters, my clan relatives, the womenfolk do the same thing as the men folk do. They have bows and arrows and they are the warriors at that time - the women folk of my clan. And when their ceremonies are over, they are back in the system again and then the men folk take care of the whole ceremonials and everything that goes. In my village, right now I'm the chief warrior. And so, with my nephews, with my uncles, I set them to do certain types of tasks. Then there comes education. If there's a person that's responsible for a certain part of the ceremony, we have the right to go over there and tell them, 'Hey. You need to learn that a little bit more. You are not doing what you are supposed to do.' We are always helping each other. If there's a person in poor health, we go and talk to them to get them out of their misery. We tell them, 'Look into the better life and you'll get out of it. Don't dwell on your illness. Get out of it.' Those kind of things we do as a people. If people are short-of-hand in building a home or building a field or fixing the trail or cleaning out the spring, then we have to go in and help them. That's the kind of responsibilities that we have because we are members of the village."

"Wouldn't it be a good idea for some of you from the protector clan to run for tribal council so you could steer the tribe in the right direction?" I asked. "The new Havasupai tribal council is very conscious and value their Covenant and it has made a difference."

"The tribal council is made up of representatives from all the villages," Radford answered, "but from our village. We at Shungopavi don't have representation because we believe in our old traditional ways of government. So we don't even go into that government. And there is no representative from here, from Hotevilla. So that's where we are having this real tough task to change the tribal council ideas."

"What I hear Robert asking," Elaine said, "is, 'Is there any worth tactically to actually train someone to go into the tribal council, like how you would send a warrior as an advanced party to look at the advancing enemy, to attempt to influence, to turn, the tribal council into a council that would then be more representative of true Hopi ways.' In some of the African indigenous tribes, they do the same thing of sending ones that are named to go out of the tribe to learn to come back in. Strategically, they have a group of people that do that but they don't give up their ways."

"I'm talking about just one village that I'm responsible to," Radford said. "We have other clans that are in the same situation that I am. My leaders don't want any representation in there, but others could do that. So we've been talking to other villages like First Mesa and Second Mesa, to do the same thing. At least try that. We are talking to some of the young people about Maasaw. This is the education they want me to do, my uncles to do. So I have done that so now I'm trying to give what I found out from the outside world to my fellow workers in the village. So now we are working with a young group that has gone out and now has come back and want to continue with their own clan duties. It's hard, but we are working on it."

"It is hard but it can be done," I said. "The Peacemaker showed that you *can* reason leaders into higher levels. He was able to convince the Iroquois leaders to stop a centuries-old blood feud. The Hopi tribal council could be reasoned into the Hopi Way. So maybe even if you do not actively participate on the council, you could greatly influence them."

"We need to do that in the schools, too," Dawn added. "They tell you, 'Get an education and move away from here.' I think that's why I wanted to become a teacher because my ultimate goal is to learn as much as I can. He told me that [pointing toward her father]. My uncles told me that. I want to go to law school so I can know these laws that affect us - to help him because they are always needing lawyers. I want to teach the young people that there *is* a reason that we stay here. There is a reason for us *being* here in the first place. And show them you can go away and learn but you don't have to live that way because that's not our way. That's not for us. Whatever they do out there, that's not for us. We already have a way to live. We already know what's good and what's bad. We've had thousands of years of experience telling us. We are a communal society, always giving to each other. We have thousands of years of experience telling us *this* is where it's at. There was a reason why we were brought *here* and this is where we are supposed to be."

"It is not by accident that we are all here in this room together," I said. "There have been almost seventy reggae concerts here. This reggae music coming from Jamaica has blown a strong wind over your fire of love and peace, and it has kept a lot of your youths from listening to slack music."

"Yes," Dawn said. "We have that One Love here very strongly - that you're supposed to be loving to everybody because if you're not, you're not loving yourself."

"That is what we mean by 'Hopi,' " Radford added.

" Also, I want to give you some of the other books that I wrote. I have one called *The Complete Disaster Home Preparation Guide*, that shows you how to live without power, and my *Building Your Own House* book is the best-selling book on building your own home. Maybe they can help you be more self-sufficient. Also we have some of our how-to DVDs in the car that we'll leave with you. It shows you everything about working on your own home - drywall, wallpaper, flooring, plumbing, electrical, everything. We started a company twenty years ago to produce these. They've been on PBS, the Learning Channel, USA Network. That's how Julia and I pay our bills, selling our DVDs to schools and libraries and on the Internet. Also, in the seventies, I founded a school in California that taught people how to build and remodel their homes. Every summer we had a housebuilding camp in the Sierra Nevada Mountains. We would take people out of the city and put them in a relaxed environment and teach them solar energy, composting toilets, wastewater recycling, wind power - everything that was sustainable."

"That is my dream, too," Dawn said, "to make a video on how to build Hopi-style."

"And the gardening, too," Julia said. "Your way of gardening is so unique."

"I would like that. This is what I have been telling my village that we need to go out there and start teaching these kids at a younger age how it is done. We have not been doing that for a long, long time. What we are doing is weaving," Radford said, pointing to the beautiful loom where he was weaving a delicate natural white cotton wedding shawl, "but it is done mainly for ceremonial purposes. In our history, they were using looms to have clothing made for the family. We don't do that any more because like you were saying, we can go to Wal-Mart and get our clothing

there. But we can still do that." (As does almost everything in Hopi practical life, weaving embodies a spiritual dimension. For generations, it
has represented the regeneration of the world. Like their basketry, it is integral to their ceremonial life. Each part of their woven patterns has
meaning, often encouraging rain and fertility.)

"And that's what I was telling Robert and Julia when they first came
to the school with Abijah," Dawn said. "They were telling us, 'Keep your
Covenants. Remember why you are here.' And I told them I think that's
the best thing to do for *us* because we've become clouded. Our minds have
become contaminated with Babylon. Sometimes we have to hear from
somebody else, 'You guys have something that's important. It's unique.
Remember it.' We tell that to our kids but they don't want to listen sometimes because it's the same thing over and over. But when someone from
the outside recognizes what's special about us, what's good about us,
and reminds us what we're supposed to be doing, it's more powerful.
It's always good to be reminded by someone else."

"And in the reggae world," I said. "Hopi and Havasupai are well-
known and respected."

"That is true for the traditional reggae," Carol said, "as opposed to the
more current, modern dancehall phenomenon. The traditional reggae
world has had a long history of relating to native people, whether it's
Hopi or another group. But there is an interruption now with the dancehall music. What is occurring here now with us, and I know it needs to
occur more, is the cross-cultural exchange, so that there is that clarity
that the worldview occurred in different parts of the world and that that
worldview has served to protect important practices, knowledge, etcetera,
in different parts of the world. And that in this time, as the universe is
cycling into a period where the risk is there of self-destruction, that these
different places where the knowledge has been kept, that it's important
now for those places to encounter each other and to realize that in fact
there are these very similar, very, very similar, worldviews occurring."

"That's what I meant," Radford said, "when I was saying there is a
group of people that don't see it that way. They always so develop themselves so that they wanted more - supreme power - among the rest of
the nation. That's where the struggle is. They are thinking about them-

selves only, and not thinking about the rest of the nation. And that's where we have the problem. United States wants to have the power. Russia wants to have the power. Germany wants to have power. And all of these powers, are coming up so often and us people aren't even recognized. We have knowledge, too, that we can provide. We can share that with other people but it doesn't ring a bell with these people who have so much control. They don't want to listen to that. We call ourselves 'Hopi.' We don't believe in fighting. We don't believe in war. We believe in maintaining and sustaining ourselves in *this* world. Once we get those people to understand where we are coming from and what we know about the world, forget about being powerful and work with the people, make your people richer and more healthful. That's what we say."

"I have been thinking about what it would take to get your family and other Native American elders to Jamaica to reason with the people there," I said to Radford. "Just as Jamaica has had a big impact on your tribe, I think Native Americans could have a big impact on Jamaica. Hopefully, one day that will happen."

"Once you start the cross-fertilization that Carol is talking about, in a very peculiar way, the opposition is diluted," John said. "Take Dawn. Because once you know Jamaica functions this way, it already empowers you to go forward and make a case to win the battle against casinos. If we keep cross-fertilizing, each person will bring a single worldview but a different context to solve the problems. So we all rise and the obstacles gradually start to fall. We have discovered one another."

"We need to talk to people like Robert, like all of you," Dawn said. "When we can all come and sit here and think about how we can make it better for *all* of our people. That's all that we want. I told my father, he needs to start talking to people. I finally got him to go to the United Nations with a daughter from the elders of Hotevilla. We need to talk to people."

"We are all tradition-based people and there is power in the talk," John said. "If there is power in the talk for us, then for the people that we represent, there's power in the talk for them, too. So we need to develop the talk, like a council, and sanction the talk. And then have everyone participate in the talk. We are all tradition people."

"When I put on my workshops in Jamaica for companies," Elaine said, "the core thing that all the people are looking for is 'How can I be better?' Not just for the company, but 'How can I, as a human soul, find my way and have life?' What I am leaving here with is the reminder that your work is to keep the sacred laws aflame and alive because everybody needs them and all teachings of the sacred laws say the same thing. There is no difference of opinion as to what those laws are. People are dying because they haven't heard them in a way that has them make a connection to transform their lives."

"The other gift I leave with is reminding us of the beauty of giving and receiving - which we know - but to practice it with such consistency is so absolutely beautiful," she continued. "I really just want to thank you. Yesterday when we went to the sacred site, Carol got the message of acknowledging the warrior spirit, which we make wrong a lot. But the warrior spirit as you know it and as you've spoken, is not about fighting or violence. But we don't know that. So we made warrior wrong. And warrior says, 'I have a gift and you need to acknowledge me because if you don't, the anger gets misrepresented.' There is an importance for us all to speak our truths because we never know how many others agree with you until you do. And then if you're called, that creates the call for the energy to gather, of the like minds. And then there's a surprise and it's beautiful when it happens."

"We belong to a group of people in Jamaica that want to transform our country. We don't know how to do it but we got together anyway," Elaine continued. "One of the things we discovered in trying to vision the country we wanted, was that we didn't want to struggle. We didn't want to strive. We didn't want to feel like we were beating our heads. And we came up with a little phrase called 'effortlessly in love.' That's how we wanted to work, to make things happen effortlessly, easily but with love. We are here for a divine reason. Spirit has set up this meeting and we just need to effortlessly and easily and in love to take what it is leading us to create. We want to bring to our country the examples of indigenous people living in truth and in harmony and in love and so we will talk to Robert about how to make that happen. We know you will come to Jamaica. We declare it right now, that you will be speaking, that we will be learning from you; that you will be learning from us. Because Jamaica is to do something for the world. In the same way that you are keeping energy for the planet, there is something that Jamaica has to birth. We are just forty years old. We've come out of four hundred years, but sovereignty is just forty two."

"A little piece of this," Radford said, "you find is going to be good so you take it into yourself and include that into your system and somehow it does."

"It is also important to make a difference in how the tribe eats," Elaine said, "because that creates your entire energy."

"And I learned that from some of what your people told Robert about Ital food, vegetarian eating," Dawn said, referring to *Rasta Heart* which has a section on the benefits - to the planet, to the animals and to humans - on a vegetarian diet. "In the past we were mostly vegetarians. We only ate small game like rabbits and prairie dogs occasionally. We eat a lot of meat now. And now being conscious about food, seeing what we are eating, what we are feeding our guests, is kind of sad. We have a lot of pastry, a lot of processed foods. Learning about the food is really important to me now."

"The other thing that Elaine and I have committed ourselves to doing," Carol said, "is to start a cable channel that is focused on the 'Good Mind.' This will be an instrument for this cross-talk. This journey for us has been amazing in what it has been presenting as another piece of the picture that we have in our minds. You speak what the picture is that you have in your mind, but how you're going to get the puzzle to fit, you have no idea. And then you come on a trip like this one, you go 'A-HA!' It has been a series of *A-HAs!*"

Before we went separate ways, we all gathered in a circle and held hands in their living room and Radford said a prayer in Hopi. As we drove away, Julia asked me if I noticed Dawn's and Lorna's tears of joy after Radford's prayer.

Chapter 10
The Final Journey

"I am always looking forward to see what the Creator has in store for me."
—**Travis Terry**, *Native American flutists, composer and recording artist*

"Me only have one ambition, y'know. I only have one thing I really like to see happen. I like to see mankind live together - black, white, Chinese, everyone. That's all!" —**Bob Marley**

After our journey to Arizona, we returned home and I started working on the chapter about the trip, thinking it would be the last chapter; however, as I spent hours watching Radford on video as I transcribed his reasoning, I found myself drawn to be with him once again.

"You know," I said to Julia one night as we sat by the fire, "I think I want to go back to see Radford again before the book is completed. We never set out to write a book about Native Americans and One Love. We were guided. When you think about it, the Hopi hold the light of Native American wisdom and Shungopavi is the heart of that light and Radford is one of the spiritual leaders of that village. And Dawn, Roland and Supai Waters, too. We could not have found better sources for our book and they've been gently brought to us. I have no particular reason for going but I'm just feeling like drawing wisdom from these deep wells one more time - for myself *and* for our readers."

I called Radford and he said he really didn't know if he had more to say but that when I was there we could go over the previous Hopi chapters I had just sent him for corrections and additions. I also called Roland and told him I would drop by the canyon and visit with him. I wanted to contact Supai Waters to see if he wanted to join me but he didn't call before I left, and he has no phone. If it was meant to be, I'd find him in Supai.

A few weeks later, in early November, two months after we visited Arizona with our Jamaican friends, I flew to Phoenix. As I watched CNN on the airport monitors, I realized yet again how much these messages of love were needed now. I rented a car and drove from Phoenix to Flagstaff, and checked in to the historic Hotel Monte Vista in the downtown area, avoiding the heartless motel chains that dot the landscape. The next morning, I headed out for Hualapai Hilltop before dawn to catch the first helicopter down to Supai village, planning to stay the day and take the last helicopter out.

Looking into the Grand Canyon as I flew in, I felt blessed for our journeys that took us to so many beautiful places to be with so many remarkable people. As I landed in the village, it no longer seemed like an alien world. I felt I had a place here - a role to play. I found Roland in his office in the village center, behind a mound of paperwork. We headed out to sit by the creek near the sweat lodge to reason together.

As we walked, I realized how much I had come to love this gentle but powerful man and to respect his path. So much rested on his broad shoulders. In addition to raising seven children, he had his paid work as the environmental and solid waste manager of the canyon plus the many tasks he had volunteered to undertake to help his people. The grace and determination in which he shouldered all these sacred responsibilities was inspiring.

"What was it like here when you were a youth?" I asked him as we settled down by the clear, bold Cataract Creek, a few yards from their sweat lodge. The day was cool and pleasant, the oppressive heat of the summer only a memory. It was good to be there together.

"Nobody said you had to wear swimming attire or anything," he said. "We went in the nude and it was normal for us. We would get the water from the creek. There weren't any stores."

"So how would you get food?" I asked, already knowing the answer. "Did you hunt and fish?"

"Yea, we did a lot of fishing. The tribe worked with the forest service or one of those entities and they would stock the water here with fish. So we used to go and catch the fish and we used to have a cat that used to chase us when he saw us picking up our fishing rod. We didn't have a fishing line or the fancy reel. We made them on our own. My dad even made a hook using wire, just bent it in and molded it like a fish hook and we put some fishing line on and we went fishing with it. We caught quite a few fish with that homemade hook."

"So you had people bring in flour, sugar, the basics down here from Flagstaff?"

"Yes. A lot of people would save their corn for different ways to prepare the corn. The deer meat we'd make into jerky and we had the nuts and beans, dried figs, apricots and peaches. So there was a lot of food that was grown and that was dried, so even if you didn't hunt, you had relatives that had a garden or something and they would share what they had."

"What were the houses like?" I asked.

"Before the government housing came in, a lot of the people began to adopt four-walls type of construction like modern homes. They started getting whatever they could like cardboard boxes and patch homes that way."

"Before that, was it mostly wickiups, earthen homes?" (Wickiups are their ancient building style of a spacious and clean earthen dome-shaped structure made of branches covered by earth, with a fire pit in the middle and a fire hole in the roof.)

"Yea. As I was growing up there was a lot of the wickiups and earthen structures. Kind of like the sweat lodge with earth all around it and fire pits in the center. That was still here."

"As children, how much did you know about what was going on outside the canyon? Would you go out once a year and see Phoenix and say, 'Oh! That's another planet?' "

"No. I didn't see anything about the outside contact. I didn't even know there were white people or black people or Mexicans or any of the other nationalities. We heard that there was the great ocean and that there were people on the other shore. We heard there was all kinds of different people and they had their own languages but we had never seen them live until I would say '65 or '64. I was getting a little older. I was born in '54. I would say the first contact I had with white people was probably 1958 when I was sitting by the trail and people would go by. The first hikers that came in, and it wasn't like 100, 200 people a month or anything like that, it was just rare when people came through, maybe eight people in one year. That was until *National Geographic* came in, *Arizona Highways* came in. Then the postal service came in and it was like the prophecy said. We were hidden from the public eye for a long time. Even Indian tribes that lived in Arizona didn't know there was an Indian tribe living in the Grand Canyon still living off the land."

"And your prophecy said that you were intentionally hidden away."

"Yes."

"For what purpose did the prophecy say you were hidden?" I asked.

"Because the prophecy said that these resources, the water, the environment, would be devastated, contaminated, degraded, polluted for one's gain. Whoever that one person was, had a lot of power, had a lot of money and that isn't the way it's supposed to work, you know. It's supposed to work in a way where the gains go to everyone - the children, the elders, with respect to the past, the present, and the future. But that isn't the goals that I see projected by the businesses that are on the plateau today. They use and abuse left and right. They don't care what happens to the cultures that were here first and what is sacred to those cultures. In the sixties, the influence from the outside was starting to come in and it was important to learn who these people were and to learn to use the tools that they had. I think that's when the houses first came in. But when the houses first came in, the people that brought these proposals of new homes, of better houses, and luxury and everything, did not tell our people back then that they would face solid waste issues, leaks in the homes, how do you repair the plumbing problems, electrical appliances going out. They didn't tell us that we were going to have these problems."

"You didn't have these problems before? You just had a wickiup and food to eat?" I asked.

"Yes. And those things didn't require too much maintenance. You were living with nature and *in* nature and living according to the things you saw, like the animals behaving certain ways. Like my daughters, they're young but they are gaining the knowledge. When we hear a ringing noise in our ear (he cups his large hand around his ear), it means that a spirit went through you. In our level, our perception, our understanding of what is sacred, goes to that level and it involves everyday beliefs. My daughter had this experience yesterday, of ringing in her ear and she said, 'What does it mean when we get ringing in our ear?' My other daughter, the younger one said, 'Oh I know! I know! If a spirit goes by you or something like that?' I said, 'Yea. When a spirit goes through you, whether it is a good spirit or an evil spirit, but these spirits go through things. They move all the time.' And it's to that level that our children are taught. It's something invisible, but you hear it and only one individual can hear that connection. And that's the way it is with the practitioner, the shaman. It isn't like because a shaman sees a revelation, the whole tribe heard it or felt it."

"Most people outside do not understand that level," I said.

"Not many, and sometimes I think that what is sacred to the government is usually a burial site, a pipe, a medicine man's gourd," he continued. "But that's not where it ends. It goes beyond that and that's what we are trying to convey in the courts. We're trying convey that without really releasing too much of the information but we are beginning to release some of that. We live so close in the environment that we feel related to these things. They are a part of us and that's missing with the people going two blocks for an orange or some corn. They never sow the seed and watch it grow for months and nurture it and begin to develop respect. All they do is run around the block and get whatever they need and that the way it's always been for them."

"And that's the kind of energy you are talking about, that exists here still?" I asked.

"That kind of sacredness and spirituality exists," he answered, moving his hands in a circle above his heart, "at a level that the white man can only relate to in materialism, an altar, a burial site. He can only relate to a physical object because the spiritual part is lost on him. That is true and yet the Native American or indigenous people, have so much respect in spite of all the rivalries, the different cultures, the different ways warriors were developed or puberty rights or the peyote meetings and all the unity ceremonies, sweat lodging, all this. If one was to travel east to a tribe that he never affiliated with or never knew them, but if he saw that they were holding a ceremony or that they were having respect for whatever the ceremony was about, this one person would also recognize that in a respectful way. That's what indigenous people do worldwide. If we went to Europe and we came to a native village, we would honor that if they said that this feature, a little hill or big hill or whatever, was sacred to their people, we would make offerings there and recognize that it's all a part of this Mother Earth. It's all one. This wind that we see that blows against the leaves, they're breathing it. The water is a part of us. We're all connected. And that air, that breath of life, the wind, it travels around the world to all these different cultures. The wind goes to everyone. The Creator is fair and equal to all of us. That's the way it is with the wind, the water, that is flowing by. Sometimes I hear people say 'Oh, man, it keeps flowing and going by. I want to turn it off, dam it up.' For what? This is nature at it's best. The only people that I see damming it up, are the ones that want to profit off every drop for gain or power. But it shouldn't be that way. The Creator gave it to all of us, even the fish, the plants, the people that fly, for all of us to enjoy," he says with quiet reverence.

"When you say people that fly," I said. "I've heard that people living here had many powers that you wouldn't see outside this canyon.

"Yes."

"Back in your history? Even presently?"

"Yes. There is a lot of power here. The spirits, the shamanism, the medicine man, the singers, the drum keepers, the pipe carriers, the sweat lodge people, the fire man, all these different roles that these people had were, I would say, at level one. Then there is another level that is much higher than the one that has knowledge of the medicine that this plant is for venereal disease, this one is for diarrhea, or this one's for diabetes, for soreness, or this is for strep throat. That knowledge is at a lower level and that's kind of like the medicine man level. Then it goes to a different level where these practitioners have connections with the patterns of the climate, nature, the wind, how to bring floods or tornadoes. Then there is another level (gesture with one palm above the other, a few inches apart)."

"So at the second level, they actually learn to control the forces of nature?" I asked.

"Yes. The forces."

"So they can split the clouds? They can bring the rain?"

"Yes. And then it goes to another level where it breaks open another barrier where you can communicate with the spirit world," he says reverently, his hands open wide, three feet apart. "You can't attain that level until you've mastered these other levels and you have proven that you can take care of this knowledge and not abuse that knowledge for one's gain."

"So when they can see that you have learned how to manifest on the physical planet," I said, "how to control the forces of nature, but that you are not going to use that for selfishness or attack, then the ancestors and the other spiritual beings connect directly with that person?"

"Yes." he answered directly, a note of certainty in his voice.

"Is that still going on in the tribe now?" I asked.

"That experience people are having, especially the people that are descendants of the shaman, the practitioners, the medicine people, the singers, the chiefs, a lot of individuals that came from those spirits. The spirit that they had is still here. It didn't leave. Because the individual that was the powerful shaman, his spirit came down and is still here."

"And it is now starting to manifest through his direct relatives?" I asked.

"His relatives, one that is in each family, one that is going to be responsible, that has learned maturity, that is committed and dedicated to take this responsibility and live up to the charge that they now have the power, that what they have has to be protected as well. For me, I've seen some of the revelations come to me personally. Nineteen ninety-one was the year where the sacred Red Butte glowed like amber. That was an experience that I had that people would say, 'Ah you're crazy. Things like that don't happen.' "

"So the sacred Red Butte on top on the plateau was glowing?" I asked.

"It was glowing amber and this was like four in the morning as I was singing the Dawn Boy Song and that song was sung there by our grandma who lives forever now. I sang that and right after I finished singing, is when that butte glowed. I called to my wife and I was telling her get out - you got to see this - and she was trying to hurry the best she could but she did not get to see it. So I prayed that I needed the Creator to show my wife that there was a connection between me and Him and that there was a goal, that I was predestined to do certain things in my lifetime and I wanted the Creator to prove that to her. I know I am not supposed to play with that power that way, but the Creator approved that for me. Only with his permission it happened."

"Did He answer your prayer?" I asked, knowing that He had.

"Yes. One day we were over on the wall (gestures behind him across the stream), over near the falls. We live over by the falls and me, my daughter, my wife went over to gather some wood kindling for the fire. You know, each one gets the fire going and then I do my prayer for the offerings on top of the stove. We went to get some wood, some fire-starter, and there was adrenalin flowing through my body and it was so powerful, I knew something was going to happen that day and I knew that there was no doubt that what was going to happen that day was going to happen. And we went over, me, my wife and my oldest daughter, and started to gather wood but I stood there and looked over the ridge and there was a hawk flying around and I knew that it had something to do with what was going to happen that day. I kept looking up at that hawk and my wife was still picking up wood and kind of noticed me and said, 'What's wrong?' I said, 'Do you see that hawk over there?' She said, 'Yea,' and I said, 'I am going to make that hawk come over above me. Fifty feet above me, it's going to circle four times and I am going to talk to that hawk.' My wife had that 'Are-you-alright? Are-you-O.K.?' type of look but that didn't even faze me because the adrenalin that was flowing in my nerves and veins was so strong that I knew that I am going to prove something to you today and I don't care if you criticize or think something about me. You might think I am crazy but that didn't mean nothing. There was nobody on this planet that could have told me that, 'Ah, you don't know what you are talking about.' There was no one. I knew it was going to happen."

"I lifted up my arms like this," he continued, his arms full wide above his head, his voice reflected the same rapture he had experienced that day, "and my adrenalin was flowing and it was like a vacuum and I stood there like this and that hawk, that was almost a quarter mile away, flew and came right above me like I said it would. My wife saw that and she said, 'Whoa!' And my daughter was getting so excited she said, 'Look!' and I wasn't listening to them. I was hearing them but my concentration had to remain focused on what I was doing. I knew that they were seeing, witnessing something a lot of people don't witness these days. The power is here. It is still here. The shaman power is still here. For me, it's like to take that next step, that next level, is going to commit me more to not make any mistakes when I heal people because we are accountable for all our actions. If we abuse that power, then our relatives will start getting sick or death will come, even to myself."

"You know Bob Marley said if you can be corrupted you are corrupt," I said, enchanted by his story. "But that it is not a concern for you. From what I can sense, nothing would tempt you at this point in your life, at this stage of your evolution - not ego, not money, not power, not sex. What could ever tempt you to do anything but give back to the planet? So corruption is a non-issue, not because you're not having to resist temptations, but because you're not even tempted."

"Yes," he said, his voice relaxed. I sensed some healing had occurred for him. Maybe he needed someone to tell him what he already knew. "After that experience that my wife and my daughter witnessed, if I woke up at three o'clock in the morning and I told my wife I needed to go pray, she knows something is bothering me and something's going on, there is going to be an evil spirit in the community. It could even be death, could be one of our distant relatives. You feel those things. When it is death, you feel a part of you forgot something, something is missing. You know you have that feeling and it is strong. People have this globally but say it's just intuition or just say it's nothing."

"What I am beginning to think," I said, "is that when we started this journey, we never thought we would come and find out what Native Americans knew about One Love. We were working in Jamaica but we came here because of Bob Marley's connection. Even when we were first here three years ago or even last summer, it wasn't yet clear to us that we would write this book. We only decided we were going to do this book about six months ago. Then we could see that we were guided to the two tribes that were on their original land, most out of the way of the modern world and still reflecting the vibration of One Love. There is an innocence and an elegance and a humility in the Havasupai people that only outsiders who know what they are looking at can see. The Creator put you here. It's as if He was saying, 'I am going to put you down below. You are going to be the last one's the outside world gets to.' Many of you knew a time when most the vibes here were loving, caring, when you lived off the land and took care of each other in the ancient way - with almost no intrusion from the rest of the society. And if you were too young to know that time, you were raised by people who knew it."

"Yes," he said. "I saw dissension came in when people started getting barbed-wire fences. The law-and-order court started to change and especially passing laws and this started coming in and alcohol started coming in. It started causing friction among the families. I saw it as it started to come in the sixties, and that is when the families started to fight each other because of the different rules that were being applied to our culture. One would share their crops, one would gather a little kindling and take it to the elders or take spring water to the elders. All these practices still existed in the sixties until the law code started to change. And the new products came in. Someone once said when the white man came in they brought four white things with them: flour, sugar, lard and salt. And those are killers. There are good for you if you use it in certain ways, as offerings. You pray that it nourishes you. I think the main thing, no matter what food you are taking or sustaining yourself with, you need to give thanks for whatever it is. That food could be poison but it won't hurt you. It will nurture you because you recognize and give thanks to the Creator for what little you have."

"Me and my son were sitting on our steps," he continued, "and there was no one else there but me and my son. Little Sage was about four years old then but he could communicate with me. He said in Supai, 'Dad, why is it that the birds, the horses, the cats, the dogs, those guys, they never change their clothes? We always change our clothes or we buy the newest shampoo or the latest bar of soup or we're always trying to outdo each other. Why don't they ever change their clothes?' That made me think for a bit and I looked at this deep thought that he had and the best answer I could give him was that these creatures didn't have to go home to a refrigerator or a soft pillow or anything like that, but they were proud of what they had on and the Creator provided for them in spite of the conditions weatherwise - winter, spring, summer, fall - and yet they have a place to come to and they are really happy to be a part of the environment. Every time the birds sing, they teach us to be content with what we have. It's not about outdoing each other and having the latest Mercedes Benz or Cadillac or limo or whatever. Just be content with what you have. You have water. You have love. You have people before you that share these ways with you. You hear laughter. You hear music. You hear birds singing, the wind, the thunder. It is a lot to appreciate where you are at right now. I think that really taught my son a lot. So he never asked me for money (laughing) when he got older. He is shy to ask me for money and a lot of times when he chops wood for me and does what I ask him to, he doesn't have to ask me for money. All I do is say, 'Here is a ten or twenty dollar bill. Get yourself a burger or whatever you want to do.' I hope I am bringing him up in a good way."

"You are," I said. "As we've been talking, I've been thinking that the Hopi carry the strongest, purist ceremonial cycle and knowledge and wisdom but in many ways the Havasupai are not only the 'Guardians of the Heart of Mother Earth, you are also the 'Guardians of the Heart *Vibe* of Mother Earth.' No one has such a sweetness because you've been so removed. This is an inspiring place to live and you were brought up by people that loved you, where it was safe and you could play all day and fall asleep where you were and you didn't worry about crime or loneliness or bills. You were brought up in the Garden. Before the commercial culture and all that stuff started, this was as close to the Garden as it gets. Few have more of a connection to the Earth than Havasupai. No one is more removed from that commercial vibration than you. Everyone else is connected to a road to somewhere. I see that many have their health problems and I see the alcohol. I am not blind too that. A lot of this is because you have such a strong heart vibe, you're having problems functioning in the modern world. So you guys are very close *experientially* to the true Native American vibration."

"Because of that," I continued, "you are in a perfect position to pull above the insanity and heal yourself physically, emotionally and spiritually. I'm not talking about perfection. I'm talking about healing. Almost all other cultures are in a decline. The modern world is in a downhill slide. Some society needs to show how it's getting better and your tribe is in a good position to do that. The healing has already begun. The more you believe in your healing, the more healing will continue because just believing it, creates it. If you embrace this perception, you'll always think of yourself differently. The tribe would have a new vision of themselves. Maybe that's why we were sent. We can see from the outside what you may not be able to see as clearly from the inside. Even reading this book will be healing for the tribe. You have everything you need for your healing. You have conscious leadership and are isolated. You have a beautiful home and reggae music has become your drumbeat."

"That sounds pretty accurate," Roland said after some thought. "I think the people here related to Marley's music because of the message, the revelations, prophecies. That's how that fit in and then the relationship that we have with the plants, the wind and the water, the love that we have, not only the human kind of love, but the love that we have for the land, the wind, the birds, the grass and all the legends and stories we have of all these things. We're so close to them, more than the society that is in the red-yellow-green light, fast lane. Some of those people will read about it but they may never really understand the true spirit of love for the environment because their hearts, their minds, have been so poisoned by luxury and materialism and the competition mode that just having a little dirt on their pants like this (he takes some red dirt and smears it on his pants leg) is taboo. For us, it's natural. You come out of the sweat lodge and you just lay down on the sand. This is where I come from. This is where I'm going to go back to, but the spirit that is invisible, it's going to live forever. That's why that spirit that existed - shamanism, the songs - they're still here. It's just a matter of the right people that these spirits will manifest themselves again."

"So as people here become more conscious, they can work with them more?" I asked.

"Yes. It's like in a classroom. The teacher knows who is the best mathematician, the best speller, the best reader, the best artist, the best musician, the ones that whine a lot, the one that's disabled and the one that is the eldest in the class, to the youngest, the skinniest, the fattest. The teacher recognizes that as the group he is working with. And the Creator recognizes the human race like in a classroom, the same thing, which ones are whining more. And we see that even from here, living in this environment. We see the ones that are whining for this or sniveling for this or that. A lot of them are getting their ways and going back to what happened hundreds of years ago as part of their reason for whining. It's like a little baby in a family setting, like with my children. In my home, my young ones are perceiving me burning sage, keeping the fire going to warm the home. This is what we do to bring forth watermelon, corn, apple, plums, peaches, pears. They love those fruits and I always tell them that this is how I relate with Jesus Christ. When Jesus Christ said, 'The fruits of My spirit are like the fruits of your labors,' I can relate to that because the labor that I've done taking care and irrigating my apricot trees, my Alberta peaches, the plums, the pears, the grapes, the apples, all these things, all the years I've watched the water irrigate, moving it to the next tree, and watching it as it begins to ripen and it's harvest time again, you appreciate it more, and me as a gardener raising my children, nurturing them and trying to take care of them and teaching them and trying to keep poisons out of the garden, which is my children, my family. They're seeing me do this."

"It's a house full of love, isn't it?" I said.

"Yes. It is. It's like a little battle zone sometimes. It's like the climate. The weather changes. Sometimes it's stormy, sometimes its windy, sometimes it's flooding."

"And with nine people, you going to have people at different places in development - physically, emotionally, spiritually," I said thinking how much simpler it had been raising two daughters separated by seventeen years. "A loving home allows everyone to grow from wherever they start."

"That spirit that we were talking about earlier," he said, "the one that is ignorant, that doesn't have too much respect for other's feelings, how much rate of pay one's getting or how much they push someone who's getting four bucks an hour and they've got to work every minute of that hour, I think that spirit is beginning to come into this village. That's why we have the sweat lodge. That creates a buffer zone for all our people no matter if they're spiritual or not. They're still family and it also creates a buffer zone for all our visitors that come here, from abroad, overseas, people in the States, from small towns and the cities, wherever they are, all walks of life, they come through here. And whatever spirit they're bringing through here, whether it's an evil one, whether they're having AIDS in the family, whatever problems they're bring in, the spirits that we're praying to here will watch over our families that are here, including the people from the outside that are coming in that may be subject to others that are coming in that may create problems for them."

"These are things that are into the invisible level but we pray to that level so that there are no unseen spirits that may jeopardize those families that are walking this road like myself, Toby, Cleighton, Fidel, Bob, Goofy, Supai Waters - those of us that have chosen to walk the path of spirituality. Even if we have confrontation with these spirits coming across our path, our prayer is strong enough that it does not go into the family, especially the innocent ones, the young ones, the pure ones; the ones that don't know a dollar bill from a thousand dollar bill, that don't know the value yet. That's how society is right now. They can't decipher the value of water, the air, the land, all these good things. They're just using it. They're like a child. You know, you throw a dollar bill and a thousand dollar bill to a baby, they don't know which is more valuable. So people use everything up while they can benefit off of it and no matter who comes along, they'll clean it up. And that's the spirits that are coming in - the ignorant one. That's the one we're telling, 'Back off!' "

"It's coming into the tribal members?" I asked.

"It's coming into tribal people's minds. That's where these spirits come in, through the brain, through fashion, through music, through video, through attitudes. We're beginning to see that. I told Rex, Carletta,

Diana, the leaders, that now that we have all these different influences, different spirits coming in, it's up to us now to really, really pray and to pray from your heart and your mind with real sincerity about what you're saying because this *is* reality. It's not something that you do each day just so you show off to other people and say, 'Hey, Roland is doing his certain ceremony.' It's not an ego thing. This is *reality*. We must pray. It's universal. And we pray and acknowledge the Creator for everything, whether it brings good or bad. Let us learn from these two things and hope that our prayers are being heard by the Creator, God, Jesus, JAH, Allah, whatever name you give Him, whatever nationality or culture you are. It's still the same Being. It's still the same power that gives us the sun, the water, the air that we breath, that makes it all one."

"If you could find a way to help people transmute that spirit that is coming in," I said, "that could help many others on the outside who are having that same struggle."

"That reminds me that as a young man I felt that not having TV and luxuries, felt like we were poor. But now I feel that we are one of the richest tribes even though we don't have the gaming or cattle industries or anything like that. The beauty and nature that we have and being away from traffic and the mainstream, I realize that we have a treasure. I feel real proud and different from the way I felt as a youth. I feel so privileged and empowered by the Creator to continue keeping this place the way it is - natural, the way He made it."

"And you're doing a great job," I said.

"Yes. But it's hard at times when you have leaders that come in just for the dollars for their family. And it's hard to work with people that way. I just wrote a statement to the election board because I heard politics was sticking its ugly head in there. For me, it's not about politics. It's about working together and mending and healing each other, heading in the same direction to recleanse this place and re-purify and regenerate our consciousness to that level of spirituality. We may never go back to the bow and arrow and the ways our ancestors lived but *spiritually*, we can. That is one goal that I'm hoping that I can be an influence and be an example to the youths because I went through some really rough times when I was younger."

"You're right," I said. "We're not going to go back to the bow and arrow but the real problem is people's worldview, seeing themselves as separate from nature, from each other, from the Creator. We can heal that so that people see themselves as one with all that - as all indigenous people did and many still do. As people heal their mind and hearts, the problems get solved by infusing love into them. After all it was the lack of love that created them in the first place. And when a person heals their mind, *their* world will definitely show the results."

"Ho!' he said.

"By the way, Roland, I wanted to read you something from this book, *He Walked the America*," I said, taking the book out of my backpack. "It says that Jesus or a Christ-like prophet visited Havasupai long ago. Let me read it to you. 'To the land of the Havasu the Healer came one early dawn. Climbing down the steep trail into the Great Dividing Canyon, with the sunrise behind Him, they saw He of the White Robe coming. The flame of the dawn touched His golden sandals, and long before they saw him raise one arm in greeting, meaning Peace and Prosperity to You, they whispered to one another: 'He comes to us! The Great Tacobya! The Mighty Master Miracle Worker!' Then with the whole tribe watching, they saw him stop and tap a large rock in the midst of the desert dryness with his long staff, and behold, there gushed forth water. He stooped and drank from the Sacred Water which is still called the Spring of Tacobya.' Have you heard of this legend from your foreparents?"

"OHHHHHH!" he said slowly, softly. "AHHHHHH! Yes. My dad told me that there were stories of him coming here and that he hid some gold tablets underground and that these tablets told of his relationship with The Ones Before Us. The biblical teachings that people brought down here later are the same teachings that this individual taught the people when he came here. He taught the people that if they didn't treat this land, this Earth, with respect, then it was going to turn against us - the water, which is happening now through the floods, the wind, in the form of the tornadoes and hurricanes. It's turning against us because these people that have power, money, the corporations, the banks, whoever it is, they don't have roots. Their goals are not the like the goals of a Christian person or a hiker or someone that loves nature. Their goals are so different. There's a wall there and that wall can't be penetrated. This is what we're dealing with. That's why I keep saying prayers are like a defense. It's like a force-field around you all the time. Like I tell my kids, 'Don't forget there's these angels that are with you all the time. There's these warriors, too. It's not only Jesus that you pray to or God but you pray and let these guys know that, 'Hey. Help me out. Sometimes I have problems with a bully or something. Do something.' "

"Do most of the tribe know that your foreparents said this person came here? Is that common knowledge in the tribe?" I asked, curious as to how vibrant this legend still was.

"I think to most of the elders, that's common knowledge, to some people my age and back," he said. "If they were told and taught that, it would be common knowledge to them."

"Is their anything else you want to say for the book?" I said, sensing the reasoning had come to a close. He had a big work load and a tribal member had come up to start the fire for the sweat lodge.

"I want to emphasize, like I do with the children, that no matter how your prayer is, *when* you pray doesn't matter. It doesn't have to be right at daybreak. That's a practice that our people did years ago. Thousands of years ago, they'd rise before the sunrise. That would be a plus but the main thing is that you acknowledge your Creator for what you have, no matter where you are. When you pray, doesn't matter. There's no one way that I was taught by my spiritual leaders, the different elders like Lakota, the holy medicine people, people on the peyote road, but I was taught by these people that there's no one correct way. It ain't like you have to carry a pipe to make your presence known or wear a certain shirt or sit in a certain spot like a vortex point. It doesn't have to be there. The Creator's everywhere. The wind blows everywhere. The sun shines everywhere. He's everywhere. I would just emphasize, no matter who you are, how much trouble you've made in your lifetime, just say a prayer for yourself and your family and the environment that continues to sustain us as a human race, the love that some of us have given to this place. This Mother Earth deserves the respect that we all have shared with each other, respect for the environment, for one's culture. That's all I ask. Thank you very much for permitting me to share this knowledge with you.

Many blessings."

As we wandered back to the village, we saw Supai Waters near the lodge. He was taking a lunch break from his job. He had been working for a few weeks helping cleanup solid waste, especially broken appliances which would be transported by helicopter out of the canyon.

"I'm on another journey," I said to him, both of us glad to see each other. Julia and I had come to love him like a brother and felt relaxed in his presence, even on several days travel with him sleeping on the floor of our motel room. "I'm going to see Radford and Dawn and I'm going to go to Chaco Canyon and Canyon de Chelly. I'll be out for five days. Want to join me?"

"Yes, I," he responded, using the Rasta term, "I," meaning the "divinity within," "let me get my knapsack."

We walked to a nearby shed and he got his small, almost-empty knapsack and we headed out to the helicopter pad. *Incredible*, I thought. *All he needs for five days travel is the clothes on his back and that knapsack.*

After a night at the Hotel Monte Vista in Flagstaff, we headed east a few hours to visit Chaco Canyon, an area of several ancient Anasazi ruins. I had been wanting to visit the canyon since I saw a PBS special on it several years before. What it presented was that whoever built these villages had a very high level of sophistication and knowledge.

Until recently, the ruins were thought to be just more ancient abandoned villages like hundreds of others that are spread over the Southwest. In 1977, an American artist, Anna Sofaer, was visiting the area near the summer solstice. Quite by chance, she happened to notice a spiral drawn on a rock face hidden behind three large slabs of sandstone. Around noon, a dagger of sunlight created by the space between the slabs exactly split the spiral. Her discovery of this "sun dagger" lead her to spend over two decades researching the ruins of the many villages of Chaco Canyon.

Over the years, she discovered that these ruins, built between 850 and 1150AD, comprised not only impressive architectural feats, but also served as a vast astronomical reckoning system as well. Even the small spiral she initially discovered, proved to not only capture the sun's cycle but the complex moon cycle as well. No other ancient astronomers were known to use such a lunar device. Eventually, many of the villages that dot the canyon were professionally surveyed and what was revealed was astonishing. It is now accepted that these villages were erected with the same accuracy and celestial understanding as Stonehenge in England and the Great Pyramid on the Gaza Plain in Egypt.

The main three-acre, D-shaped village, Pueblo Bonito, was a series of four-story houses surrounding a central plaza with over 3000 rooms that could have housed over 6,000 people. It took over 250 years and 12 generations to build. It involved cutting and hauling thousands of tons of rocks from the mesa above and carrying over 225,000 large timbers by foot from 50 to 70 miles away. Thirty-foot wide roads, probably for trade, span out from the ruins, covering an area of over 95,000 square miles. One main road ends at a deep canyon. It is thought that this represents their returning home to their place of emergence.

Given the lack of windows for light and ventilation in many of the rooms and the scarcity of hearths, graves or trash mounds, it is believed that the village of Pueblo Bonito may have been more of a ceremonial village than a fulltime residence. This is further supported by the 15 subterranean "great kivas" in the village, some holding up to 400 people, and the 100 smaller kivas, holding between 50 to 100 people.

The survey further revealed that many of the main walls in the villages are aligned along an exact north-south or east-west axis. Others are aligned to the solar or lunar cycles (these buildings are the only ones on earth except Stonehenge known to align to the moon cycles). It is as if the builders were trying to impose the orderliness of the heavens onto the earth. It was also discovered that the villages were not only part of a grand astronomical design but that they were also exactly aligned with each other, a feat that took seemingly impossible surveying work that involved calculating location of villages miles apart and separated by huge cliffs and mesas.

What is even more unusual, is that around 1150AD, after 250 years of building the complexes, the people abandoned all their efforts in an orderly and efficient manner. They sealed up all the openings with fine masonry work and disassembled the massive kiva roofs and burned the timbers inside the kivas, an effort that is thought to rival the actual construction of the kivas. From then on, no one ever built in this grand Chacoan style.

It is hard to understand how a civilization without even the wheel could have built these precise celestially-oriented villages. The buildings, along with the associated Chacoan roads, ramps, dams, and mounds, required a great deal of well-organized and skillful planning, designing, resource gathering, and construction. These ancient people combined pre-planned architectural designs, astronomical alignments, geometry, landscaping, and engineering to create an ancient spectacular urban and ceremonial center - one that still amazes and inspires us a thousand years later.

Archaeologists do not know who the Chocoans were or why they left. Enemy attack? Crop failure? Drought? However, the Hopi believe this was their last stop of their millennia-long migrations before their final arrival in Hopiland. As during all their migrations, they believe they were guided to leave Chaco Canyon and continue migrating. Their view is supported by the fact that it was only a few years *after* the abandonment of Chaco Canyon, that the Hopi arrived in Hopiland where the morning star appeared to them - their long-awaited sign that Maasaw had promised them at their Emergence.

As Supai Waters and I walked around the Pueblo Bonito, a foreboding site that almost overwhelms you, I noticed he looked rather tense.

"What's going on with you?" I asked.

"Something heavy happened here," he said thoughtfully. "It's O.K. I have said a prayer of protection."

"Maybe this is where the Hopi came to connect with the *kachinas*, the spirit guides. I read many Hopi believe that the villages were abandoned because the leaders had begun to misuse the powers that they had developed," I said.

"That is the vibe I am getting," he said.

"What do you think of the book so far?" I asked as we sat in the central plaza of the ruins. I had sent him the manuscript a few weeks earlier.

"It's very strong, very full," he said and then lapsed into his comfortable silence. Just five words but all I needed to know everything he was thinking on the matter.

From Chaco Canyon we headed to Canyon de Chelly, a two-hour drive west. That night we stayed at another historic inn, the Thunderbird Lodge, at the entrance to the canyon and the site of the original trading post in the area. I had wanted to visit Canyon de Chelly for several years after we started to listen to the music of Native American flutist, Travis Terry, especially his CD "Echoes of the Canyon Wall." Travis, a member of the Gila River Pima Nation, now lives in Chinle at the canyon's entrance. I had read on his CD cover that he credits Canyon de Chelly as the inspiration for his beautiful, almost-transcendent flute music, as well as being the place where he met another of his inspirations, his Navajo wife, Cara.

"I've been thinking that when this book is ready," I said to Supai Waters that night over dinner, "I'd like to put on a concert in Hopiland and give the tribe hundreds of books. We'll invite your tribe and give them books, too. I think it will really help when they see themselves through our eyes. This time I'd like to use Native American conscious artists. I'd invite Casper and the 602 Band, Uproot, Travis Terry, Tchiya Amet, and others."

"That would be good," Supai Waters said. "They are our people. We need to hear their voices more."

"What would you be eating back in the canyon tonight?" I asked as I looked at his meal of roast beef, bread, squash, potatoes, cake, coffee and a small bowl of red beans. For over two decades, Supai Waters had been living either under the stars or in a small tent on his family's land in the village.

Without a word, he tapped the bowl of beans twice and continued eating with relish.

"What would you do after supper?" I asked.

"This time of year, I'd crawl in my tent and get in my sleeping bag and read for a while. In the summer, I'd get *on* my sleeping bag," he replied and we laughed together. "But when I get back, I'm setting up a full-size tipi. It's the one my friend brought me at our concert last summer."

"If you could change anything about your life," I asked him, as we wandered the property after dinner, "what would it be?"

"Nothing."

I thought, *Here's a guy with no money, no home, no job, almost no posses-sions, who's been living in a small tent in the Grand Canyon for years, and yet he wants nothing. He has less than anyone I know and yet he wants less than anyone I know.*

The next morning, we took a four-hour jeep tour from the lodge into the canyon, the only way to view it from within unless you get a special permit. There are no roads or utilities in the canyon, just sand washes that you can maneuver only with a four-wheel drive vehicle. Canyon de Chelly is considered by many as one of the most beautiful canyons in the world, a reputation that is well-earned. This comparatively little-known canyon, comprised entirely of Navajo Tribal Trust, is one of the longest continu-ously inhabited landscapes in North America and still sustains a community of Navajo people, most of whom farm and herd during the summer on the valley floor, which is green and fertile all year round. The canyon's sheer beauty and the protective feel of its high red and orange rocky walls, easily explains why it has been inhabited for so long. Other than this beauty, its primary attractions are cliff ruins of Indian villages built between 350 and 1300 AD.

About two hours into the tour, we stopped at a small rest area with some clean outhouses, a small snack-bar and six or eight craftespeople selling their wares. As I looked around, I heard one of Travis Terry's CDs playing on a portable player on a table where a tall Native American man was selling the CDs and beautiful handmade flutes.

"I'd like to buy these two CDs," I said to him, finding two we did not have.

"Would you like me to sign them for you?" he asked.

"Are you Travis Terry," I said quickly looking up at him for the first time and then down at the picture on the CD cover. He was a handsome, powerful-looking man with a long jet-black ponytail and smiling eyes.

"Yes. I'm Travis," he said, laughing.

"What a pleasure to meet you!" I said, enthusiastically. "My wife and I have been listening to your music for years. Its one of the musical backdrops of our lives."

I told him about the One Love Concerts we had been hosting and asked if he'd like to perform at the next one in Hopiland.

"I'd love that," he responded. "I've got a full band. Just let me know when."

"This is my friend, Supai Waters, from Supai," I said as Supai Waters wandered over.

"I remember going into your village when I was a kid," Travis said. "They were showing Elvis Presley movies on a sheet with an old projector run off a generator. I loved it."

"I was probably sitting next to you that night," Supai Waters said laughing.

After buying the CDs and a flute for Julia, we headed out for the rest of our tour conducted by a Navajo man, David, who had been taking guests through the canyon for over twenty years. By mid-afternoon we left the canyon and were on the road to Hopiland, about a two-hour drive west. As we drove across the reservation toward the lodge at the Hopi Cultural Center, I noticed a thin Hopi man walking along side of the road with a cane and what looked to be a heavy bag of groceries. We stopped and offered him a ride.

"How's it been spending your life out here?" I asked after brief introductions. He looked to be in his late fifties, thin and fit except for a limp.

"Not bad, I guess," he answered. "Could have been better. When I was a kid they took me away and put me in elementary school. I hated it. Then I got to come home but they sent me away again to high school. I was so lonely, I just kind of snapped and kept running away. I walked home, over a hundred miles, but they caught me and sent me back."

"Have you been here since after high school?" I asked.

"No. I was drafted in the Vietnam War. I did two tours there. It was hell. A mine blew up and smashed my hand and leg. Been having problems with it ever since. They gave me a medal. I've been here since they discharged me after the accident. It was the white man's schools and the white man's war that caused me my pain. I'll never leave home again."

We dropped him at his home in Second Mesa and checked in the lodge. I called Karen Abieta to see about getting together for dinner that night. It was Friday and we weren't meeting with Radford until Sunday.

"I'm glad you called," she said as we ate together at the Cultural Center's restaurant. "I'm on the air tonight. Come on down and hear some good reggae. Also tomorrow is the Women's Basket Dance in Second Mesa. You and Supai Waters can come as my guests. It starts at dawn and goes to dusk but come anytime. It's a social dance and it's open to visitors. Only the Kachina Dances are closed."

(Author's note: If you go to Hopiland and want to attend any of their ceremonies, be sure you ask at the Hopi Cultural Center first. Many are closed to outsiders. You should also check even before visiting their villages, as each village has its own visitor rules. No photos, videos or sketching is allowed in the villages. Also, please respect the privacy of the people in this book. Should you desire to contact them, please do so through us at the contact info at the front of the book. We always love to hear from our readers.)

After dinner, we joined her at the station for a few hours, talking between some great reggae music. Back at the motel room, Supai Waters and I watched *Gandhi* on a small portable DVD player I travel with. I had brought the movie with me as it is always inspiring to watch his story. Supai Waters knew little of Gandhi and his life.

"It was good to watch that," he said as we got in our beds after the movie. "I learned something. He didn't hate the English that had oppressed his people for so long. He made friends with all the English leaders he dealt with but still told them they had to leave. He never used violence and trusted that the Creator would settle things if he didn't. He is a good teacher for Native Americans."

"Gandhi really understood that the people who we think are our enemies, are really our best teachers," I said, cutting out the light. "More than our friends, they teach us to love and forgive."

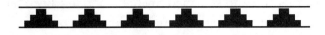

Around mid-morning the next day, we headed over to Second Mesa, home of three Hopi villages: Mishongnovi, Sipaulovi, and Radford's home village and the most traditional of all Hopi villages, Shungopavi, the "Mother Village." Mishongnovi and Sipaulovi, separated by only a few hundred yards, occupy the east-most edge of the mesa-top, while Shungopavi is located southwest of these two villages about a mile away, also atop the mesa. Though Mishongnovi and Sipaulovi, like the other Hopi villages, have representation on the Hopi Tribal Council, Shungopavi, by its own choice, does not. It operates under their ancient traditional system and is governed by a *kikmongwi* or village leader.

The Women's Basket Dance (the English name for their ceremony) is performed in several Hopi villages in the late fall. That day it was being held in the village plaza at Sipaulovi. Baskets themselves are sacred to the tribe and Hopi baskets are considered some of the finest indigenous art in the world. Made from all natural vegetation grown on or near the mesas, they are colorful, with intricate designs of humans, animals, the earth, *kachinas*, the sun and moon. The basket weavers of Second Mesa specialize in coiled baskets; basket weavers on Third Mesa on wicker basket and on First Mesa, where basket weaving was never extensive, it is mostly plaited basket. The knowledge of the weaving is past down through the women - from mother to daughter, from grandmother to granddaughter, from clan mother to clan daughter.

Baskets are used in many of their ceremonies, often holding sacred cornmeal, prayer sticks and prayer feathers or *pahos*. Though they are also used for utilitarian purposes such as the gathering, sifting, storage, drying and preparation of food, like almost all things Hopi, the baskets significance goes to many levels. Indeed, they are called "sacred baskets" or "sacred trays" in their language.

The fibers of the baskets represent the many fibers that hold Hopi life together as a cohesive tribe. To the Hopi, the basket is a sign of generosity and love between individuals, clans, villages and religious societies. They are an integral part of their social interactions. A bride will weave a basket for her husband which he will keep his entire life and it will be buried with him. Gifts of baskets are offered to initiate, strengthen or heal human relationships. It is an art form that creates strong human and social bonds.

The Women's Basket Dance involves the women's societies in several villages (for the most part, women's and men's ceremonies are kept separate, both to avoid the distraction of sex and because some of the men's rituals are physically strenuous, involving up to four nights with no sleep and thought to be too intense physically for the women). Like all components of the Hopi Ceremonial Cycle, extensive and enjoyable preparation is involved. For months beforehand, the baskets and plaques are woven and new initiates are taught the rituals and the meaning of the ceremony. In this case, the central theme is generosity. Secret rituals are held for several days before the dance. The night before, the women retreat into their kivas for fasting and prayer. Though solemn, it is also a festive, playful time for them as innocent kidding and playing is a constant among the Hopi, no matter how sacred their task. It is the social lubricant that has helped them live peacefully, packed so closely together in small villages surrounded by a demanding environment. At dawn, they emerge from their underground kivas and proceed into the village's central plaza, where hundreds of their clan and tribal members anxiously await their arrival.

By the time we arrived at Second Mesa in mid-morning, the cliff-top village was crowded and we parked our car about half way up and walked the rest of the way. Approaching the central plaza, we spotted Karen on the roof of one of the rows of low-slung houses that border and surround the plaza. Each row belongs to a separate clan. They are built from local stone or from concrete blocks covered with a stucco facing. Like Hotevilla, where the Butterfly Dance was held two months earlier, this village too looked ancient - complete with its narrow dirt lanes and see-forever cliff-top views. As we passed by a window, I looked inside. There in the clean, well-lit large kitchen area was a table full of food - mutton stew, chicken, homemade bread, corn, piki bread, squash, fry bread, beans, desserts - surrounded by fifteen or twenty clan members, all involved in an animated and playful conversation. It was a warm and welcoming scene.

From our rooftop perch with Karen and her daughter, Faye, we had a great view of the plaza ten feet below. It was about the size of a small basketball court with the ground worn down to solid rock with centuries of ceremonies exactly like the one we were about to witness. There looked to be about 200 people in the plaza, mostly men, teenage boys and young adults. On the rooftops, there were maybe another 200 people, mostly women, elderly, and young children. I soon discovered why these group were separated.

When we got settled, I noticed that some men were carrying in very large boxes and garbage bags and placing them in the center of the plaza, which was clear and open. I couldn't tell what was in them. This continued until there were six to eight bags and boxes. When this was completed, I heard a stirring coming from my right. Immediately, the crowd grew quiet, reverent. Then the women dancers started to file into the center from a lane between two rows of clan houses.

Around thirty women filed in, with the youngest first, around five or six, then the oldest, perhaps in their eighties, maybe nineties. Each was wearing a beautiful traditional dress covered with a red, black and white cape. Each was carrying a beautiful woven plaque, facing out, their hands on either side. They were powerful, strong women - secure in their reverence, secure in their ceremony, secure in their tribal world. Unlike my world, this was a matri-linear world where the female and her ability to create new life is still held sacred.

They walked in and formed an oval in the center, with their plaques facing in. On an silent signal from one of the elders, they began their slow rhythmic dance with a quiet, peaceful chant, their feet caressing the Earth with small tight steps. Their somber dances and songs continued for a long time. It was like a meditation, soothing your mind and body. With downcast eyes and soft feminine voices, they sang while slowly raising and lowering their baskets in recognition of the four directions, their up and down arm motions symbolically shaking down the much-needed snow.

No one spoke or moved, the only sound the young children playing happily in the background. I looked around the crowd. Except for one other young woman and middle-aged man, I was the only white in the crowd but I felt welcomed. Their dance continued for a half-hour, maybe longer. It was mesmerizing and I had lost my sense of time. Then again as if on some unspoken cue, four of the women wearing distinctive head-dresses and carrying feathers, peeled out of the circle and started loading their baskets with things from the large boxes and bags. A low murmur of excitement went through the crowd. Then something amazing happened!

The four women turned toward the crowd and started throwing things - plastic bowls and spatulas, boxes of cornbread mix, macaroni and cheese, and Brillo pads, rolls of toilet paper, soap, kitchen utensils, pie-pans, boxes of matches, every small, inexpensive household item imaginable - and the crowd erupted in joyful glee, each striving to catch a prize. Things were getting thrown in every direction, into the crowd in the plaza and on the rooftops. Sometimes they would fake a throw in one direction and throw it in another, all to the delight of the crowd. With the younger men in the plaza, it was a mad, but good-natured, scramble for everything. A teenage boy would hold up a plastic spatula as if he had caught the game ball at the World Series.

Every now and then, they would throw out a handmade basket that might sell for a thousand dollars in a local shop. Occasionally, the women would go into the crowd and place a gift, maybe even a priceless hand-made piece of pottery, in the hands of an elder, someone in a wheelchair, or a young child or a favored man, usually eliciting good-natured "boos" from the excited crowd. And all the time, the other women continued their slow, mesmerizing singing and dancing. It was symbolic of what indigenous women do everywhere, keeping the peace and staying focused on their sacred daily tasks while the young men fight, often needlessly.

Another thing that amazed me was that a strange social protocol was observed by everyone. The taller people were in the back and the shorter ones were in the front. Except for the young boys and men, who jostled and kidded each other for everything that came their way, no one was greedy, grabbing something from the winner's hand once it was caught. This was especially true on the rooftop, where pushing and shoving could have lead to a fall. And no matter who finally claimed the prize, their success was greeted by laughter and applause from everyone. People stored their catches nearby with no thought to theft.

I had never seen so many people of all ages have such innocent fun - non-commercially, non-electronically, and simply. This went on for over an hour. It was one of several "giveaways" of the day. Similar ceremonies are common among Native American tribes. Coming as it did right after the harvest and before the winter, in former times, the Basket Dances helped to distribute much-needed provisions so everyone could make it through the cold months. In addition to celebrating generosity, they serve as a leveling effect, keeping everyone in more or less the same economic status - a condition valued by many tribes. These ceremonies were about generosity, in *many* forms - between friends, between strangers, between clan members and relatives, and especially to the very young, old, and sick. As you struggled for the prize you wanted, you also had to be kind and generous, allowing others a fair opportunity and quickly conceding with a "good heart."

"Let's go over to my cousin and get some lunch," Supai Waters said around mid-day. "He lives next door at Mishongnovi."

"I didn't know you had relatives here," I said as we walked over.

"Yes," he replied. "There are many Havasupais here. I spent a lot of my youth here. This place is a source of strength, of power. When I was going astray, being here would pull me back."

"Do the Supais have ceremonies like these?" I asked.

"We used to, but now everyone watches the golden calf - the TV," Supai Waters said laughing.

"Are there any special days there to look forward to? Do you celebrate Christmas or Easter or New Year's Eve?" I asked. "Everyone needs celebrations to look forward to, especially the kids."

"We do no ceremonies in the canyon but the sweats. The Hopi are holding our dances and songs for us - over fifty of them. When we are ready, they will teach them to us."

We wandered over to his relative's house, a simple two-room stone home, comfortable and clean. The view from the front porch was awesome. It had electricity and running waters but I noticed outhouses in an area below. Several pictures of relatives in military uniforms hung on the walls. His cousin lived with his mother - kind, humble people, glad to have unexpected guests. After lunch at his cousin's of mutton stew and homemade bread, we decided to drive over to Walpi to tour the village. Walpi is one of the three villages on top of First Mesa, the other two being Tewa and Sichomovi. Polacca is a Tewa village at the bottom of First Mesa.

Walpi is the oldest village at First Mesa and was established in 1690 when a village at the foot of the mesa, Koechaptevela, was abandoned out of fear of Spanish reprisals for the 1680 Pueblo Revolt. Though both Walpi and Sichmovi have representatives on the Hopi Tribal Council, they are governed by the same *kikmongwi* in the traditional style of Hopi government. Walpi recently underwent restoration to preserve the beauty of the village and to make it safer for residents to live and perform their religious ceremonies. Visitors are allowed to tour the village only with a Hopi guide that meets you next door at the Sichomovi Community Development Hall.

As we waited for the guide to take us on tour, I read the Walpi mission statement:

Walpi's mission is to create a dignified participatory environment from which emanates consensual community values as a covenant to meeting feasible village jurisdictional needs while protecting and preserving the cultural and natural environments. Walpi will strive towards finding a delicate balance to co-existing with other Hopi villages, the central government and global world to accomplish what is manifested in our destiny.

I also bought a beautiful *kachina* doll from a women selling them off a blanket on the porch. These dolls have no spiritual powers as such but are used to familiarize the Hopi children with the different *kachinas*, of which there are over two hundred and fifty. Some of these hand-carved dolls are sold for thousands of dollars.

After a few minutes, our guide showed up, a twenty-something Hopi man who had recently returned from living off the reservation. The tour consisted of myself, Supai Waters and three people from Paris who did not speak English but seemed fascinated by all they saw - as we were. In a way this worked well. For the most part, we slowly toured the village in quiet reverence, broken only by our guide's occasional comments.

Walpi is the most pristine of the Hopi villages, with cliff-edge houses and vast scenic vistas. From Sichmovi, you enter Walpi by crossing a fifteen-foot wide, two-hundred foot long walkway with sheer drops on both sides. There are no utilities in Walpi but a small bathhouse has recently been built on the Sichmovi side of the walkway. The entire village is maybe a hundred and fifty yards long and fifty yards wide, perched precariously on its narrow rock ledge with steep, dangerous drop-offs on all sides. A natural stone fifteen-foot wide lane circles the village and widens on one side where the kiva and ceremonial plaza are located. Steep stone steps are carved into the rocks for access to the gardens and orchards far below.

Walpi is the only ancient Hopi village totally untouched by modern times. Even in ancient Oraibi, which also has no utilities, there are the occasional signs of modernity like a television antennae, a generator or a vehicle. There is none of that in Walpi. The multi-level stone houses seem to grow out of their rock base and are stacked several stories high around a central courtyard. For safety, strong walls were constructed without ground-level openings.

The houses, the kivas, the small cliffside ceremonial plaza, have been restored and look exactly as they have looked for hundreds of years. There is no garbage or debris around, no plastic jugs or food boxes or metal gas cans to bring you back to the present reality. There is only a deep sense of power and antiquity merging together. It is very roots, very ancient, and perhaps this is why there are only five elderly fulltime residents.

We stopped at the home of one of the residents who looked to be in her eighties or nineties, with lots of energy, smiling eyes and a friendly, welcoming vibe. She invited us all in her small dwelling which was amazingly clean and light inside with whitewashed walls, a woodstove, kerosene lamps and a new vinyl floor. It was comfortable and welcoming. I could see myself living there. She lived alone and was selling small pieces of pottery she had made. When she told us she needed money to buy wood for the winter, I bought several pieces knowing they would make great gifts for friends back home.

"That's my grandmother," our guide said after we left. "Sometimes she can be a pain but I love her. I live next door in Sichomovi and she comes to get me whenever she needs anything. I guess I'll be carrying her fire wood soon."

"How do you like living up here?" I asked, wondering how a young person who had experienced the modern world would handle such isolation and lack of stimulation. "What do you do at night?"

"I love it here," he replied with enthusiasm. "It's great. At night I read or write or play music and there are always neighbors to visit. It's never lonely or boring. I may never leave."

As we headed back to the community center, there was a middle-aged Hopi couple on the walkway connecting the two villages. They were scouring the desert floor below with binoculars. Our guide spoke to them in Hopi and they all laughed.

"What was that about?" I asked.

"They're my clan relatives. They lost two sheep so they drove up here to look for them. They found them and they invited me over for mutton stew tomorrow."

Just another everyday interaction in a cliff-top village in the Center of the Universe, I thought.

We headed back over to the dance and as we pulled in our parking spot halfway up, we saw about twenty people shouting encouragement to the runners who were nearing their destination in the plaza. They had begun their run hours earlier twelve miles away on the desert floor. The most grueling part was the last few miles uphill on the very steep grade. In the past, and in some cases even today, Hopi are famous for their running stamina. It was said that before the tribe had trucks and cars, men would run from Third Mesa to Moencopi and back each day to water their gardens there - a roundtrip distance of almost one hundred miles!

As we rejoined Karen on the rooftop, we noticed that the women dancers were temporarily gone and in the cleared center of the plaza was a row of handmade plaques and beautiful store-bought Indian blankets - a prize for each runner. As each runner came into the plaza, they proudly claimed their prize to the applause and shouts of approval of the crowd. The youngest runner looked to be around ten; the oldest in his seventies.

"That's quite a feat," I said to Karen, as we settled near her. "I was winded just walking up half the hill."

"Running is very important here," she said. "I am training for the

2006 H2OPI Run to Mexico City this March. Runners from all the Hopi villages will run some 2,000 miles. We'll start in Moencopi and run through all the villages, through New Mexico, then Texas and finally into Mexico. We will run for two weeks until we reach Mexico City where the Fourth Water World Symposium is underway. I have been preparing myself physically, spiritually and mentally for this run."

"Why are you going to the symposium?" I asked.

"Water is life," she answered, "and sustains all life. We are delivering a message of water. Also, there are many Hopi clan migration symbols in Mexico. The youngest runner will be twelve, the oldest in his late seventies. To see this elder run along with us during our training as a team and to feel his vibes is heartwarming. He is always smiling even when he is running. We are all one big family, related somehow. As you are being dropped off on the side of the road, runners in the back of the truck are encouraging and yelling, 'Hopi, push yourself! Use your strength! Don't give up! Thank you! Qwah, qwah! Es-kwa-li!' They are thanking you for getting ready to run and thanking you for just finishing your run. Down the road, they thank us again for our next run as we await the ear of corn we carry as our baton. As I run, I think of Hopi prayers and I also sing the Luciano song, 'Lord give me strength to face another day. Give me strength, Oh Jah, to carry on.' This is the most amazing and spiritual relay. Makes you want more."

After the runners received their prizes, someone took out a one-foot diameter inflated rubber ball and a new game began. The object was to keep the ball from hitting the ground and the hundreds of people made up one huge co-operative team. The ball would be hit from rooftop to courtyard and all around with anyone welcome to try to keep it in the air. If it hit the ground everyone let out a collective "AHHHHHH!" If someone made a good save, everyone applauded and shouted their thanks. This went on for well over an hour until the dancers returned. Here were hundreds of people having a great time with *their* people, on *their* land, with a cheap fifty-nine cent ball. As far as I could tell, everyone was in a "good heart" at this ceremony - just as they had been instructed to be in *all* their ceremonies.

As I watched their game, I began to see that even this seemingly

simple activity was part of their sacred cycle. It was teaching cooperation, not competition. Unlike most ball games, there were no winners and
losers, no stars and weak players, no score to make you feel worthy or
inadequate. It was inclusive, never exclusive. All could play with equal skill
- young and old, healthy and sick, male and female - and every tribal
member was needed and every tribal member was necessary. Everyone was
responsible to keep the ball in the air and no one was responsible.

This was the second public ceremony I had witnessed and I was
beginning to feel the incredible power and clarity of their Ceremonial
Cycle. It is the heart and soul of their tribe and of their religion - a religion that the Creator's messenger, Maasaw, instructed them never to
abandon. Incorporated in this mystical and moving cycle was thought to
be their history and all human wisdom, expressed in easily understandable presentations of dance, song and drumming, each accompanied by
a sacred - and fun - preparation period of costume making, basket
weaving, initiate instruction, transfer of knowledge from the elders and
the kachinas, and finally prayer and fasting.

It reflected a system of thought and activity always honoring the
Creator and centering on respect for life and everyone being happy
together and never losing sight of the love of all beings. Like the ball is
kept in the air, everyone has a part to play.

As Frank Waters writes of these ceremonies in his Book of the Hopi:

What they tell is the story of their creation and their emergence
from previous worlds, their migration over this continent, and the
meaning of their ceremonies. It is a worldview of life, deeply religious in nature, whose esoteric meaning they have kept inviolate
for generations uncounted. Their existence always has been
patterned upon the universal plan of world creation and maintenance, and their progress on the evolutionary Road of Life
depends upon the unbroken observance of its laws. In turn, the
purpose of their religious ceremonies is to help maintain the
harmony of the universe. It is a mytho religious system of year-
long ceremonies, rituals, dances, songs, recitations, and prayers as
complex, abstract and esoteric as any in the world. They remind

us we must attune ourselves to the need for inner change if we are
to avert cataclysmic rupture between our own minds and hearts.

Every village had their own cycle and every clan was responsible for
a part of the cycle. Each person over five that chose to be initiated, had
a specific part to play in a ceremony - their own personal piece of this
ancient and consecrated Cycle. Almost every week, part of the Ceremonial
Cycle was being expressed somewhere on the reservation. In the Mother
Village of Shungopavi, the Ceremonial Cycle has endured almost
completely intact for almost a millennium. Above all else, it was a
reminder of their Covenant with the Creator - to stay on this land and
practice their religion and become Hopi, the Peaceful People, and to do
this for all humanity.

The next morning, Supai Waters and I drove the short distance from
the lodge to Hotevilla to meet with Radford and his family. As we drove
over, I felt a peaceful sense of excitement to be with them again. I had
come to feel very bonded to them, as a family and as individuals -
Radford's wisdom and clarity, Lorna's quiet calm and ever-present support
for her family, Dawn's passion and her heartfelt commitment to help
her people, Duane's vigilant aura of protection and concern, and Rad's
joyous playfulness and innocence.

On the way, we stopped at the small store in Kykotsmovi to pickup
some groceries as a gift.

"Do you think we should see if Radford wants to go outside for this
reasoning," I asked Supai Waters as we drove over. "It would look better
on the video."

"Don't break his circle," he answered.

I had also brought some small colorful bags made by Tibetan monks
in exile in India. In a phone conversation a few weeks earlier with Radford,
I had asked him who were the other people that were holding the planet
in balance.

"I don't know," he answered, "but we feel very close to the Tibetan

Buddhist Monks."

The next day, Tami Parnell, a friend of ours and a big-hearted teacher at our local university who is always challenging her students worldview (and the editor of this book), called to invite us to a nearby small college, where several Tibetan Buddhist monks were completing five days of lecturing and the construction of a huge sand mandala. To represent the transient quality of all life, the mandala was to be swept into a pile of colored sand and ceremoniously emptied into a nearby river once it was completed. There we met Geshe Gelek Chdha, one of the four monks. We talked to him about our journey through Jamaica and Native America and gifted him a copy of *The Gathering of the Healers*. We told him what Radford had said about feeling very close to the Tibetan monks.

"That is interesting," he said. "When we were in New Mexico, we visited a lake. We had a vision of a tribe of people praying around the lake. They looked just like us! Later that day we found out that the lake was sacred to the Pueblo Indians near Taos. I've seen pictures of the Havasupai. They look just like my relatives."

The small bags we gave to Radford's family were made and sold by them to help support their "Peace Tour" or "Shiwa Tour" - a tour that presented their wisdom as a gift to the world. By now, we had come to see people like him and Radford's family and Roland and Supai Waters and so many of the Jamaican people we worked with as fellow teachers of love - each with our own assignment and yet connected together in an often unrecognized worldwide spiritual network. When we meet, there is a happy recognition that often leads to working supportively together and sharing knowledge that might be useful to each other. As we drove to Radford's, I looked forward to more of this sharing.

After warm greetings, we settled in their comfortable living room. Only Lorna, Radford and Dawn were there. Duane and Rad were in Flagstaff where Duane was attending North Arizona State University. It felt good to be back, knowing the next few hours would be remembered forever. I gave them the groceries and the Tibetan bags, telling them of the encounter with the monks. I had also brought young Rad, an avid Marley fan, a gift of a Bob Marley "One Love" flag I had bought at Bob's home in Kingston, now a museum. As I left the museum, I ran into Rita, his wife, as I was leaving the grounds and we chatted while she held the flag, so I told Dawn to tell Rad it was from Bob's home and blessed by his wife. She said he would be thrilled to get it.

"I came one more time, not with any real agenda other than just feeling drawn back," I said. "I spent time with Roland a few days ago and we had a great reasoning especially about his love of the land. Yesterday, we went to the Women's Basket Dance and as I walked away I said to Supai Waters that this might be the highest point of evolution humanity has reached, at least in the U.S. in modern times. I saw hundreds of people that all had a sense of tribe, all had a sense of land. Few in my world have a sense of tribe and land and I don't think you can live sanely on the Earth without it. It's just too difficult a planet. So once you lose your tribe, your homeland, all kinds of strange behavior starts to happen. The other thing, as I watched them throw the gifts out, it noticed no one was greedy. This was a gathering of people that had a great time for hours in an innocent way, from four to ninety years old. Nothing in the commercial world could offer such a rich human experience. Your people seem to be at peace, both within the tribe and with people outside the tribe. Not that you're perfect but you weren't told to become the 'Perfect People.' You were told to become the 'Peaceful People,' with all the flaws of human nature. It looks to me like the covenant is completed - or very close to it."

"It's a strive towards that," Radford said. "We're still in the process of reaching that and as long as people *outside* see it like yourself, that you think we have met the Covenant, that's good. But within ourselves, we still need to make it much better than what is seen on the outside."

"Well, Hopi has always been very demanding of itself," I said.

"Yes. Yes," he continued. "Because we are a group of people that are just holy, holy people that depend on one another and as long as we have that friendliness and friendship between one another to do something good, that's what counts and as long as we are doing it to make the people from the outside see it, that's good but yet we feel that we have not really reached the Covenant one hundred percent."

"What do you see is the real work left?" I asked

"Well, it's going to be our younger generation to reach that," he said, gesturing toward his daughter. "As elders, we need to keep preaching that to them. We have got to instill that idea to the younger generation to keep that going, so it's always there. I would almost say it is *their* responsibility from this point on to keep that going."

"How effective have you been in bringing that to the youths?" I asked.

"I think we are pretty effective. Like you say, you saw that at the dance. We feel the same way, even though there might be a little bit of friction there. It used to be you would have drunks and we had people that hate one another in these kinds of dances. It used to be really, really rough. You wouldn't imagine there would be fights. There would be all kinds of stuff going on." (Hopi are severely warned against performing any of their sacred rites while intoxicated.)

"How long ago was that?" I asked.

"About ten or more years ago," Radford answered.

"So in the last ten years there has been a healing?"

"Yes, a lot more respect," he said.

"Yes," Dawn said. "In the eighties and the early nineties, I remember not even wanting to go down in the plaza because there were drunks. For awhile you couldn't even go down there unless you didn't mind getting beat up and stuff but it has not been like that for awhile."

"What do think happened?" I asked.

"I think the parents of the villages began to really talk to the kids," Radford said. "Really talk about that this is not Hopi and you've got to respect Hopi, one another. We have relations in other villages and we have really started to talk to one another. We have marriages going from village to village and so we have really got relations there and that's the way the Hopi clan relations are, the ones that gather together to complete the ceremony."

"So that helps you heal the relationships between the other tribes, too, the Navahos, the Tewas, the bahannas, because once they marry in, they become part of your clan?"

"You would have to respect the clan," Radford answered. "If the mother is Hopi, the children are clan members. If the father is Hopi but the mother is not, the children are not members of the mother's clan. The in-laws are not clan members but they're relatives in our family."

"As I watched the women come in, I realized how empowering it has got to be for women to know that the children are of *their* clan. You seldom see that kind of self-assurance in women in my world. If thirty American women of all ages came together, all would have experienced being treated as a second-class citizen and as a sex object and many of them would have been sexually or emotionally or physically abused. What I saw there were women who seemed to feel secure in their society. I could see the pride in the faces."

"Sexual abuse is a lot less here," Lorna said, "but it happens and its often not reported or widely known. It's not talked about."

"And that abuse has a tremendous warping effect in my society," I said,

"I think that happens when the population is just too big," Radford said, "and in our culture, we still talk to our adult children and counsel them and give them advise but I noticed in the white world, once a child become 18 or 21 years old, they're out the door and there is, maybe, just a conversation or a telephone call or just a little form of communication, is about all that's there."

"But there is no more mentoring," I said in agreement.

"Yes. That's true," he replied. "With Hopi, there is mentoring. The tribe includes them in different things that are all clan related. If it can't be done, we just let it go but that is another difference between our culture and the Anglo culture - we keep talking to our kids even though they're adults."

"That chain's been broken in Supai now," I said. "Supai Waters was talking about the how chain of the elders bringing the wisdom to the kids has been broken. This started to happen when they took the kids out from the tribe and sent them off to schools. Now there are few elders to give guidance to the young and the young proceed without their instructions. That's really what's happened in the entire country. There are few elders to give instructions to the young."

"Our elders really fought the idea of taking the kids away from here," Radford said. "I think that's how we still are clinging to what we have.

That's what happened here. They tried to take the children away from the tribe to never come back. They took the adult men to prison because they didn't want the kids to be taken away. Even when they were released from prison, they still fought. They came back and said, 'No. Don't take the kid's anymore.' "

"Because you knew what would happen," I said. "You knew the hoop would break?"

"Yes," he answered. "That's the very thing that when we came to this new world, we were told to *never, never* forget our religion; *never, never* let the tradition and culture go. That's the only thing in the future or whenever that's going to be there, the way to survive. There was a big, big problem amongst the other villages when Oraibi split because all the rest of the villages know it's not supposed to happen. We're not supposed to do that but because that village became so big, it grew so fast, they didn't know one another from one end of the village to the other."

"Even in that small village?" I asked, remembering that Oraibi looked to be only five or ten acres.

"It wasn't so little then. It was bigger than any of the villages," he said.

"And some of the Friendlies and Hostiles asked others to move there?" I said.

"The reason that the Hostiles were pulled over there was because they wanted them to give their ideas about the tradition, but the Friendlies just didn't pay attention," he said.

"That was actually part of your struggle to become 'Peaceful People,' " I said, "to see how well you did in that conflict, under the huge pressure created by the bahanna culture, with all its temptations. You could see the split as a failure but it's really not. It didn't escalate into violence, even though it almost did. It was settled by a shoving match."

"Some people went to the houses and took the guns so it wouldn't happen like that," Dawn added. "Our family had to leave. The Friendlies were getting mean. They would taunt the women when they would go get water. They were mean to the kids from the different families and a lot of it was the people that were siding with the government that were the mean ones. The Friendlies were really the hostile ones and the Hostiles were like, 'We just want to be Hopi. Just leave us alone.' It's still like that when you get with people that believe that the Hopi ways are gone. They're the ones that get real violent and mad. When we had that thing at the council about the school, the people from Kykotsmovi (the non-traditional village where the Hopi Tribal Council is based), they couldn't contain their energy and they left the council chambers because they were so angry. It was over the building of the Second Mesa School. It would have been built on another sacred site and the *kikmongwi* wanted it to stay where it already was. It's these guys [pointing towards her parents] that are calm, the traditional elders, the ones that know the religion. They're trying to talk real calmly, without raising their voices. It's the other ones that don't believe in the Hopi ways that are yelling, pounding their fists, waving their arms around. It's weird."

"I'm sure they feel a certain amount of guilt and that guilt manifests in anger," I said. "At some deep level they know they are not following the instructions. When you wake someone up before they're ready, they get mad at you."

"We were talking about the influences like the TV and the radio but one of the main influences still are the schools," Dawn said. "Our schools are still trying to force that mainstream belief on the kids, that they have to leave Hopi before they can ever be happy. That's still in there. The tribe acts like they really want the kids to learn Hopi, to learn their culture, but it's not being done in a way that's sensitive to the culture. To me and the way I see it, it's not a real push toward Hopi. It's more like the icing on the cake. And that's one of the things that has to change. That is still one of the main forces of change out here."

"Is this an issue among the teachers?" I asked.

"No," Radford answered. "It's just instilled in them that this is the government school and the U.S. government wants to acculturate all these Native Americans into the Anglo society."

"Are these Anglo teachers?" I asked.

"Mostly," he answered.

"The tribe has been trying to increase the number of Hopi teachers in the school," Dawn said. "I was a part of a program like that. It was supposed to have Hopi teachers teach the language and the culture. But then once our group finally formed, we got all the members to talk about the importance of the Hopi life, the Hopi culture, the Hopi language, in forming these kids and making them Hopi. The majority of the group did not understand Hopi religion, did not understand the Hopi ways, could barely talk or understand Hopi. One of our group members would say all that was important but the kids really needed to learn about lasers. I would get into arguments with them about why are we really here - why do you want to teach the kids to talk Hopi and *be* Hopi. My reason is so my son will go to the dance and understand what those basket dancers were singing about, what the *kachinas* are talking about, what his *qua-ah* [grandfather] says to him in the kiva. Not to go out and say, 'Oh. I can read in Hopi and I can write in Hopi.' Because that's the push now to be able to write and read in Hopi but the real subtleties and nuances of the language are pushed to the side and the whole purpose of it is because according to Hopi, our spirits only talk Hopi, so you only can converse with the spirits if you can speak to them in Hopi. They only understand the Hopi language. To me, those are the real reasons why those kids should be learning Hopi language and Hopi culture and Hopi tradition. Instead it came out from our director that it will raise test scores. Studies have shown that if you're knowledgeable in two languages, it helps you to get better test scores. It got to a point where me and my husband felt this is not where we belong. This is not our reason for being in the schools - to keep the system as it is. We wanted to change it. We ended up quitting that program. One day, we want to go to Supai and teach down there."

"The elders have the knowledge and the wisdom or a least have the prophecies," Radford said, "then they [pointing to his daughter] are the ones that have to take it on from where we leave off. They have to be the ones that have the energy and the belief to keep it going."

"It seems like a dichotomy because what I witnessed at the dances was a society that seems to be working," I said. "The people looked healthy for the most part, they looked like they liked each other and were having fun together. There was an innocence of play among all ages. There was a beauty and simplicity to it and yet what you're saying is when the kid's walk into class tomorrow, it will be a world with a very different value system. It's like they're living in two worlds. There are two worlds going on here."

"Yes. We know that," Radford said.

"But the kids seemed to be really enjoying themselves," I said. "I didn't see a lot of kids that looked like they didn't want to be there."

"Because those kids weren't there," Dawn said. "What you saw was the families, the people that believe in the Hopi Way and are still participating in that. There was probably at least ten families from that village that went somewhere else. The grandma might have gone to the casino. The kids might have gone to Flagstaff. There's always families that are not there. We, as Hopi, know who is not there."

"So the struggle between the Friendlies and the Hostiles continues to this day," I said. They both nodded in agreement. "What percentage would avoid these ceremonies?"

"About twenty percent," Radford said. "They know who they are and they want to be a part of a Hopi ceremony and so they would go, but in their minds they are not really believing. What I am saying is they are there because they are Hopi and that is what they are *supposed* to be doing."

"They feel peer pressure and they are afraid to step out and say I am not into this anymore?" I asked.

"That is right," Radford said.

"That's why there are still those people that still live here but don't believe in the Hopi Way," Dawn said. "If you don't believe in it, you are free to leave this area because this area is so permeated with the Hopi beliefs and the Hopi system. You can't go outside without feeling what you are supposed feel - that covenant with Maasaw to take care of the land. How can you walk around out here and not feel that it is what you believe. But they can't leave because they want to live in that way. They want to live like a white man but they are afraid to because they know they are not supposed to, or they know that is not what is really expected so instead they stay here. They try to change everything to make it so that they can still be Hopi and still be bahannas at the same time, which is what we don't want because if you're not sincere in your beliefs and your thoughts and prayers then what you're trying to get done is not going to happen. So what's going on now is that there's people that don't believe in the Hopi ways that still live out here that are trying to make these things happen, trying to build stores, trying to develop land, so we can have economic security, things like that and that's basically where the council is at."

"So actually those people are more corrosive to the ways because they want to stay here and change things?" I asked.

"Yes," Dawn said. "Because they're the ones that are willing to get on the council. They're the ones running for chairman. So they're the ones that get the positions and those are the people that go out to other tribes, other places to the U.N."

"To represent you?" I asked.

"Yes," she answered "To represent us and say, 'We're Hopi. We're peaceful but this how we are. We want to mine our coal but we want to do it in a way that is O.K. with Maasaw or whatever, or we want to build a shopping center, an office complex. We want to build a renewable energy plant on our land.' To me this flies in the face of Hopi beliefs. Do you, as a Hopi, really need to have that here? The only reason you are putting that here is so the tribe can get money."

"So if the consciousness that is promoting this is doing it for the money, it is splintered," I said. "Then no matter what they come up with, even if it's solar energy, the consciousness is greed and separation. On the other hand, someone coming from the right consciousness could do solar energy and it could be a healing thing. So it's not *what* you do but *why* you're doing it. You guys are conscious but you have a TV and a truck. It's not like you have to live fully roots. So again it goes into changing people's hearts and minds to remember who they are."

"Yes," Dawn said.

"Radford, are you satisfied with the progress?" I asked.

"I think so, as far as having the culture and the religion still going, I am pretty satisfied with what we are doing. When World War II erupted, that was the biggest change to the Hopi Way because a lot to the men went out and came back with the ideas of whatever they experienced in the outside world. They were all over the world and when they came home then there was this big push from the government to incorporate their ideas in the Native American ways."

"So that was another big threat?" I asked.

"Yes. A big threat fifty years ago."

"Especially because we are people of peace and these men had to go to war," Dawn said.

"Yes," Radford continued. "Because we don't believe in wars and our elders really fought the draft. The elders and the religious leaders fought the draft. 'Don't take the men!' But they didn't have any power to hold them back and so they went. All of my uncles went to World War II."

"So that generation suffered a big blow because they were ripped out of Hopi Way in a very visceral way and said go shoot and kill and that must have reverberated throughout the tribe," I said.

"Yes," Dawn and Radford said sadly in unison.

"So you've healed from that?" I asked.

"Yes," Radford answered. "Some of the families that lost their family members in that war were the ones that really felt it."

"So that represented the insanity of the *kahopi* way?" I said, thinking of the man we had given a ride the day before.

"Yes," he answered, looking off as if remembering lost friends and relatives.

"So in a way that really served to strengthen the tribe," I said, "because they said, 'Look we left the Hopi way and they sent our family back in a coffin.' It revealed the *kahopi* way."

"Sort of," Radford answered. "Then there is the peacetime between World War II and the Vietnam War. It was a time when the majority of the men in their high school years were sought by the recruiters, the different armed services. During the peacetime, a lot of the kids went into the armed services. The enticement was you can get your degrees or your graduate degrees after you finish your years in service and you can have the GI bill and you can travel the world."

"They'll teach you a trade," Dawn said.

"All these things were out there," Radford continued, "so a lot of the high school kids, Hopi men, went into the services."

"So it was the second blow?"

Yes," he answered, "the Vietnam War."

"How about the Iraq war?"

"The same thing," he said, "but I don't think we've got that many in that war."

"So it's been diluted," I said. "That warrior concept, the noble concept of the warrior going out to protect the clan through aggression has been weakened?"

"Yes," he answered.

"People aren't buying it like they used to?" I asked.

"No," Dawn said. "I think they are because a lot of people my age are saying, 'Well, my uncle was in the army and my whatever was in the army and so I am going in because that's what they did.' "

"It seems like Native Americans take great pride in their people in the armed forces," I said, "because traditionally they knew the warriors were a very important part of the tribe, very honored. However, now the chiefs, the political leaders that direct the warriors, are misguided, maybe worse."

"I think a lot of these people," Radford said, "that push for the celebration of the veterans are looking outside Hopi. They're looking at the Navajos, they're looking at the Plains Indians, who were warring types of people. Like the Navajos were the codetalkers in World War II and the Hopi came back and said that we have to use our language because that would help the army."

"But it wasn't your covenant to use your language for war," I said.

"And it wasn't just the Navajos," Dawn said. "All the native tribes used their language for code."

"But Navajos were the majority," Radford said. "There were many in the war."

"So for the Sioux or the Navajo to be a soldier is not the same as for a Hopi to be a soldier?" I asked.

"That's right," Radford said. "When some of the Hopi people who had their relatives go into the army, they were looking at the outside tribes and were saying, 'Well, we have our soldiers, too.' But those are the ones that don't really understand what Hopi is."

"I think a lot of people when they read about your life here," I said, "are going to long to have something like this in their life - a life with family and clan and tribe all around on our own land, but most of us can never get that and we've never had it. We're going to have to create it as best we can in our minds, in our hearts, and in our lives, even if it's only with our own family. We're going to have to see *everyone* as our tribe and *everywhere* as our home. We really don't understand the importance of land and tribe because most of us have never had it and I'm not sure people can stay balanced without it. To date, there's no evidence that they can. Your work here will remind us of where we need to head. I was really amazed to see how the teenagers had such a great time at the dances. They didn't resent it or think it was corny. They were glad to be there all day. There were having a great time."

"It is the ingenuity of the ceremonies," Dawn said. "The spirits that brought these rituals to us knew you have to have fun. You have to be happy. If you really know the Ceremonial Cycle, there's a lot of fun put into it that makes the whole thing so that you *want* to participate. You go to the kiva and these guys [pointing towards her father], they tease each other. They have fun while they're doing things. Women do the same thing. The way the relationships are laid out, you get to tease your nephew. Maybe he's your brother's son or your uncle's son. They're your boy friends so you get to have that element of teasing. Then your uncles tease you in certain ways and those are ways that you show each other that you love each other. This ceremony, the Basket Dance, the reason that they're throwing things out is that they've been doing something that they want to cleanse themselves of, to purify themselves. But at the same time, it adds an element of fun to the people outside because they have to grab those things. Everything that Hopi does, there is an element of fun and energy. Whoever it was, the Creator, that gave us these things to do, realized that you can't just be there and have to do these things without having that fun in it. Everything that we do is like that so that we are happy. It's not like that puritanical type of Christianity, where everything is prim and proper and serious. You can't laugh. You can't do things like that. The way that the Hopi society was put together makes it fun. Ultimately the Creator knew, *My people must be happy in order for them to do what I want them to do.*"

"Prior to the entertainment," Radford said, "there's that seriousness, that ritual that the elders, and the older religious men, do in these ceremonies by themselves. When that's done, then comes the public view.

That's where everybody, the kids on up, are able to enjoy what comes out of the ritual."

"So everyone knows the underlying serious statement that's being made?" I asked.

"Yes," he answered.

"And many of these ceremonies involve the *kachinas*, your spirit guides?"

"Yes," he continued. "We believe that there is the Creator and Maasaw, His Messenger - just like in Christianity. If you believe in Maasaw then you are much more spiritually connected to the Creator. From summer solstice to December, the winter solstice, is purely Hopi religious activities. Then, from December it goes back to the summer solstice. That's the *kachina* religious ceremonies. That's a supernatural series that we believe in. So that's more of a way to make the people enjoy the life of a new birth every year and the *kachinas* are the ones that are spirits that bring happiness to the people, for the people, including the children because at that time, they become initiated into the *kachina* societies and there's a lot of different things happening to them."

"So these *kachinas*, when they initiate the children, they come and play? They appear to them in a friendly, approachable manner?" I asked.

"They come back to make friends," he said.

"You know how the bahannas way of doing everything is to compartmentalize everything," Dawn said. "With Hopi, you don't compartmentalize everything because everything is related to each other and how can you put anything into little compartments? The way that Hopi has evolved into what it is now is based on what it *was* in the past. And in the past, the *kachinas* were real spirits that came to us at certain times and then things happened to how it is now. That's the whole point of the initiation - to understand that process that you go through as a Hopi person, to go from a child to an adult and what happened to you in between. What's sad is that not all of us have that training anymore. My dad is the only one in our family that knows all those steps that you have to take to become a Hopi adult. They talk to you forever when you get initiated, hours and hours of telling you, 'This is what we were. This is how we were. These are the things we've gone through. These are the ways you need to understand the world so that you'll be able to fulfill these steps.' It's hard for the people that don't live the Hopi Way to understand how we are without compartmentalizing."

"It must be very comforting to know that this divine assistance and guidance is there and that your people have been chosen as one of the repositories for their guidance and wisdom?" I said, once again awed by the beauty of their ways.

"We know that and so we pray to those superbeings," Radford said. "We believe that. I keep telling my family [he gestures toward Lorna and Dawn], you can do *anything*. There's these beings out there to pray to. At night you can go out and pray to the starpeople that are out there. They're even looking at you right now. You can go out there in the morning and pray or at noon. *Anytime,* you can pray to these people. If you're down with something, pray to these people and they'll help you. They will take you out of your misery and make you happy and you go on."

"And every Hopi knows that concept whether they follow it or not?" I asked.

"Some that are born off the reservation won't have any information about that," he said. "Those are the ones that Dawn is talking about that want to come back and change the Hopi Way into the outside system."

"Yet, there was a struggle with human corruption before that outside world came here so it didn't come on the back of the white culture," I said. "It looked like you were finally getting a handle on your inner struggle when the bahannas showed up, and later the Navajos, and they gave you your next lesson - your struggle with the corruption *outside* the tribe. Yours was a struggle that took constant vigilance."

"That's what the elders say in our religious practices," he said. "You're going to be going through all the turmoil. We are Hopi but yet there's visitors coming with different characters. You're going to have to deal with their character and make them understand *who* we are and that's friendship. That's peace. Because they don't know that because they are from different cultures. They don't know that. We have to bring that out to them, to make them see that we are peaceful people. That's what they say. You're going to have all kinds of turmoil with these people but just keep at it and don't give up. You'll make these people understand *where* we are, *who* we are."

"And people like ourselves and others will come looking for that wisdom?" I asked.

"Yes," he said. "Even some people will come crawling back to you, crawling on their knees to get advice."

"When I was a hippie, I heard that one of your prophecies said that your people would be reborn as the children of the white people and that we would have similar names- hippies, Hopi - and wear beads and feathers. I've never seen that prophecy written. Was there one?"

"No," he said gently laughing.

"Oh well," I said. "It made good late night conversation when you were laying around the commune in Northern California. In any case, I'm glad we were guided here, to bring this information, this knowledge, out. It is calming and encouraging to me to know that this worldview that once encompassed this entire continent is still so vital here and I'm beginning to understand that it is in many other Native American people and tribes as well. Thank you for that. You kept your Covenant. You kept it alive. We need that hope and encouragement now."

"Tell them about your trip to Japan," Lorna said.

"I was in Japan about two weeks ago," Radford said. "It was interesting because I never knew that Japan had indigenous groups among themselves and that they have a peaceful people in Japan. One group that I met are from Okinawa and the peaceful people on that island never had any weapons."

"Did they ask you to come to speak to them?"

"Yes. They had this celebration coming up, the remembrance of the bombing of Hiroshima. They have a yearly remembrance. The person that put this together is from Okinawa. He is a well-known musician. His name is Shokichi Kina. Through his music, he has been going through different parts of Japan, and I think he was in the United States too, in San Francisco and in New York at the Onondaga Nation. He is part of a group of people that are working as peacemakers or seeking peace from all nations. There was a seat, a senate seat, in Japan and he was called on to run for the seat because people knew that he was seeking for peace. The prime minister there is wanting to change that peace in Japan. In the Japanese constitution, they have an article saying that there will be no more wars. This happened after World War II."

"That Japan would never again take part in a war?" I asked.

"Right. But now this prime minister is saying that he wants to take this article out and make the Japanese a more active army. Kina is from the peaceful group and he did not want the prime minister to take that article out. So he did become a senator and then there was another senator that already had the same philosophy. Now there's two people in their senate that want to keep that article in to have no wars at all. So he had invited some people from different nations. There were people from China, North and South Korea, Thailand, India, Vietnam, two or thee groups from Africa. Onondagas were invited. Over two thousand people were there. There were singers and dancers to perform, also. There was a person there demonstrating karate because the peaceful people used that to protect themselves. These were all people who wanted to have peace around the world. This was in remembrance of Hiroshima and they don't want to have anything to do with nuclear weapons. They also want to just ban wars the world over. That's how I got invited to go over there, to talk about the Hopi philosophy. Onondaga was invited because they have almost the same philosophy but it's deeper than that. Kina knew that this Onondaga nation was the one that had the democratic system and that when the United States was just being established, they used their system of democracy to make their constitution. He's even thinking of making Okinawa an independent nation from Japan."

"He's a singer *and* a senator?" I asked. (I later learned Kina was a close friend of Bob Marley.)

"Yes. And how he campaigned was through his concerts throughout Japan. His motto is, 'No wars but celebration.' The other is 'All weapons into the musical instruments.' "

"Even Steven Seagal, the actor, was there," Dawn said. "He has a band and one of the people in his band use to be a Wailer with Bob Marley."

"So this is another people that were meant to hold the world in balance along with Hopi?" I asked.

"Yes," Radford said. "I could call these people in Okinawa, 'Hopisinumu, Peaceful People,' because I know now they are people of peace."

"And the Tibetan Buddhists were one of those people?"

"Yes," he said.

"Do you know who all the wisdomkeepers are?" I asked. "The other people keeping the Earth in balance?"

"No," he answered.

"So you're just discovering them as they're revealed to you," I said. "That would be very powerful if all those wisdomkeepers on the planet joined together."

"That's right," he said. "We know that when we started migrating in different directions, some people stayed in different areas and that's how we know that they are part of us."

"So even the white race was Hopi," I said. "Did they get their instructions?"

"Everybody got their instructions prior to the migrations," he said.

"Was it because we took the witch with us that we have strayed?" I asked. "That we have forgotten our instructions?"

"Yes. They knew the Covenant but because of the negative temptation they took it and went ahead and made use of that power. We already know that they're going to become very powerful and use that power to change the world."

"Which we've done," I said, feeling no remorse for my skin color (*Hey, trying to stay conscious in the white world is a lot tougher assignment than being Hopi! We can't even agree on what our wisdom is!*).

"Which you've done," he said. "and they're going to be the ones that ask, 'Why is this happening? Let's really investigate. Let's really dig into it and find out if it's true.' They're going to be the ones to really find out what is Hopi like - for everything."

"So you're saying that the white race would come to find the Hopi knowledge?" I asked.

"Yes. If it's really true what the Covenant is. They're going to be the ones. We believe in them as a brother. So they're going to come if there's is a dire need to survive. They're supposed to come together and we're supposed to make that survival together."

"And you think that's what might be coming up?" I asked.

"That's what we believe," he said, nodding his head.

"Sometime soon?" I asked.

"Maybe not soon but sometime. When we are nearing that need, then it will happen. We don't know when it's going to happen."

"And we'll complete our knowledge at that time?" I asked.

"That's about it," he said. "We are told to keep our religious activities and our traditions going before we do that. Amongst the villages, even though when they let go of their practices, they're going to still find out later on that, 'Hey. We are still Hopi.' "

"Do you have a son in Massachusetts?" I asked, sensing that it was time to change the subject.

"Yes," Dawn and Lorna started laughing.

"I got an email a few weeks ago from someone who read our books and gets our email updates, Liz Bailey. She's a teacher at Berklee College of Music in Boston. She said that this Hopi student came to see her about a class almost by accident. He was supposed to meet with another teacher. When she heard he was from Hopiland, she told him that she knew people that had done concerts there and had taken some Hopi to speak to the Havasupai. He told her that his family had gone down there last summer to speak."

"Yes," Lorna said. "That's our son, Blair. He wanted to get his courses in order. Somehow the Hopi thing caught her attention."

"Blair called us and told my mom it was 'Ras-something,' " Dawn said, laughing. "He couldn't remember your name. Apparently they don't normally meet with students like that but somehow it happened. We told him what had happened and then she emailed you. That was crazy."

"That was a nice sign that we were meant to work together," I said. "And there was more. When I was getting ready to send you the manuscript a few weeks ago, I was filling out the shipping label but I couldn't remember how to spell you name so I reached across my desk to get my address book and as I did, I glanced at the computer screen and the emails were on the screen and the top email, the one my eye went to, said 'Radford Quamahongnewa' in the subject line. It was this email from Liz."

"I think one of the things to know is that all of us here have experienced living off the reservation and coming back," Lorna said. "You appreciate being back out here. We both went to the boarding school [pointing toward her husband] and we both lived in Phoenix for several years before we came home. We've experienced that. We can go there for a weekend but you don't want all that running around, all that traffic, pollution, and stuff. It's nice to be out here. Even our son, who is in Boston, says he can't wait to get back home and be in the wide open spaces. He's appreciated this more being there. I think once he gets back home, he'll be here for good."

"I'll send Blair our books," I said. "Also, Elaine and Carol want to try to bring you to Jamaica for their wellness event in April. Are you interested in going?" I asked.

"I would like to go there if I can make it work at the school," Radford said. "The principal is real tight on staffing." (Radford is the librarian at two Hopi elementary schools).

"That might work," Dawn said, unwrapping her mom's 2006 Bob Marley calendar. "Got to have my Bob Marley. On the back of my shirt [she is wearing a beautiful Bob Marley tee-shirt] is 'If the Cap Fits.' That's my favorite Bob Marley song. I've been listening to 'One Drop' lately, over and over again. My little boy, he's so funny. Even he likes to listen to Bob Marley. His song right now is 'Iron, Lion, Zion.' Ziggy Marley said that his father was always regretful that he never made it to Hopiland and Ziggy says he wants to come one day. He's been waiting for an invitation."

"Maybe I can invite him through his sister, Stephanie," I said. "I'd love it if your whole family could go to Jamaica. They need to see more families working together. I think one reason we had a big impact is that we brought our message as a family. I'd like to see you greeted as a head of state, which you are, and have the Governor General, who is a real One Love guy, host a reception and then do a full media tour so that everyone hears your message. It would be like a diplomatic mission of love. It could help Jamaica heal to hear a message of peace and forgiveness from another oppressed people. In Jamaica, like so many people who have been oppressed, they take the anger out on themselves."

"That would be good to go there," Radford said.

"And if the Jamaicans appreciate us," Dawn said, "it would show our people here that they should appreciate us, too. If other people can understand what we're talking about, why shouldn't our own people."

"This would be in line with your prophecies," I said, "that said you would help other people become peaceful. Through the reggae, there's already a deep connection between Jamaica and Hopiland. Their conscious music has helped you keep your Covenant. Now you could go there and help them. What was designed out here, your entire Hopi Way and your Ceremonial Cycle, really is brilliant. All you had was this land and each other to do the work for the Covenant. And you lived very close together in your villages so you *really* had to love your neighbors."

"The way our villages are set up," he said, "is that we are set by clans, in rows. One clan stays together and then another clan and then a related clan. They're all together. That's how it was set up."

"So not only did you have to get along with your neighbor," I said "you had to get along with different clans."

"Much more easier to live with your clan than another clan," he said. "I think that's the idea - so that you know one another. In the Hopi way, we have to marry into a different clan. When we go to the ceremonies, like the one yesterday, and we meet someone new, the first thing we would ask is, 'What clan are you?' Then someone would say, 'I'm a Water Clan,' and then you say, 'I'm a Bear Clan.' Somewhere in those clanships there might be your mother or your father or your grandfather - related in some way. So then you would say, 'Oh. Then you are my brother,' or 'You are my niece or nephew,' or 'You are my grandson.' That's how we make connections."

"So there's always a cross-fertilization," I said. "Is everybody related to everybody through the clans?

"Yes," he said. "Everybody. Everybody. You know your relatives. You know your brothers and sisters. If someone's from a *different* clan, you can have a relationship, a marriage, with them. We also have godparents. When you're born, your parents will look for godparents for your according to what clan or religious society you will belong to. This way, there are no orphans within the tribe."

"That's such a difference from my culture which is designed in such a way that it's always pulling us apart," I said. "Your society is always intertwining you together. If you want to teach humans to love, it's a brilliant system. After all the migrations, you take a tribe of people, the

most committed spiritually, the descendents of the ones that were willing
to keep uprooting to follow their spiritual guidance, and you put them
on a piece of land that is almost barren so they stay physically strong
and have to trust the Creator and pray for enough rain and snow to
survive and that all you have is each other, living closely together, to
work through all the human dramas. And when you're just getting that
down, outsiders are introduced. Everything was in place for you to
continue purifying yourself to become Hopi - to become the Peaceful
People. And always the spiritual guides, the *kachinas*, are their to guide
you."

"One of the individuals, Oliver LaFarge" Radford said, "a govern-
ment-paid anthropologist, who was working with the government on
establishing the constitution for the Hopi tribe back in the thirties, was
talking to different village elders and leaders and after getting some information about the Hopi system and the Hopi government, he was so
amazed that he reported to the government commission, 'This tribe has
government structures so unique, why do we want to change this? They
have their government structured in a more civilized way than any other
that I know of.' He knew that the government was intertwined with our
religion and that the religion is already in there with the civil system.
He said, 'Maybe we should not change it,' but it was the U.S. government that changed it. The first draft of the constitution he wrote is almost
like the Hopi system but when it went to the commissioner, he said,
'Change it to the way the United States is - with separation of church
and state.' In the beginning when the first draft was explained to the
leaders, they were pretty well satisfied with it because it was almost like
the Hopi Way. When it was changed, then they said, 'No!' "

"And the traditional elders have washed their hands of that system to
this day?" I asked.

"Yes," he said.

"Which means that only those with the bahanna worldview gravitate
to the tribal government and the tribal council," I said. "Let's make sure
every tribal council member gets a copy of this book. It may change their
hearts. We would do it out of friendship, to encourage them to use their
leadership skills and power to teach the people love, to teach them the

Hopi Way, even as they do their duties as council members. It's the highest form of leadership. Gandhi did that. Supai Waters and I were watching his life story last night. He never made the English leaders wrong - no matter how much they were unable to understand. He felt they were caught in the system, too. We all are. Gandhi felt that if he could demonstrate the injustice in the system, people's higher nature would be willing to see it and change it but he knew to do that he would have to take many blows and still remain non-violent - just as your people have done for centuries. Martin Luther King understood this. He said Bull Conor, the racist sheriff in Birmingham, really helped the civil rights movement by releasing the dogs and water hoses on young children. It revealed the true nature of racial prejudice to many who really didn't understand. He showed *this* is what segregation is *really* like. They both showed that they could change people's hearts. And then Mandela followed their model."

"Ho," Supai Waters grunted from the side.

"It may be similar out here," I said. "When I was in Jamaica, I began to think that maybe they could be the first society to heal themselves with love and forgiveness. Like with Gandhi's model of non-violence, some society must one day show that living in peace as a society, especially as an oppressed society, is possible. I thought it might be Jamaica but now I know it's Hopi. Your tribe has always known that, too. That's been your goal since you entered the Forth World - to become the Peaceful People for *all* humanity, so that *everyone* would have a model. Your prophecies say that you were the *first* people out in the Emergence and you would be the *first* Hopi - the first Peaceful People. Hasn't your prophecies said that other societies will become peaceful after you have completed your Covenant?"

"Yes," he said, nodding. "That's what we believe."

"And that you would set the pattern for the entire planet?" I said. "Is that coming to a completion?"

"Towards it, yes," he said, willing to answer the same question three times.

"I think for the young people," Dawn said, "there's always going to be mainstream out there, but roots reggae is always going to be better, a better choice than rock or hip-hop or rap or techno, because roots reggae is all about the oppression that makes people suffer and how they got through it. Rastas didn't have to feel oppressed. They didn't have to feel sad in the conditions they were in because JAH *loved* them. He loves them and He knows that they're there and doing what they can to do whatever it is that they're supposed to do. We, as Hopi, have lived through all the same things and we know that our Creator still loves us because He's still here with us and helping us. Like my dad said, you go and you pray to these beings, and when you pray to them and you're filled with that calmness and that happiness that you're supposed to have. You realize that they're still out there watching you and taking care of you and if you have that kind of belief and if you believe in it and you pray, you see good things happening, like the connection with Blair and you. It really shows that they're out there listening to you."

"That's how I felt when I got her email," I said.

"While I have been student teaching," she continued, "and in the past, I noticed that even my little kindergarten students when they listen to roots reggae, they calm down. It's not hyper and frantic. There's this one reggae song that totally is the frame of Hopi mindset. It asks the women, 'Where are your skirts and your blouses?' Because in Hopi, women are supposed to wear dresses, too. And I asked my mom, 'Why do you have to wear a dress when you go to pray to the *kachinas*?' And she said, 'It's because the spirits need to know that you're a female so that they know that those are the kind of thoughts that are going to be coming from you.' And this reggae song says the same thing. 'What happened to your dresses? What happened to your womanly thoughts? Why are you so aggressive behaving like this?' When I become a teacher, there will be reggae in my classroom. It's the same thing with the Hopi songs, talking about the beauty of life, the things you can make happen if you're happy, if your thoughts are in the correct place and the things that you yourself can manifest if you're just pure in thought and pure in your Hopi Way and your belief system. We can still be happy. We can still be proud."

"I hope you and Duane go to Havasupai to teach," I said. "I think you would bring a great healing there. I also wanted to mention that I think the revival of the Havasupai may be very connected with the Hopi. The ceremonies are not going on in Supai, but there are some very conscious leaders now, like Roland, like Supai Waters, like Rex and Carletta Tilousi, Toby, Diana Sue and others. They could draw on your strength, especially the youths. Maybe one day there could be a Hopi-Havasupai youth exchange where kids from Hopiland visit Supai and swim in clear water and ride horseback and Havasupai kids can come here and go to your ceremonies and talk with the elders and visit your craftspeople. Both could draw strength from each other."

"That would be good," Dawn said. "We are doing that already with Yaqui Indians in Mexico and indigenous people in Hawaii."

"Robert, they've already merged that acquaintance," Supai Waters said. "The Hopi kids from Bacavi came to Supai when the flu epidemic was going on in 1918 and after the epidemic was over, they came back here. Other Hopi kids were just in Supai a few weeks ago."

"Yeah," Dawn said, "Those were the kids from the cross-country team that went to Supai. They're from Hopi Day School, the school that I'm student teaching at right now. The assistant coach and the head coach took the kids down to Supai a few weeks ago. They said they really enjoyed it."

"It intrigued the Supai kids," Supai Waters said. "They don't know what's on the outside. The kids from Hopi brought their school work and taught the Havasupai kids."

"I made a point to go out there and say 'bye' to them," she said. "They walked in and walked out. It's kind of like a dangerous thing to be going down there where there is so much spirituality that resides there. I told them that, 'You guys need to behave in a way that's Hopi and proper. I don't want you guys to be yelling around and acting in a way that's all dumb. You have to remember *who* you are. You need to be really aware of *what* you're going down there for. That place is special and there's no place like that anywhere in this world. Make us proud. Be real Hopi boys and girls. Everyone watches us closely. And see how they all speak their own language, even the little kids. You can learn from that."

"Havasupai has some traction now and if they keep connecting with you, it will reinforce it, quicken it," I said. "The children raised consciously here and at Supai have a lot to offer their generation. They're more removed from the intensity of that commercial world than almost anyone in this country. It's spinning out of control out there. We still think that if we're the *richest* country, we must be the *greatest*. Few are even questioning all this. I hope this connection increases. I know Roland is looking forward to the time that the songs and dance that you are holding for them can be given back. This wisdom is needed in my culture badly, too. My daughter's only eighteen and she's buried five friends - from drugs, from drinking and driving, from suicide. The kids out there are very lost. They're awash in alcohol. It's tearing up that generation. It's not really an alcohol problem. It's that the society is spiritually lost in so many ways. It's out-picturing with the youths."

"Same here. I've lost three or four friends," Dawn said, her eyes tearing up.

"Alicia's always the designated driver because she doesn't like alcohol," I said. "But it would be too lonely to only hang out with kids that don't drink. Almost nobody would be there."

"I totally know what that feels like," Dawn said, "especially being raised by these two [she gestured affectionately towards Lorna and Radford]. A lot of my friends don't have dads, some don't live with their moms. They live with their grandparents and they don't have any control over the kids."

"There's was an Anglo guy that came here a few years ago," Lorna added, "and he said he wanted to be a Hopi. We told him that he couldn't. That there was a warning that you can't be. He was so fed up with the white society that he was willing to give up his citizenship and move somewhere else. He came one day and we talked to him and then he left and he came back later and said he was leaving. We don't know where he went."

"I understand those feelings," I said, "but I wish he would know that even though you might not be able to become a Hopi and live here, the Hopi Way is available to every human being. The path runs by us always. You don't have to *be* a Hopi to *live* the Hopi Way and as you said, many Hopi here don't live the Hopi Way. If you step on the path of the love and forgiveness, the path of The Peacemaker, you're living the Hopi Way. You're on the Beauty Path and it doesn't matter how far off the path - how far *kahopi* - you went in the past. We were just at your Prophecy Rock down the road and it shows the two lines, the Hopi Way and the way of materialism, but there's a line - a short line - connecting those two lines to remind us that we can change at any time. Once you've done that, you're living Hopi. You're teaching love."

"Ho," Supai Waters said, quietly but emphatically.

"Radford," I said, "I know your legends say that humanity didn't complete the Covenant in the Third World. Do you think we'll make it in this, the Fourth World?" I asked for the third time. I needed the reassurance. I was heading back into the *other* world the next day.

"It's supposed to be the world that will be pure and paradise," he said.

"The fact that all of us are sitting here discussing this, makes me believe it can happen," I said.

"That's our challenge," he said. "If you Hopi people keep this thing going, you will see it, but if you stray from the Hopi Way, you're not going to see it. Where we are now, we are still in conflict within our people, with some of the tribal council. What we're saying is that we don't think it's right *now* that we will have that signal to release our information to the world. Every year we go through this history in November and at that time we talk about these things, about the Covenant. We are saying we are *still* in conflict within ourselves, within our tribe, even with our neighboring tribes."

"So when your bloodlines are purified, it will be completed and that signal could be in a year or a hundred years?" I asked.

"That's right. There's no way to know. We just have to keep the Hopi Way going."

"I'm glad I came back here for this visit," I said to Supai Waters, as we drove to Flagstaff later that day. "I feel the book is finished now. My goal was to encourage the reader to love and forgive and it seems like every main person in the book comes with another piece of that puzzle. Radford's knowledge and connection to the ancient wisdom, Dawn's conscious activism, Roland's love of the Earth, and the freedom and insights created by your uncluttered life. Each will speak differently to the reader but the wisdom is complete."

"Sounds to me that the sun dagger has cut the spiral," he said and we both cracked up laughing.

A few weeks later, Julia and I drove three hours down to Cherokee, North Carolina to see the fall colors. As we drove on a back road around the countryside a few miles out of town, I noticed a beautiful hand-painted sign (in Cherokee and English) indicating that the cleared mound, about fifty yards across and four feet high at the peak, in the cornfield behind the sign was the location of Etowah - the sacred mother village of the Cherokees. The site is in a beautiful valley with the Smoky Mountains on both sides and the beautiful Tuckaseegee River running down the middle. There was a man on a riding mower cutting the mound.

"Let's go visit," I said to Julia, pulling off the road into the small gravel parking area. "I read in *He Walked the Americas*, that this was the exact spot that a prophet appeared to the Cherokees and gave them their instructions."

As we sat by the car, the man finished cutting the grass and loaded the mower into the back of his pickup. As he drove by us, I flagged him down.

"Do you mind if I ask you a question?" I said.

"Go ahead," he replied. He was a healthy, intelligent man with classic Cherokee features. He looked to be in his forties.

"Have you heard stories that a prophet appeared to your people in this spot?" I said. He looked at me with a shocked expression and studied me carefully for a long time. I think he thought I was going to ask him how to get to the casino or the golf course.

"Yes," he said, having made some internal decision that it was safe to reveal this to me. "That is what our elders said. They say that he gave us our instructions here. They are like the Ten Commandments. Most of the tribe doesn't know this or they don't believe it. Only the elders still believe this. My parents and grandparents told me of him. I believe it. The old legends were fading but now they are coming back, even with the very young. I know a seven-year old girl who is learning all the legends. She has been coming to all our medicine meetings since she was four."

"Are the elders still respected by the youths of the tribe?" I asked.

"Yes. By many, not all. When I was young, I saw my father talking with some of our elders. They were very old. After that, he would take all of us children every morning to the river to bath - no matter how cold it was. One day I asked my father why we were doing that. He said, 'Because the elders told me to.' "

"Do you always cut the grass on the mound?" I asked.

"Yes. The mound was once much higher. That was before our people bought it back from the farmer. I take care of the mound to honor this spot. It is sacred. I've lived in many place but now I'm here. Whenever I come into this valley, no matter how long I have been gone, I feel like I'm home. I feel safe here."

We spent an hour talking with him in a shady grove by the river. His name was Henry Welch and he had lived on the reservation, home to the Eastern Band of the Cherokees, for most of his life. His wisdom and vision overlapped much of what we had learned on our journey. Like the Hopi Way, his tribe too had an ancient trail, a path of great antiquity, which they called the "Beauty Path."

"You know our journey through Native American wisdom has really grounded my understanding of putting One Love into action as societies," I said to Julia as we headed home along the Blue Ridge Parkway later that day. "They designed their cultures to reflect this love - love of the Creator, love of the Earth, love of each other, love of themselves, love of all living things. They have shown us a workable, sustainable pattern of living together in peace and cooperation. We need this indigenous knowledge and wisdom - not just for our health and happiness but for our survival. Most of us can't go back to living as they did in the past. We just have to find ways to merge their wisdom into our modern cultures so we can have the best of both worlds. If we can merge wisdom with technology, it's possible to have a *conscious* technological world. This wisdom is very much alive. Not just with the Hopi but with wisdomkeepers in *all* the tribes. We're getting there. It seems like people are waking up everywhere. It may not be covered by the media but its happening and we're finding each other. I think we're all Hopi - all People of Peace. We've just temporarily forgotten. We just need to stay awake ourselves and help remind others that it's always been within them."

"It's really *us* remembering to see it in *them*," Julia said smiling.

Epilogue

In early 2006, we are planning a *Completing the Covenant Concert* in Hopiland, hopefully on February 6, Bob Marley's 61st birthday and the 30-year anniversary of Leonard Peltier's imprisonment. We plan to invite Travis Terry, Uproot, Casper and the 602 Band, and other conscious Native American artists. As Radford addressed the Havasupai people at their concert in Supai, Roland will address the Hopi at this concert in Hopiland. We will also give away hundreds of copies of this book. All funds collected at the concert and all profits from future sales of this book will go to fund a Hopi-Havasupai youth exchange program. We believe this will help the Hopi sustain their Covenant by sharing their peace with other cultures.

A Message From the Hopi Elders

You have been telling the people that this is the Eleventh Hour.
Now you must go back and tell the people that this is The Hour.

Here are the things that must be considered:
　　Where are you living?
　　What are you doing?
　　What are your relationships?
　　Are you in right relation?
　　Where is your water?
　　Know our garden.
　　It is time to speak your Truth.
　　Create your community.
　　Be good to each other.
　　And do not look outside yourself for the leader.

This could be a good time!
There is a river flowing now very fast.
It is so great and swift that there are those who will be afraid.
They will try to hold on to the shore.
They will feel like they are being torn apart,
　　and they will suffer greatly.
Know the river has its destination.
The elders say we must let go of the shore,
　　push off toward the middle of the river,
keep our eyes open, and our heads above the water.
See who is there with you and celebrate.

At this time in history, we are to take nothing personally,
　　least of all ourselves!
For the moment we do, our spiritual growth
　　and journey comes to a halt.

The time of the lonely wolf is over.
Gather yourselves!
Banish the word struggle from your attitude and vocabulary.
All that we do now must be done in a sacred manner
      and in celebration.
We are the ones we have been waiting for.

The Elders,
Oraibi, Arizona August 2002

ORDER PAGE

To order copies of this or our other books, visit our Website at:

www.onelovepress.com

or contact us at:

One Love Press
PO Box 2142
Blowing Rock, NC 28605
(828) 295-4610 FAX: (828) 295-6901
Email: roskind@boone.net

Also check our Website for DVDs with video footage of our travels, including our reasonings with many of the wisdomkeepers featured in our books.